DATE DUE		

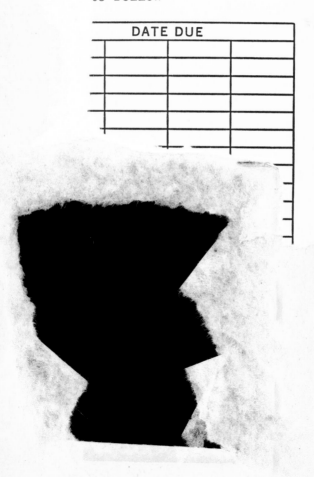

RISE TO FOLLOW

Violet Oakley
1928

ALBERT SPALDING

RISE TO FOLLOW

❧

AN AUTOBIOGRAPHY

❧

New York
HENRY HOLT AND COMPANY

Copyright, 1943, by

HENRY HOLT AND COMPANY, INC.

Published, November, 1943
Second printing, December, 1943
Third printing, January, 1944
Fourth printing, June, 1945
Fifth printing, December, 1946

PRINTED IN THE UNITED STATES OF AMERICA

To

M. P. S.

ON MUSIC

Many love music but for music's sake,
Many because her touches can awake
Thoughts that repose within the breast half-dead,
And rise to follow where she loves to lead.
What various feelings come from days gone by!
What tears from far-off sources dim the eye!
Few, when light fingers with sweet voices play
And melodies swell, pause, and melt away,
Mind how at every touch, at every tone,
A spark of life hath glistened and hath gone.

WALTER SAVAGE LANDOR

RISE TO FOLLOW.

CHAPTER ONE

THE half-bent figure suddenly straightened. The orchestra, holding its breath for one tense moment, waited for the initial down beat. I was holding my breath, too, as I stood watching from the corner of my eye that aquiline profile, carved out of granite, over which was stretched a yellow and seamed parchment that had once, perhaps, been human skin. No warmth appeared to animate this head: only a kind of smoldering blaze in the half-closed eyes, the eyelids heavy with age. But fire there was, and a kind of sardonic humor that commanded the attention of every musician on the stage.

It seemed right that Karl Muck should have found a place for his last years of activity in Hamburg, that proud city of the North whose character reflected his own. He was loved and revered there. The orchestra, indifferently good under other leaders, always contrived to outdo itself under his direction. It rang with a voice not ordinarily its own—warm, vibrant, flowing. Rhythmic vitality coursed through its tired limbs, communicating and compelling, a rhythm prompted rather by nature than by the discipline of a metronome. And all this accomplished with the economy of means which is the secret of great leadership, shared by few, the wonder of many. Muck's phenomenal technical resources were servants to a simplicity of purpose that gave irresistible eloquence to performance.

The poised baton signaled its first decisive command. Four detached raps of the kettledrum modestly announced the opening of this Beethoven masterpiece, the most serene of all violin concertos. Unique from his pen, it reflects, perhaps, the one unclouded period of that master's cyclonic life. With the Fourth Symphony and the G-major Piano Concerto it shares a confident faith in what life promised to hold for him. Prometheus had stolen fire from heaven; but Prometheus was as yet unbound.

The long orchestral introduction which precedes the soloist's first entrance is at once a challenge and an invitation: a challenge to the nerves and an invitation to memory. Waiting your cue, you relive the past and anticipate the future with a kind of lightning rapidity; the spur of heightened excitement lifts your imagination over the barriers of time and space. At least, it was so for me.

What does the violinist think about at such times? I have asked myself this question over and over and discussed it with many of my colleagues. Their reactions are curiously alike in general and individually varied in detail. Common to all is an absorbed preoccupation with the opening problem. The violin must break its silence with an ascent of broken octaves which are pitiless in their discovery of any impurity of tone or pitch. The orchestra has died down to a sustained dominant chord which supports but in no way covers the slightest imperfection. Many a violinist's neck is broken on this opening. It is not strange, then, that a man's thoughts may cover a wide panorama of defeats as well as victories while he waits for such a trial. You say to yourself: "Plague take the heat! How much warmer it is here than in the dressing room. . . . The strings must be sagging! Tune them when the orchestra is playing loud again and in keys with which you can make the open strings harmonize. . . . There, that's better! How soon will they start to sag again?"

You think, too, of many less relevant things: a neglected telegram; a needed haircut; a pair of tickets you forgot to leave at the box office for a friend; the man in the third row staring at you fiercely as though you were about to do him a personal injury; and the woman next to him whose hair is as tautly stretched as fiddle strings; students in the front rows, who, taking their Beethoven seriously, are armed with pocket scores.

The music progresses radiantly through its initial chapters.

The tender sub-theme piped sweetly in the major by the wood winds is answered in the minor by the strings. No other master has so shaped a diatonic scale. It remains, you reflect, the exclusive property of a genius who knows, as no one else does, how to give it an original turn by rhythmic device, by extension, by contraction, by inversion. This first movement is above all a lesson in the use of scales as melodic material. A simple figure which to the ordinary mind merely traces a monotonous and utilitarian pattern can, in the hands of a master, emerge invested with the freedom of originality. It is the triumph of craftsmanship in transcendent disguise. A miser with his motives, but a prodigal in his fertile and creative development of theme. The five-note scale of the seraphic sub-theme, rising from the major third to the octave, is matched if not surpassed by the haunting episode in G minor, still built on a scale.

As you stand waiting, you remember how you used to rebel at the interminable scales prescribed by your old teacher. How dull they were and how useless, you thought, especially as you were not even allowed the fun of playing them as fast as you could. And suddenly, etched clear, is the portrait of yourself as a small boy arrogantly arguing the point with your long-suffering master. "Scales?" he would say. "Why, they are the bread and butter of violin-playing!" Bread *without* butter, you used to think. That same small boy had experienced a kind of ecstasy when his master, as a reward for good work, had permitted him to tackle the Beethoven concerto. You recall his odd sense of disappointment—not that the work was too difficult; on the contrary, he almost resented the ease with which it first flowed. A great work ought to impose a more demanding task at the outset.

"So," observed his teacher, "you find it simple—too simple. In effect it is. Profoundly simple, and truly profound. In the future when you play better you will have more doubts than you have now. Its difficulties, like the dangerous parts of an iceberg, lie two-thirds submerged. But good mariners recognize the perils of icebergs however calm the sea that surrounds them."

Well, here they are, the scales and the icebergs, staring you in the face; and now, even now, after countless public performances, after prodigal public favor, you wonder, "Can I, will I, do half justice to these 'Stairs to Heaven'?"

Next to you the Mephistophelian figure, so sparing of gesture, so commanding in dynamic control of a hundred players, gives you a sidelong glance as the music arpeggios its way down to the dominant chord that is your cue.

"Der Amerikaner," he had called me. This, from him, should have been a term of disparagement for he had, or thought he had, a full measure of grievance against my country for his internment during the War. We had all thought it was for espionage, though later I knew it was for something quite different, an absurd device for bowing to the hysteria of the moment. Yet it was this very Amerikaner that Karl Muck had insistently demanded as soloist for the Beethoven Festival at Hamburg in 1927 on the centenary of the composer's death. The orchestral committee had argued, the Bürgermeister had demurred, the public had protested with indignant letters that this, of all occasions, demanded a German violinist, but all to no avail. Muck had still called for "der Amerikaner"—Spalding— and Muck's will generally prevailed.

This was my first orchestral appearance in Germany in many years; indeed, since well before the First World War. I was delighted, flattered, and also somewhat puzzled by this engagement, not knowing until long afterward all the details that had led to it. That very morning, after rehearsal, Dr. Muck had invited me to join him in a cup of tea—he drank tea almost as consistently, although not quite so consecutively, as he smoked cigarettes. This was a signal honor which I didn't half appreciate at the time. The rehearsal had gone well, but personal relationships were kept in a refrigerator so far as Muck was concerned. Icy politeness barred any attempt at cordiality. You would sooner try familiarity with a sphinx. On this morning, however, he was talkative between alternate sips of tea and long, inhaled puffs of a cigarette. He wanted to talk, and to talk, of all things, about America. There was bitterness in what he said, and an angry resentment, and yet coupled with them was an almost pathetic turning back to the old, happy days in Boston where, with an

[4]

ideal instrument at his command, he had stormed the very gates of Parnassus.

Happy days, I reflected; "happy" was scarcely a term applicable to any part or parcel of that enigmatic man's life. But artistic satisfaction, freedom from preoccupation, and the power to indulge his almost licentious disregard of public opinion were enough to justify the word.

I was embarrassed and almost tongue-tied when, after his third cup of tea, Muck broached the painful subject of his difficulties in the United States following our entry into the war in 1917. I didn't even have a third cup of tea with which to mask my distress. Fortunately, he had a great deal to get off his chest, and all "der Amerikaner" had to say was an occasional "Yes" or "No" or sometimes "Indeed!" The metallic voice went monotonously on in the excellent English he spoke, retailing this grievance and that, this and that privation, and with such a mounting bitterness against everything American that finally twelve generations of Yankee ancestry began to react within me. I waited for a pause when he obviously expected something more than a monosyllable and managed to find my voice.

"I can't tell you, Dr. Muck," I observed, "how distressed I am, how distressed all your admirers are, that you should have suffered such difficulties, and in my country, too. Of course during all this time, you will perhaps remember, I was under arms and abroad serving with the American Air Force. I beg you, though, to ask yourself what would have occurred in like circumstances had the country and the individual been reversed. Suppose you had been an American conductor officiating with one of the major orchestras in Germany when the war broke out. Would there have been, do you think, fewer difficulties?"

"Have another cup of tea," snapped Muck; and the incident was closed.

The concerto went on. The perilous octaves at the solo entrance had taken their flight upward with surprising ease, and once launched on its course the violin was threading its way through the delicate pattern that Beethoven has woven into the symphonic structure. The lovely G-minor phrase had, it seemed to me, been given full liberty by the gentle checkrein of Muck

[5]

which allowed it to become tranquil without, however, changing the tempo as is so often done. We had agreed at rehearsal, to his obvious satisfaction, as to the treatment of this passage. And the almost imperceptible animando which followed it had stolen in with the "modesty of nature."

Decidedly, one always played at one's best with Muck.

Hamburg's 1927 Spring Festival appeared to celebrate not merely the great Liberator of Music. That happy year augured well for those who loved peace. The Locarno Treaty was enjoying its honeymoon; Germany was now a welcomed member of the League of Nations; a flood of foreign loans was pouring in to her from erstwhile enemy lands. You could not travel many miles through this country without observing its extraordinary rebound from inertia and despair to productive activity of the most enviable kind. A few days before, in the train, a British traveler had commented on this paradoxical achievement. Noticing the imposing array of modern buildings of all kinds springing up, he said: "We see nothing of this sort at home or in France. Perhaps it is an advantage to be defeated. To the vanquished belong the spoils!" He said it without bitterness, almost without irony. He did not imagine, no one wished to imagine, that this productive field was being sown with dragon's teeth. The leaders of the Weimar Republic were not then in reputation sick; in honor bankrupt. They enjoyed good credit. Germany was henceforth to be a prosperous, a friendly, neighbor. How far away then was the shadow of Hitler. . . . Indeed, with Beethoven speaking, only a deaf man would disbelieve in the brotherhood of man. And the celestial music of the violin concerto was somehow an earnest of democratic Germany's place in the sun.

The slow movement, which ascends to astronomical heights, is one of the most cherished pages of all literature. Over the simple song of the orchestra the solo violin traces a thread of abstract embroidery that floats in suspension between heaven and earth. The Gothic angels incline their heads from a cathedral niche and smile. You scarcely want to breathe while phrasing these illuminations. When you are abruptly returned to reality by the compelling rhythms of the Rondo, you resent for a moment this violent transition. But the last movement goes with gusto, with pulsating élan, and the audience responds in true festival spirit.

At the close of the concert the thronged greenroom exploded with excited, red-faced, perspiring groups, all shouting their approval. Muck insisted on presenting me personally to each and every one. Deathly pale from fatigue, and with a mocking smile slightly curving the thin lips (only the eyes betraying flashes of his inward satisfaction), he introduced "der Amerikaner" with an aloof air of proprietorship. It was plain that I was his discovery. It was plain that he was pleased but unastonished by my reception. To me he said only: "Herrlich, was?" But as he gripped my hand the mummy seemed for a brief instant to come to life. For Muck it was a moment of incredible warmth.

There is no immediate sense of fatigue after such a concert. On the contrary, thought is quickened and there is an exhilaration that postpones the eventual relaxation of sleep. And you are ravenously hungry.

We had supper at Schümann's, where they specialized in marine delicacies. In recent years it has been somewhat shunned by all right-thinking Nazis, for was there not a suspicion of non-Aryanism in its management? "Ach, Schümann's!" said one conductor with zest. "Do you know, Spalding, I have a regular and unfailing ritual on returning to Hamburg after a long absence. To Schümann's at once, and I say to the Herr Ober: 'Please bring me relays of oysters for the next half-hour; and follow it with a continuous half-hour of caviar.'"

Lordly ideas! I was glad to reflect that a successful American season had provided him with the wherewithal to finance such an order. Oysters were listed at two or three dollars a dozen in Germany. And caviar!—well, caviar is caviar and commands its price no matter where you are.

"Why is it," my wife asked a prosperous industrialist when we had been particularly self-indulgent one evening, "that the best caviar obtainable outside of Russia is to be found in Germany?"

[7]

"Gnädige," he replied, and there was a twinkle in his eye as well as a chuckle in his voice, "we detest the Bolsheviks, we fear Communism, we proclaim the Reds as our chief objects of detestation. Nevertheless we do trade with them; perhaps more than is generally known. There are ways and means—" He broke off suddenly as though not wanting to say too much, and added, "In any case the fruits of our tireless industry are steadily invading Russia and in return . . . in return, at least, you see what excellent caviar we can boast of!"

"Better," agreed Mary, "than the best tables in Paris, London, or New York can afford."

Back at the hotel I prepared for bed. As I threw open the windows which overlooked the Alster, it came over me how superb Hamburg could be under its black mantle of night. The shadowy buildings of the proud Hanseatic city rose in dark and silent splendor. And with the gentle approach of spring Hamburg always shed some of its austerity. . . . I found my room crowded with memories. In a state half asleep, half awake, you could review a procession of events and figures that did not seem to emerge from the past: they claimed the present. Linked somehow with the silver chain of sound still throbbing in your ears, they turned page by page and recited chapter by chapter the sequences of a life that you only vaguely recognized as your own.

A small boy with avid, questioning eyes, and a mop of unruly hair, drawn from his toys by the sound of the piano—during his waking moments his mother was never far from it.

The calm, tolerant figure of Father, an Olympian presence that insured against fear.

Aunt Sally Guest, marooned in her rocking chair, quoting Scripture and excoriating Democrats.

Grandma Spalding, a majestic portrait from pioneering days.

"Martie," the boy's maternal grandmother, a precursor of the modern business woman.

Brother Boardman, struggling with a cello but relaxing with mathematics.

The picture slides of life flashed silently on.

Home in the Navarro Apartments in that vanished section of New York which was monotonously brownstone.

Migrations to Italy where an abundance of flowers made up for the absence of central heating and the scarcity of plumbing.

Adventures in music and the betraying quicksands of an over-ready facility.

First contacts with the public. A boy's wonder at finding that here was a friend, not an enemy; a source of strength, not weakness; a spur to best endeavor, not a checkrein.

Saint-Saëns with his lisp. Richter with his growl. Damrosch with his daughters.

The magic of Joachim, of Ysaÿe, of Kreisler, of Sarasate.

The Gordons at home in England; and the England that always traveled with them abroad.

Janet Ross and Lady Paget facing each other with hostile respect and aloofness from their villas providentially isolated, one on the southern and the other on the northeastern hills of Tuscany.

Early successes, early failures.

The cavalcade of Tsarist Russia. The frugal values of Finland. The poetic silences of Norway. The symphonic pattern of all Scandinavia.

War . . . A complete reversal in the conduct of life.

LaGuardia . . . You would have to remember him.

Marriage . . . "Worth what's dearest to the world."

The concert stage again, and the essential readjustment of early facility to maturity.

Conceptual music . . . Pieces that build cathedrals in the mind . . . the *Chaconne* of Bach. . . .

CHAPTER TWO

MY mother used to say that a hearing of Bach's *Chaconne* always reminded her of the Sermon on the Mount, and that the introduction of the major variations represented the Beatitudes. If a purist objected to the analogy on the ground that the Beatitudes open the Sermon, the objection was brushed aside as inconsequential. Mother was never one to cross the *t*'s or dot the *i*'s, even in her handwriting.

It was bold calligraphy, abrupt, angular, and defiantly rebellious against the confines of the letter sheet. You had the impression that years of arduous self-discipline had been at work before any semblance of conformity was achieved. My mother was utterly unpredictable in her moods, in her likes and dislikes; her reactions had the quality of quicksilver. Her small, regular features alternated from frown to smile with the capriciousness of Irish Sea weather, and her diminutive hands expressed a restless activity that would have been unendurable had it not found a release in music. She respected mathematics, but had an altogether unorthodox approach to it. She admitted the decimal system as an academic entity, but for herself she had her own technique. Etched clearly in her mind was a pattern of numbers which governed her economics. It might have been baffling to a bank teller, but it would have delighted a surrealist painter. A line ascending vertically to the number 17 represented that amount in the aggregate and in its individual parts. From there to 26 it moderated its flight to an angle of forty-five degrees. From 26 to 43 the patch was almost horizontal; then it rose vertically again. It continued in this fashion, growing into a statistical diagram that was deeply satisfying to her.

She had the power of inspiring both devotion and affection without any apparent effort on her part. A friend once said to me: "Your mother is unique in this way. I find myself irresistibly compelled to do things I do not particularly want to do, to think things with which I do not altogether agree—and to find myself enchanted merely because it happens to be her world. In anyone else it would be irritating."

She dominated, as far back as I can remember, a large household. There were often many extraneous additions to bed and board besides the immediate family—my father and herself, my brother and me. They ranged all the way from grandparents (on the distaff side) through aunts and uncles to cousins, the titles sometimes genuine, often merely honorary, but always numerically generous. Mary, the old Alabama mammy who first tended Boardman and myself used to hunch her shoulders and protest: "Nevah, even in de South, did Ah see chillun with so many kinfolk!"

Mary Jackson was a snob if ever there was one. To her rearing of us she brought many of the traditions of the deep South. Architecturally she was built somewhat like a Byzantine cathedral, wide-spaced and bulging heavily with domes. Majestic of movement and imperious in command, she was an excellent lieutenant to my mother in planting the first seeds of discipline. There was tenderness, too, plenty of it. She would croon us to sleep in a husky voice, mixing strange African words with more intelligible ones in her improvised cradle songs. She was vigilantly jealous in preserving an equality of attention for both children. When my brother Boardman, by both seniority and good looks, drew compliments in which I could not share, Mary would rebel at the neglect of the younger one and would say, pointing to me, "Dis yere chile may not be so handsum, but he knows a heap!"

One of her chief objections to too many kinfolk was indiscriminate kissing. Without the advantage of modern clinical ideas on the rearing of infants, Mary trusted to her traditions, and no one would have dreamed of overruling any dictum of hers. " 'Tain't fittin'," she would decide.

Then, one day, she went south on a visit, promising that it was only a leave of absence and that she would surely return. My mother was in despair when word came that her family had persuaded Mary to remain in Mobile. Her post was not easy to fill. Where was another such to be found?

The new incumbent, however, was a worthy successor. She was Nanny Harris of Virginia. Nanny was very young when she came to us—only seventeen. Unlike Mary Jackson, she was all bone and no flesh. Her sable skin was drawn taut over a skeleton frame suggesting but scarcely realizing three dimensions. But she, too, had dignity and tradition. She inspired confidence. She filled a dual role: besides being custodian of the children she was maid to Aunt Sally Guest, a lady of remote antiquity.

Aunt Sally was my mother's great-aunt. Her permanent residence with us had dated from before I was born. Presumably my father and mother had had a honeymoon to themselves, though I am tempted sometimes to doubt it. My father must have been a somewhat bewildered man on discovering the extent of the more or less permanent clan he had taken on with his marriage vows. In addition to the fully established Aunt Sally, there were many familiar faces at the family table: "Martie," my maternal grandmother; Grandma Spalding; Uncle Charlie Sargent, a great-uncle by marriage; his son, Harry; and Cousins Walter and Elsie Pell, to speak of only the real kinfolk.

Many of these paid us what were termed visits. But in our family a visit was of prodigious dimensions. Not by days or weeks was it measured, but by months or years. Like a Procrustean bed the house or apartment expanded or contracted. How it was accomplished I don't know, but accomplished it was. To my mother's way of thinking, the limitations of space never served as a valid excuse for refusing an extra relative.

Aunt Sally Guest sat always in a favorite rocking chair near the window, her hands industriously making one patchwork quilt after another. Short and impressively stout, she had a special gift for militant inactivity. I used to watch her with awe. Her self-imposed task did not, however, prevent her from noticing everything that went on in the street below. There always had to be a street, and a busy street, under Aunt Sally's window. She was urban in the extreme and followed us to the country only under protest. Probably her favorite location was the apartment house in which we lived for a few years during the early eighteen-nineties, from the time I was three. The Navarro Apartments stood at Central Park South and Seventh Avenue. Here Aunt Sally was completely happy. Her window looked out on Seventh Avenue, a busy, hustling street where from only the corner of her eye could she see a patch of the uninteresting green of Central Park. Thus there was a minimum of distraction from metropolitan activity.

A focal point for her concentration was the saloon opposite. She would scrutinize the comings and goings here, and it was a colorless day that didn't offer her at least one drunken brawl. Prohibitionist in principle, the swinging doors to iniquity nevertheless provided her with constant bulwarks against any suspicion of boredom. Aunt Sally was devoutly a Baptist, intransigently a Republican, obstinately a Northerner, and vindictively a New Yorker. In the abstract she consented to be an American also, but this was only in her broader moments. "New Jersey, indeed!" she exclaimed when my father proposed that we spend the summer months on the Jersey coast. "How long, Walter, will it be before you grow up and learn never to trust a Jersey man?"

She had a swift and trenchant way of summing up people at a glance and was unashamedly dismayed when called upon to revoke her judgments. To think that that charming man who had come unexpectedly to dinner—such nice manners, too— could be a Democrat! Once, after having been enchanted with a newcomer, she learned with a shock that we had been harboring a Papist. I think that aromatic spirits of ammonia had to be resorted to. Aunt Sally eyed even Episcopalians with deep distrust. There were many roads to hell, but only one path to salvation.

Sally Guest had grown up in a Manhattan that was a world in itself, comprising city, country, and even wilderness. When she was first married and went to live in the old Dutch homestead with the Guest family, her new home was a considerable distance from the New York where the men of the family went to business. At this time the stage traveled once a week to the city. Later, when a daily route was inaugurated, the Guests thought they were made. Their home, with its outlying farms, was situated at what is now Fiftieth Street, between Fifth and Eighth Avenues. They must have been a rather profligate lot. The land would have meant eventual millions to all who inherited it—as the city marched north at an ever-increasing pace it changed wild country, rocky hills, and woodlands first into sparse suburbs, then thickly settled suburbs, and finally to uptown—but the need for ready cash whittled away this wide domain piece by piece. By the time Aunt Sally came to live with us her entire estate consisted of a few houses of diminishing value on upper Sixth Avenue. Even the little income that they represented was deflated by the coming of the Elevated, but nothing, it appeared, could deflate the incurable optimism of this old lady. She cheerfully and invariably spent in excess of whatever her rents netted her—generally, I must say, not on herself but on others—and just as cheerfully would part with another house at any sacrifice to meet the unpaid bills. Her clothes, fashioned to last a lifetime, were of heavy silks from the richest looms of Lyons. You couldn't say they draped the figure—rather, they stood like a scaffolding around it.

"When I am gone to glory," she would say to Nanny, "be sure you lay me out in my black moiré." Clad in such armor she could confidently meet her Maker.

Grandma Spalding was the same age as Aunt Sally. She was as tall as Aunt Sally was short; as bony in structure as Aunt Sally was padded. Born in Batavia, New York, she had married when she was very young a second cousin, Austin Wright, in whose household she had been brought up. It was a large family—in fact, in those days it appeared scandalous to have a small one. Grandma used often to visit her Uncle James Tiffany whose children were so numerous that it seemed as if the usual Christian names had been exhausted.

"What were they all called, Grandma?" I would ask.

"Well," she would say, "there was Sara Ann, and Juliet; then there was Harriet (named like me) and Lucy, Ruth, Laura, and Betsy. . . ." She would pause—the best was yet to come: "Then there was Delue, Reclue, and Deguile."

I would howl with delight and unbelief.

In 1839 the young Wrights set out to make their fortune in the wide West. When they reached Chicago, which was then a settlement of some four thousand, they remained for about a week, debating the possibility of settling there permanently. But, as Grandma said, "We were not favorably impressed. We found the place low and marshy; many people were down with fevers, and some were suffering with ague." They traveled on to the Rock River country, where they were more pleased with the lay of the land.

"What was it like, Grandma?" I could hear her tell it over and over again.

Her eyes sparkled with almost a renewed youth. "It was a wide, lovely country," she'd say; "the rivers clear as a well-washed window, river banks high and dry, and the prairies covered with wildflowers."

Aunt Sally sat in silent disapproval. All these virtues were too distant from her beloved New York. And it was not, she reflected, just the moment to quote Scripture.

"But, Mother Spalding," my mother would suggest, "life must sometimes have been very difficult."

Grandma chuckled again.

"There was," she recalled, "an eccentric old lady who kept a tavern near Galena. She was quite famous as a cook. One day a gentleman stopped there and had dinner. She was rather inclined to talk, and told him that she had been in that part of the country for two years. He asked her what she thought of the great West. She replied, 'The country is big enough in all conscience—it's heaven for men and horses, but hell for women and oxen.'"

This totally unexpected excursion into profane language would make us squeal with pleasure.

Austin Wright lived only a short time, and some years later the attractive young widow married my grandfather, James Spalding. They lived in Byron, Illinois.

The Spalding family had been American settlers for many generations. The original pioneer of that name, Edward Spalding, ventured from his Lincolnshire home in England and came to the little colony of Jamestown, Virginia, in 1619. One of his three sons, another Edward, migrated to New England. This line descended by way of Edwards, second, third and fourth, by Simons one and two, with a John and a Harry thrown in, to my grandfather. Simon the second fought as a captain in the Revolutionary War, and was elevated to the rank of brigadier general in the Pennsylvania Militia. He was, likewise, a founding member of the Connecticut Society of the Cincinnati. They were a sturdy lot; and they married sturdy women. One in particular, whose name always intrigued me, was John's wife, *circa* 1800, Welthey Anne Gore—despite the spelling, it suggested an affluence that no other record substantiates. The unions were staunchly Anglo-Saxon, though the name of one ancestress, Mary or Marie Brachet, indicates French extraction.

Grandfather James died shortly before the Civil War. Widowed a second time, Grandma Spalding was left with three young children to bring up. Though burdened with a great deal of property, she lacked ready money. But Grandma was practical, courageous, and cheerful. She would say: "I have sometimes felt pinched, but never poor."

Making her permanent home with her married daughter, Aunt Mary Brown, she made frequent visits to her other children. She was convinced that their equals were not to be found. Boardman and I could not help noticing how scrupulously Mother disciplined her habitual teasing of Father while the majestic matriarch of the family was with us. She would scarcely have understood.

My other grandmother, Martie, was of another generation and of a totally different type. She was young enough to be Madame Spalding's daughter, and the Chicago she lived in as Doctor Boardman's wife had blossomed from the unhealthy marshland to a city of sizable dimensions and aggressive ambitions. My Grandfather Boardman was a surgeon of distinction and, in the thriving young Chicago of the sixties and the early seventies, they lived a life of what must have seemed reckless affluence in those days. Dr. Boardman was many years older than his young and beautiful wife. When after a long sickness he died, their capital reserves were all but exhausted.

Everyone in Chicago expected Martie to remarry. She did not lack opportunities. But she had been romantically happy. She preferred facing a world of insecurity, armed only with her keen intelligence and resourcefulness, to the doubtful advantage of material comfort for which memories of a fixed ideal would have to be demoted to second best.

She confided the care of my mother's education and upbringing to Uncle Frank and Aunt Sally Guest, who, childless, accepted the task as if it were a cherished boon.

Martie was a pioneer, two generations in advance of her time. She had ability, acumen, and initiative. Deciding that the most promising field for the exercise of her talents lay in providing lodging and food, she resolved that it should be unique in Chicago. She disclosed her plan to some influential friends of her husband's, and succeeded in changing their hesitation and doubt to acceptance. They advanced a modest capital for the initial trial of this venture—unprecedented in the 1870's—and Martie opened a private hotel. It was situated on Michigan Avenue, and she called it "Maison du Lac." She was shrewd in the choice of her clientele and the quality of her offering. The business thrived under a personal supervision that was as unrelaxed as it was canny. It became a matter of distinction to be transferred from the long waiting list to actual residence at the Maison du Lac.

Martie's visits to us were frequent, but of briefer duration than was usual among our other relatives. The running of her little hotel always suffered in her absence. But their shortness only added to the excitement of her visits. She had a passion for moving furniture. And Mother always had to accept with a kind of resigned dismay the complete rearrangement of the drawing-room which she had, till then, thought quite satisfactory. A stifled protest would give way to the reluctant admission that Martie's eye was as keen as it was commanding and that the new disposition of the peripatetic furniture justified the upset. Only Aunt Sally's chair remained inviolate. Even Martie would have quailed at suggesting its displacement from the old lady's favorite window.

Martie looked like a handsomer and scarcely older sister of my mother. Her fine features had classical regularity, and her large dark eyes had depth and fire. Best of all, her conversation had originality and spice; she had a gift for metaphor. A picture in words would be etched clear and convincing—sharpened with an individual turn of humor that made it long remembered.

I remember thinking, as a small child, that all of her acquaintances must have come from the Zoo or the Aquarium. With a deft line Martie would draw Mrs. W's portrait until it was impossible not to recognize the lady's cousinship to a turkey. Mr. P, with his sagging, colorless lips, resembled nothing so much as an oyster without benefit of pearl. That esteemed member of the Legislature, Congressman van H, had an unruly imperial sprouting haphazardly from his chin—"A goat in everything save his morals," quoth Martie, "and I'm not so sure of those!"

When the family roof sheltered all these ladies simultaneously, it took the combined tact and ingenuity of both my parents to keep the waters smooth.

"There is nothing like old age," commented my mother, "for bringing childish emotions to the surface. Would you believe it, Walter? Mother Spalding was up extra early this morning. She was determined for once to be first with the *New York Herald*. But Aunt Sally had beaten her to it. I sensed a situation at once."

"Never mind," consoled my father. "At breakfast your coffee was good and strong. Mother has never nurtured a grudge against any household that started her day with satisfying coffee."

"All the same," decided my mother, "I shall be prudent and order two *Heralds*."

There seems to be no reasonable link by which Central Park South and Seventh Avenue in the Gay Nineties can be related to the fantastic skyline of today. Ambitious pioneers had penetrated this far north to build their inevitable brownstone homes with the serene conviction that they were secure from any possible invasion by the commercial world. Many trees on the rocky promontories of the Park could be seen above the roofs of the three- or four-story dwellings. The Navarro Apartments, where we lived, was a daring intruder into this homogeneous world. Towering above its neighbors, it soared to the incredible and uncomfortable height of nine stories. It boasted modern, almost irreligious, conveniences, including elevators. These were, it was agreed, of doubtful advantage to the digestion, especially when descending at a dizzy speed.

I can recall the excitement caused by the installation of a private telephone. Aunt Sally didn't think it was quite nice . . . such an affront to privacy. She accepted it, however, without too many protests, for she had a high regard for my father in spite of his modern tendencies. Aunt Sally was devoted to Father, she was even a little in awe of him. After she had recovered from her first resentment over his marriage to her beloved Marie, for whom no man was quite good enough, she was quick to concede to and extoll the interloper. It was no more than justice and she instinctively knew it. She lived to enjoy twenty years of their married life before she packed her bag for a journey to the Golden Gates.

There can have been but few couples who had so many years together of happy disagreement as my father and mother. Direct opposites in type, in taste, and in technique of living, they yet achieved a kind of contrapuntal harmony that belied their frequent and daring dissonances.

Father was a massive structure both mentally and physically. He was some six feet tall, a modest height for a Spalding, well built and admirably co-ordinated in movement. He carried his large head erect with a kind of proud freedom that exacted instant respect. Light brown hair and deep, wide-set gray eyes invited friendliness and cordiality, but rarely intimacy. Brought up in the little town of Rockford, Illinois, the youngest of a family of three, he had by necessity been thrown on his own resources when very young. At the age of sixteen he was working in a bank as an assistant cashier. It was one of his duties to sleep in the bank at night as guardian of the public's deposits. This was during the early seventies when the sinister figures of the Jesse James band were a national terror to banks.

"What would you have done," I'd ask him, "if the bank had been held up?"

"I should have been horribly frightened," my father confessed, "and I don't know what I would have done. Certainly my gun wouldn't have been much use to me, for I didn't know how to use it quickly enough for those gentlemen."

This was a most unsatisfactory answer, but I put it down to sheer modesty. I couldn't conceive of Father's being afraid of anything—unless, perhaps, it was Mother's displeasure.

When he was nineteen years old Father joined his elder brother, Albert (for whom I was named), in an ambitious business venture. His banking friends shook their heads when he proposed to risk his savings in such a wild scheme. My uncle, A.G., had had a short but spectacular career as a baseball player, and he asked Father to share with him in the establishment of a sporting goods store to be known as A. G. Spalding & Brother. Their joint capital was eight hundred dollars, supplied in equal shares by the two brothers. A facsimile of this agreement, witnessed by their mother in 1876, hangs in the many offices of the business of that name today. It was a modest beginning but it proved to be a notable success. The brothers complemented each other admirably. A.G. was resourceful and imaginative. J.W. was sober and balanced. A.G. inspired enthusiasm. J.W. won confidence. Above all, there existed between the two a devotion and a mutual respect that made for the most effective co-operation. The little retail store graduated to wider activities. Manufacturing was begun, developed, and expanded.

When, some six or seven years later, an attraction to a gifted young musician, Marie Boardman, ripened rapidly into romance, J.W. was regarded as one of the promising young businessmen of Chicago. It certainly was not music that attracted him, for my father had no musical ear. Though his voice had depth and richness, it would have baffled the efforts of the most tireless teacher to confine it to definite pitch. To hear him attempt to whistle defies description. No, it couldn't have been Miss Boardman's acclaimed proficiency at the keyboard or the velvet of her contralto voice that drew these two together; it must have been something quite different. This small dark girl, passionate, vehement, and complex, presented a fascinating quicksand of emotional adventure to the rational footsteps that hitherto had always sought firm ground. My father was bewildered, captivated, subjugated.

They were married in 1884. Shortly after this, they moved to New York to establish a new branch of the sporting goods business. Although my brother and I were born in Chicago, he in 1885 and I in 1888, these events took place during visits to the Windy City.

The new ménage enjoyed a comfortable income which they chronically threatened to exceed. My mother had a talent for extravagance and generally succeeded in outflanking prudent opposition by skirmishes of feminine strategy. She could tease with humor and an utter disregard for logic. Her husband found himself unable to cope with it, and found defeat enchanting. Here was a wife who was unpredictable, irrational, who outwardly quarreled with the opinions she secretly revered. She found them Jovian: if he were comfortably absent, she would quote them as unanswerable. They were devoted opposites and their friends and acquaintances, prosperous and needy, adored them both. The hospitality of bed and board was offered with a largesse that was remarkable even in those days. It was traditional from both sides of the family, and Aunt Sally would have regarded it as sacrilege not to invite a caller to stay on for a meal. That there might not be sufficient food at the moment would never have occurred to her. The dining-room table was nearly always expanding, rarely contracting. The small boys would have regarded as abnormal a reduction to the four of the immediate family.

Of our living-rooms, I remember best the long drawing-room, dominated by a Steinway grand piano. It was my early privilege and fascination to stand tiptoe and wide-eyed at the incredible sounds this miraculous instrument could give forth. This was accompanied by the scent of violets which I always associated with my mother. Once, I remember to my delight, she possessed a ridiculous hat made of violets, which she wore perched on top of the elaborate coiffure favored at that time by fashion. I found it beautiful. Colors could never be too bright or profuse for her. And this same catholic recklessness showed itself in her housefurnishings. The modern interior decorator would have shuddered at some of the combinations that delighted my mother. But even if this hybrid species had been in existence then, it would have had scant influence with her. Academically she would have admitted its authority without, however, any intention of bowing to its dictates.

How glad I am that this was so. For I have the vivid recollection of a home where the objects clashed with each other, and yet were bound by a link of character and of cherishing care. They were rooms that were lived in, where people were happy, and the memory of them makes many a modern interior seem only half alive in its conforming and submissive neutrality.

Aunt Sally, too, was partly responsible for the profuse array of furniture. She extended her love of patchwork quilts to household decoration. Vacant spaces in rooms were to her unlovely, even immodest. Often, armed with a little ready cash from a recent sale of real estate, she frequented auction rooms and returned triumphantly with a picture, a chair, or a table. Room was always found for it without discarding anything else.

Father's taste was more sober. Sometimes it sounded a warning note with effect, but too often he was outflanked. Patient beyond words, he had often to resort to Fabian tactics to make a long-desired point. Sometimes he would skirmish with telling though impermanent effect. Devoting an evening to furniture-moving, he would exile the débris of many superannuated pieces to the attic. The rooms breathed again; you could see some vacant spaces. His efforts were applauded. His will was not opposed—merely evaded. Somehow the banished articles strayed back, one by one, elbowing their way to their long-accustomed places. One of these immigrants was an old red damask chair that was the particular pride of Aunt Sally and Mother. The seat of the chair had worn threadbare, it even threatened to expose its entrails at any moment. Being a large chair, it stood in a prominent corner. At parties its shortcomings were concealed by having Aunt Sally occupy it. Once seated, no one expected her to budge an inch. Aunt Sally was no more movable than one of the lions in Trafalgar Square. Her world came to and from her. After its members came, most of them stayed, for she had the gift of making them laugh.

Once an Indian swami came to dinner. He was none other than the renowned Vivekananda. Aunt Sally found him fascinating, though she could never quite see the exalted spirituality that his fleet of admirers claimed for him. For the paeans of praise that filled the air she had pithy rejoinders. "Land-a-mercy," she would retort to some assertion of the swami's rigidly ascetic life, "ascetic life, indeed! Let me tell you that that man, Indian or no Indian, priest or no priest, that man never got such a generous figure living on wildflowers!"

"But, Aunt Sally, you know you liked him. You showed you did."

"Certainly, I liked him. I like lots of men, and I don't have to think they're Jesus of Nazareth just because I do." She would hold her breath with a kind of smothered chuckle when she felt she had been on the brink of blasphemy.

The evening parties were almost always musical ones. Even the swami did not escape, although my mother had qualms and did not let the music go on too long.

There was never a dearth of Frenchmen, Italians, Germans, even Spaniards—all with long hair and many with beards, all delighted to play or sing. Some of them were good or even excellent musicians. None of them was lacking in a picturesque quality. An old pianist by the name of Señor Villanova was altogether delightful. He never appeared without his umbrella and his fan; he would as soon have thought of leaving his courtly manners at home. His playing of some Chopin nocturnes and études bewitched me. My attention was divided between his agile fingers and the equally agile mustache which was waxed to the nth power and which was kept in perpetual motion by the trembling of his upper lip. He was pleased by my attention. "And did you like it?" he asked. Oh, I did. "Shall you want

[23]

to be a musician?" he went on. I had no doubt of it. "Well," he said, "it is a long road, but it's a nice road."

It was a sore trial to Aunt Sally when in the winter of 1895-96 a winter's sojourn in Florence, Italy, was proposed and decided upon. She had never been abroad, nor had she any desire to go. She protested, she cajoled, she begged—all to no avail. My parents had been to Florence, and my mother had fallen in love with the Tuscan city. Then, too, the panic of 1893, followed by lean years, had left my father in rather poor health. Economy was necessary. The Navarro apartment was expensive, and extravagance always seems easier to curtail in new surroundings. What is difficult at home is disguised by novelty abroad. Aunt Sally did not give in until the last ditch. She would pack her things, she threatened, and go and make her home with her brother (a not altogether sympathetic brother) in Peekskill. When this ultimatum did not produce the desired effect, she packed her things and made ready for the ocean voyage. To be parted from my mother was worse than death, and she was willing to face the Atlantic, alien lands, a Papist country, and even absence from her beloved New York, rather than suffer it.

It is fortunate that this momentous change of scene toward the close of her life never appeared to her to be more than a temporary exile. The Florentine venture was repeated year after year, and each successive year was presumably the last. Aunt Sally's faith never wavered in prophesying a permanent return to sanity and to New York. She never became reconciled to life in Florence.

However, she soon installed herself comfortably, if protestingly, in her chair beside the front window and, although she sorely missed Seventh Avenue and the entertaining saloon, she found all that went on deeply interesting. She was entertained by all the street venders with their different musical cries; had a nodding acquaintance with each carabiniere who frequented the streets; and, though she was loath to admit it, found romance in a serenader warbling to an invisible signora behind barred windows.

CHAPTER THREE

FOR no reason that I can think of, I asked for a violin for Christmas of 1895. Music had abounded in the household and my earliest memories are mixed up with the fascination of the black and white keys of the piano over which my mother's fingers had such nimble control. Her natural musical gifts had been developed to a degree that must have been rare in those days. In addition to her quite remarkable piano-playing, she sang delightfully, with a rich contralto voice. Above all, it was inherently musical singing. She thought first in terms of rhythm and of the musical phrase, and only secondarily in terms of breath control. As a young girl she had studied with a public career in mind until romance came to interrupt it. The idea of public performance was then abandoned, but not the continuance of study.

The long hours she sat at the piano were an unending source of wonder to the small boy who would stand, often on tiptoe, to watch the miraculous manipulation of the keys. As far as I can remember, however, although our house was never without music by day or night, I had never heard the sound of a violin at home. Whether it was suggestion, or perhaps a street fiddler who caught my attention, the fact remains that out of the blue I asked for a violin as a Christmas present. There was, it appears, some parental doubt about granting this request. A violin? Why a violin? Better start with the piano. Everyone advised this. Let him start with the piano, and later on we shall see. Not so, however, Aunt Sally Guest. The child wanted a violin, he had asked for it, ergo, he should have it. Her funds were too meager to allow any wild expenditure, but in Florence in those days twenty lire seemed like a princely sum with which to equip a small fiddler. It did, indeed, go far enough for a new, red, shining, half-sized fiddle with a bow of sorts. A case seemed wholly superfluous.

I was overjoyed to find it hanging on the Christmas tree. This joy was somewhat marred by the discovery that material ownership of this wonderbox was somehow not sufficient to produce the music I had expected to play and hear. Still, I was the proud possessor of a violin, and that was something. That very afternoon we had a visit from a musical acquaintance with an elementary knowledge of the instrument who showed me how to hold the violin (how unpleasantly awkward, I thought) and even to draw a squeaky bow over the open strings. For the next few days I must have driven the household nearly mad with the endless repetition of these intervals of fifths probably more doubtful of intonation than an abandoned hand organ would have been. In self-defense, no time was lost in procuring a teacher; and school, reopening after the Christmas holidays, soon brought a welcome respite to sorely tried nerves.

Ulpiano Chiti was my first teacher's name. He was a hunchback, which, in superstitious Italy, is a good omen. He was, moreover, an uncommonly fine player. His somewhat impatient temper militated against his efforts with most pupils, and many wiseacres shook their heads when their advice, that I should be placed under the more pedagogical and painstaking Maestro Faini, went unheeded. Chiti was a brilliant violinist, yes, but as a teacher. . . . Perhaps the advice was too abundant, however, or perhaps parental sales resistance had a touch of obstinacy. In any case, Chiti was called in and work was begun. He was, I am told, astonished to find a beginner who had what he called a natural position and, above all, whose bow arm was already free and straight. It wasn't possible, he said (unless this was purely family propaganda), that I had had no previous lessons. He also said much more of a nature to delight parents and no one else!

I was not to be the only débutant in music in my family. My brother, awakening to the fact that he was missing a most desirable train, proposed that he, too, should study an instrument. The cello was suggested as suitable to his seniority. In the family, therefore, there existed an embryo trio.

Boardman's teacher, Adolfo Castagnoli, was not a hunchback, but I was consoled by the fact that nature had denied him legs; he was a dwarf. Our lessons and practice hours had to be fitted in with school, and, as I look back, it must sometimes have been like a Chinese puzzle to do so. However, my mother was a good manager at this sort of thing and, of course, it was easier to do in a country where the distractions for the young are not quite so imperative or so constant as they are in America.

Chiti did not sustain his reputation for impatience. On the contrary, no one could have been gentler in his painstaking care for every detail during the initial lessons. That he had taken a special fancy to me cannot, I think, be doubted, and it was not until I had progressed a bit that I learned how swift a rap of the bow on my unprotected knuckles a momentary slip would provoke. It was a sharp reminder to be more careful in practice hours; a reminder, it must be confessed, that was not always followed. Too many times natural facility successfully cloaks a lack of industry. Out of the corner of his eye the small boy watches to see if he has gotten away with it. Sometimes he has, but momentary elation soon leads him into the inviting trap of repetition—and the knuckles sting once more.

First pieces are rapidly learned. They are received in family circles with an astonishment out of all proportion to their merit. All the latent exhibitionism of parenthood comes to the fore at such moments, and there never seems to be a lack of docile and long-suffering friends and relatives resigned to endure with appropriate cries of wonder these elementary efforts.

I must have been an abominable youngster. Undersized and frail-looking, with altogether too much hair, rebellious to either comb or curling (it was part of the torment of childhood in those days that the curling iron was used without regard to protests), I would stand up to play with an assurance I should have been far from feeling. If, once in a while, I demurred, there was a chorus of such reproach that obstinacy was soon broken; and on at least one long-remembered occasion this little brat was heard to sigh, "Oh, I wish I wasn't so talented!" This produced a laugh which I was far from understanding at the time, but, to this day, I don't remember whether it gained me a reprieve from playing.

Although our winters were spent abroad, we almost invariably returned home for the summer to the Jersey coast so highly disdained by Aunt Sally. There was an unbelievable contrast between these Italian winters and our American summers. Long school hours in Florence were not so great a deterrent to practicing as were the insistent and pressing details of outdoor life at Monmouth Beach, with swimming, baseball, and all the distractions that shower themselves with such prodigality on our young. A less determined woman than my mother would, I think, have despaired of keeping us (especially me) up to the mark with daily scales and exercises. With a patience that defies description she would sit by the hour at the piano, poised to pounce on the least infraction of intonation; but even so, it was destined to be a losing game until the services of a regular teacher were available.

They were ideally found in the person of old Juan Buitrago, a South American of Spanish parentage, who lodged near us in Monmouth Beach and gave me daily instruction. He was no such player as Chiti; but he was an excellent drill master with a perseverance that was as obstinate as his nature was mild. He had the courtly manners of a Spanish grandee, but the gentle behavior of Ferdinand the Bull. I never heard a harsh word from his lips, nor an unkind sentiment about anyone. Aunt Sally took to him at once in spite of his broken English, heavily laden with Spanish phrases. She never succeeded in teaching him bezique, her favorite game; but daily she enlisted his services in reading aloud the obituary notices from the newspaper, with an occasional account of a local murder, followed by one of the Psalms. These Mr. Buitrago would intone majestically and emotionally with more regard to sound than to sense. Nothing daunted, Aunt Sally would lean forward with absorbed interest and never fail to exclaim, "How beautifully you do read, Mr. Buitrago!"

I have often wondered about my father's rather difficult role through the years of my musical development. It must have been at first trying, and finally alarming, this headlong pursuit of a profession so alien to his own business career, and then regarded as of doubtful masculinity. I cannot recall that he ever, by word or action, opposed it and it is with a certain wonder that I pay tribute to a great and broadminded pliability toward something that he must have sensed was inevitable. As for myself, there were no doubts—no sidesteppings from the road I had undertaken. There were minor discouragements, but they sprang from dissatisfaction with accomplished results and not from any uncertainty as to what could be achieved. As I said, I must have been an unattractively pugnacious child.

In contrast to me, Boardman was much more studious at school, modest and self-effacing, with none of the egocentric qualities that gave me such a surface assurance. His progress on the cello was less marked than mine on the violin. Above all, he hated playing for people and often rebelled against it more effectively than I did, although he would join Mother and me readily enough in trios which, beginning modestly, emerged finally into the more ambitious ones. He had, and has, a quality of mind far superior to mine in its intransigent search for truth coupled with the reflective judgment of a philosopher. His superior reputation in school prepared an excellent toboggan down which I often slid with insufficient preparation. Even my mother's disciplinary technique stood a little in awe of his argumentative powers. And sure as she was that music was my destiny, she was just as sure that the law was his goal.

From time to time in Florence we were asked to perform at local benefit concerts. These were events that filled me with feverish anticipation. Fortunately they did not occur too often, nor was their importance unduly dwelt on. Once there was an appearance before visiting royalty. The Duke of Connaught, while paying his respects to his mother, old Queen Victoria, then a temporary resident at the Villa Palmieri, attended a small concert where we were performing. A trio (by Carl Böhm, I think) opened the program. I was sawing away vigorously— spurred on, perhaps, by the presence of a Royal Highness (he

[29]

was doubtless asleep)—when in the midst of a florid passage my E string broke. What was to be done? To stop was impossible, unthinkable. A term, lèse-majesté, recently read in some history book (or was it *Ivanhoe* or *The Talisman?*), flashed through my mind. What it meant, I certainly didn't know, but I was convinced that it would apply here, and with dire results.

All of a small boy's ingenuity was applied to transposing passages from the E to the A string. It took me into higher ranges of position than I could conveniently manage. I plunged intrepidly forward, but I hate to think what the audible results were like. The intonation must have been painful. The audience, having recorded the incident more with its eyes than its ears, gave us a generous accolade at the close of the trio. The day was saved. Even the Duke must have awakened, for he joined politely in the applause.

There were long and exaggerated reports of my prowess in local papers, and dazzling predictions were made. I was more pleased than I was convinced, for I knew that it had not been a good performance. Gratitude for the help of an overfriendly audience, however, persisted; the sense has never left me, that facing me from the stage is a group of allies, not enemies. It goes a long way toward dissipating self-consciousness.

At another of these benefit concerts, while I was tuning up I became aware of an uncontrollable ripple of laughter running through the audience. I looked down and saw ample cause for dismay. Dressing too hastily in the excitement preceding the concert, I had neglected to button a certain part of my short breeches. The omission was repaired there and then on the stage, accompanied by the now hilarious laughter of the entire house. I was, it must be said, more bewildered than embarrassed. But Boardman, standing in the wings, bore the mortification that should have been mine. His injured sense of modesty later took me to task. "Why didn't you come offstage to button your pants?" My stout defense was that I thought it a far worse crime to keep the audience waiting. Why, I thought, make such a fuss about a trivial part of the unconscious habits of every male? I was still several years away from the wakening adolescence which abruptly readjusts such unconcerned nonchalance.

CHAPTER FOUR

ᗷOARDMAN and I attended a Franco-Italian day school presided over by Professor Domenjé, a French patriarch whose head recalled portraits of Victor Hugo. His noble countenance, surrounded by a mane of flowing white hair and a prodigious beard, was the complete symbol of authority. A glance from his fiery eyes (more often tender with affection) commanded instant and unquestioning obedience. He had a corps of excellent lieutenants of various nationalities, but the two official languages of the school were French and Italian. The different subjects, including history, geography, and mathematics, were taught now in the one, now in the other. There were also, of course, the regular courses in French, Italian, English, German, and Latin.

One custom which I recall with definitely mixed feelings was the morning and afternoon kiss on the brow. Each pupil obediently presented himself for this prescribed salutation on Professor Domenjé's raised platform which dominated the chief classroom. I don't think I would really have minded it except for the brown-stained lips and beard which an incessant smoking of vile-smelling Italian cigars had so revoltingly discolored. Perhaps, too, a recollection of Mary Jackson's " 'Tain't fittin' " played its part.

In the school attendance many nations were represented, although of course Italian boys constituted a large majority. There were French, English, German, Russian, and some Swiss students, but Boardman and I were, I think, the only Americans. Three days a week there was an hour's recess when all repaired to the schoolyard to play Prisoner's Base. On alternate days there was exercise in a gymnasium some five minutes' walk from the school, in the palestra adjoining Santa Maria Novella. I did not shine particularly in either pursuit. Prisoner's Base found me almost invariably among the prisoners, and I must have been the despair of the athletic trainers at the various gymnasium exercises performed so easily by other boys. I would try intrepidly enough, and was generally rewarded by a skinned shin or a bloody nose. It was not, it must be confessed, a mark of courage so much as of a degree of recklessness—the same recklessness that prompted me to try on my fiddle any difficulty, however beyond my ability.

In those days Florence was an enchanting city, proudly conscious of its early years of republican tenacity. There was a quality of thought shared by every Tuscan son which tended to carry on this tradition. "Il Fiorentino che protesta" was not merely an adage; it was bred in the blood and bone of every citizen, young and old, rich and poor. Rivalry with the great capital city, Rome, was keen and sharp. It was a breach of good manners for an unwary visitor to expatiate with too lavish an enthusiasm on the glories of the Eternal City. Rome represented, it was freely admitted, the history of the world, ancient Rome, medieval Rome, Papal Rome, contemporary Rome. But, it was remarked, ancient and medieval Rome was in ruins, Papal Rome was vulgarly ostentatious, and modern Rome was not fit to speak of. But Florence was a unique entity, the heart and soul of the Renaissance. Intimate, intact, and inviting, the spirit of a reborn Athens walked the untouched streets of Florence with light feet as in the days of Angelo Poliziano and Pico della Mirandola. Botticelli's *Return of Spring* smiled down from the Accademia walls, and felt not at all superannuated by any sense of a changing world. The same magical carpet of wild anemones on which these aëry figures stood was found every March and April on the Tuscan hillsides. Among those gracious hills and sloping promontories were many of the villas so carefully catalogued by Michelangelo in his survey. You do not visit Florence merely because of its incomparable museums or churches. Those are but details—wonderful details, it is true, but incidental to the city itself. The essence of the Renaissance is spread before you and is met at every street corner. The traveler who has failed to sense this has failed to establish even a bowing acquaintance with the Tuscan Queen.

Two American schoolboys could hardly realize this. To tell the truth, visits to a gallery elicited from me more secret admiration for the garishness of a copyist's work than for the masterpieces hanging on the walls—this, too, before I learned that I shared the feeling with Mark Twain. But familiarity is an alchemy that works with invisible industry. An apprehension of beauty first stirs, then slowly awakens, then quickens to intimate and ardent realization. I remember with what astonishment I discovered that I preferred the unpretentious façade of Santa Maria Novella to the arrogantly gaudy façade of the Duomo, many hundred years its junior. The conscious recognition appeared suddenly as a spontaneous revelation. This was, however, not really the case. For, quite subconsciously, it had insinuated its laborious way, so that at the moment of actual perception it had already taken firm root.

Our family pursued a course of persistent graduation from apartment to house, from house to villino, and finally, for one ecstatic year when I was twelve, to a lovely villa with spacious rooms, a lordly park and gardens, and *podere* (farms) stretching far on all sides. I entertained a deep and personal resentment against Labouchère, erstwhile editor of *Truth,* who took a fancy to it and, by purchasing it, ended our short tenancy. He was somewhat heavy-handed in the extravagant additions he made to the fine old house, and the Italians declared that he had made a chromo out of what had once been a chromatic fantasy. After his death and its subsequent resale, it was obvious that the Villa Christina's ultimate destiny was to be an out-of-town hotel. It was being operated in this guise when I saw it last. No refashioning, however, could steal from it the glory of its position and the beauty of its grounds.

Nanny Harris, our dark factotum, presided over the large household of family and servants. To the Italian servants her color was a mark of distinction; she was always referred to as "la Signorina Nenny." Besides being personal maid to Aunt Sally, she helped my mother and grandmother, Martie. She valeted Father; she saw that Boardman and I had our baths and watched over us generally; kept the keys to the linen closet, the larder, and the wine cellar; bossed the entire personnel like a top sergeant—and was immensely popular. Many years later, shortly before her death, I said to her during a brief visit to Florence, "Nanny, I suppose you're happy to be returning to the States so soon."

"Well now, Mr. Albert, I dunno," came her considered answer. "Seems as if Ah'd grown sorta Continental."

When Nanny was preparing her for bed, Aunt Sally would say, "I'm most home to glory now, Nanny."

"Yes'm."

"And, Nanny—"

"Yes'm?"

"Will you make me a little cornbread for my breakfast tomorrow, Nanny?"

"Yes'm. What else you gwine to tote to Saint Petah, Miss Guest?"

"Well," Aunt Sally would retort, "I reckon that inside the Golden Gates they can do with a little cornbread once in a while."

"Not too good for the 'jestshun," prophesied Nanny. "Not in discumbusted bodies!"

During the nineties, the aging Victoria of England paid two visits to Florence, living in the historic Villa Palmieri that dated back to Boccaccio's days; and she used frequently to send royal commands to Chiti for private performances. Her musical taste had apparently suffered a stroke of paralysis with Mendelssohn's death, nearly fifty years earlier, and the pieces that Chiti played for her had to be chosen with due care. The revolutionary surge that was convulsing the musical world never reached her serene and somewhat saccharine world of music. She would have recoiled with horror from any unprepared dissonance not sanctioned by the classicists as a symbol of that political unrest which she had so militantly and successfully withstood. "The

Queen," she would have declared, "can neither approve nor tolerate such license. And now, Mr. Chiti," she might have added, "do, please, play one of those delicious Songs Without Words that you have so delightfully transcribed from dear Mr. Mendelssohn's pen."

It disappointed me to learn, when my teacher recounted these anecdotes, that Queen Victoria had not been wearing a crown. What was the use, I thought, of royalty without the glamour of picturesque regalia? But I was thrilled when he showed me a souvenir he had received—a handsome violin case with what I took to be gold trimmings. They later proved to be only silver gilt. The Widow of Windsor was frugal.

The firmament of Florentine society was frequently studded with kingly stars. It was, for a winter or two, the residence of the newly married Prince and Princess of Naples (the present King and Queen of Italy), and their presence added luster to social life. Even the Abyssinian disaster of 1896 was a remote cloud in the distance scarcely dimming the gaiety at hand. Wars, in those days, seemed to have little connection with everyday life. One read of them in the newspaper with an abstract interest, but with less zest and emotion than was evoked by a dramatic novel. The Carnival was not less brilliant nor the Battle of Flowers less abundant in its display and attendance. The Opera and the theater had, if anything, more than their usual attendance; concerts languished, but not more than was customary. In Florence, concerts were but anemic stepchildren; bad opera could thrive where good concerts could not.

My mother was a valiant member of a small group—a mere handful—of music-lovers who would herd themselves together fifty strong, at each and every musical event that was offered. They would aid and abet any overambitious manager who tried to catch the reluctant public with the bait of established fame. During one season, I recall, we had concerts by such international figures as Eugène d'Albert, Pablo de Sarasate, César Thompson, Feruccio Busoni, and Joachim. The empty benches gaped, row upon row of them, but the faithful vanguard were always there, moving closer together and huddling their wraps about them. For the halls were notorious for their economy in central heating; doubtless each despairing manager counted on the heating to be diffused by the multitude—and the multitude always failed him. It took inspired playing, indeed, to temper the chilly atmosphere.

These were red-letter days for me. Sarasate was a bewitching violinist. His prodigious facility was coupled with an elegance of style impossible to describe. His tone had a silvery sheen and a piercing sweetness. There must, however, have been a curious quirk in his musical approach, for here you had the paradox of a player who made trivial music sound important, and deep music sound trivial. He played Beethoven with the perfumed polish of a courtier who doesn't quite believe what he is saying to Majesty. But when he reached a piece like *La Fée d'amour,* by Raff (hardly ever performed nowadays) or his own *Spanish Dances,* he was completely in his element. The violin sang like a thrush, and his incomparable ease tossed aside difficulties with a grace and insouciance that affected even his gestures. There was a kind of studied sophistication in the way he tripped onto the stage aping the airs and graces of Watteau's *L'Indifférent.* I don't think I ever heard a *forte* passage from his bow; his palette held pastel shades only.

Joachim, on the other hand, was built of sterner stuff. I have always regretted that I never heard him when he was at his zenith. By the close of the century his bow arm had weakened; the fingers of his left hand were cramped by rheumatism (or was it gout?), and his performance was thus hampered by insecurity. However, the structure of a cathedral remained, even if the stained-glass windows had been shattered; and a great musical line was suggested, even if a trembling bow marred its complete realization.

All these giants enthralled me, each in his own way, and many were the subsequent hours spent in vainly trying to reproduce what I had heard. There was an ironic justice in the fact that at about that time I had to learn by heart for school recitation La Fontaine's fable in which the frog is ambitious to grow as large as an ox. In art, hitching one's wagon to a star requires the strong steel cables of perfected craftsmanship. Though the piano appealed to me less intimately than did the violin, d'Albert and Busoni astonished me with their thunderbolts. It was as if two Martians had suddenly paid us a visit. They disclosed a world of wonders, but it was not quite my world. Of the two, Busoni made the more profound impression. He still had his beard then; was somewhat cadaverous-looking, and enjoyed a little less of world acclaim than d'Albert. When I met him later on, I recalled some of my impressions of this concert. He said, "Oh, that concert in Florence! Never was there a time when I played to so many people who weren't there."

The financial disaster resulting from this season of stellar attractions did not discourage the indomitable fifty; promptly they set about planning ways and means to reorganize. Social Florence looked on with tolerant, amused eyes, promising better support next season—a promissory note destined to vanish into thin air. One day at Princess Strozzi's (she was one of the ardent fifty) old Giuseppe Buonamici said lazily: "It's very like the story of Vieuxtemps in a town in southwestern France. The citizens besought him to give a concert in their city on his way south to Spain. He did so. He was greeted by an audience of seventeen. The seventeen who were there were mortified and chagrined. They repaired en masse to the greenroom to express their dismay that so great a master should play before such a handful. 'But, Master,' they said, 'on your return from Spain visit us again and you shall see how the whole town will turn out to do you homage.' Well, Vieuxtemps finally acceded and was prevailed upon to come back once more. This time the audience numbered sixteen—one of the seventeen having meantime died."

CHAPTER FIVE

WHEN I was fourteen years old Chiti proposed that I go to Bologna and play for the examining board of the historic old conservatory there in an effort to obtain the graduating diploma. It was, he explained, not necessary to be an enrolled student in the school. It was customary to allow outsiders to compete for the diploma, provided the set rules for the examination were complied with. The requirements were formidable. The thirty-six studies of Fiorillo and the twenty-four caprices of Rode had all to be thoroughly prepared, for the candidate drew by lot the number he was to play from these two books of studies. Next, a performance in its entirety of one of the standard concertos (I played the Mendelssohn), a classic sonata (mine was *The Devil's Trill* by Tartini), an unaccompanied Bach Sonata or Partita (I drew the one in E major), and a reading at sight of a manuscript from the school's library.

Besides this program there was an examination in piano (fortunately for me, it was elementary), and exercises in theory, harmony, and counterpoint. The ordeal lasted over two hours and was conducted in the old concert hall of the Conservatory. It is not a large hall, but to me it looked vast. Innumerable portraits of musicians frowned down from the walls. The judges sat facing the stage behind an oblong table covered with green baize, and listened to my efforts in funereal silence. I have not to this day outgrown my dislike of green baize.

By the time the examination was over I had broken out in red spots as though infected with the plague. My mother and Chiti were anxiously awaiting the outcome. They comforted me with assurances that I had played well so far as they could judge with their ears glued to the door that led to the stage. I couldn't for the life of me have told how anything had gone; in fact, I remarked gloomily that I had made a hash of things, and that of course I hadn't passed. The modest young man who had played my accompaniments offered further reassurances. He was some ten years my senior, an excellent musician, and a student in piano and composition at the Conservatory. Years later I met a famous composer, I thought for the first time. He said to me: "My memory is better than yours. We have met before—and played together."

I must have looked puzzled.

"Yes," he went on. "Bologna in 1903—Liceo Rossini. I have never forgotten it. You were an amazing kid!"

Could it be, I wondered? It was! My accompanist had been Ottorino Respighi. His enthusiasm and optimism had cheered me at the time, but I was far from convinced that I had not invited disaster by biting off more than I could chew.

I remembered the opposition that my application had aroused on account of my age. I was too young to compete. It hadn't been done before at so early an age. Come back in two years, or better, three years—that would still be on the borderline of minority. Chiti, however, had kept insisting that it had been done, or, at least, that there was nothing in the school regulations that specifically required the age to be such and such; evidently the archives had been studied before permission was granted. But there they were—all these handicaps, staring me in the face, each one whispering defeat in those agonizing minutes while I awaited the verdict.

I couldn't quite believe it when it came. The door burst open and the judges appeared en masse. Their smiles, their tears, their embraces followed in true Latin fashion. This was all quite promising. The senior violin master of the school, Sarti, stammered out something to the effect that only once before in the long history of the school. . . .

"Does that mean, Maestro," my mother interrupted, "that he has passed?"

"*Passed!*" repeated Sarti. "Don't ask me whether he has passed, but *how* he has passed. A maximum of fifty points is obtainable. Thirty are required to pass. Your son has passed with forty-eight out of the possible fifty. But," he added, "that is far from being the most significant feature of this examination. Do you remember our hesitation in allowing it?" We did. "Well," said Sarti, "on looking up the annals of the school we found that there had been one, and only one, precedent for awarding this diploma to a candidate of fourteen. That was one hundred and thirty-three years ago, when a young native of Salzburg presented himself before an astonished board of examiners headed by Padre Martini. His name was Mozart."

It was, I thought, an incredible accident. I couldn't quite share the triumphant complacency of my mother, or my teacher for that matter, who felt that it was to be expected. Overnight I found myself front-page material, not only in the principal Italian dailies but also in the press of Europe and America. There were approaches from various managers eager to seize upon so much ready-made publicity. Fortunately I was to be spared this premature début—was to have, instead, two years of supplemental study in Paris under Lefort, of the National Conservatory. The further study of counterpoint and composition absorbed me to a degree that actually threatened my violin-playing. In Florence I undertook a serious course under Antonio Scontrino, a dull composer but an admirable teacher. He was tirelessly patient in forming a well-ordered vocabulary to express musical thought with freedom, but the very freedom he was forever proclaiming as a desirable goal was the one thing denied to him. Throughout his life he carried the burden of one of the cruelest superstitions of his gifted Latin race: the Evil Eye. Anonymous and malicious, the attribution of the Evil Eye is the type of whispered slander against which the victim is utterly defenseless; indeed, he is often unconscious of its menace until it has irrevocably smeared his reputation.

I never knew whether Scontrino himself was aware that this sinister superstition had attached itself to him; that it was considered a breach of etiquette even to mention his name aloud; that if one did so, there would be a quick clutching of amulets and talismans, and the sign of the horns would be hastily made in order to avert evil spirits. This last safeguard consisted in pointing the index and the little finger of the hand outward while clamping to the palm the two middle fingers. Often, when I was on my way to a lesson, friends or fellow students would hesitate to walk with me, fearful of some untoward accident. A tile would fall from the roof, crushing you, or you would slip and sprain an ankle; in short, any contact with Scontrino—or with any person afflicted with the Evil Eye—was enough to invite disaster.

Once, while playing a concert in the old Sala Filarmonica in Florence, I was greatly troubled by sagging strings. As it occurred in a piece with no obliging rests during which I could repair the danger to intonation, I had to struggle as best I could. That the evening was both damp and hot was enough to explain this annoyance naturally—but such a logical answer did not satisfy the Florentines. They had another answer: Scontrino had entered the hall at the very moment when my embarrassing difficulties with pitch began! Reason has little chance to make headway against such poison.

Scontrino put me through a wholesome course of sprouts. He was meticulous in exacting a mathematical observance of all established rules. Rebellious youth often revolted against such precision, and I would sometimes confront him triumphantly with an example from an admitted masterpiece whose composer had indulged in liberties refused me in the schoolroom.

"What," I would ask, "do you say to these consecutive fifths?"

"They are beautiful," was his astonishing reply. "Imbecile that you are, how often must I explain to you that rules are to be learned only to be transcended when the right moment occurs?"

"But how," I pugnaciously went on, "is one to *know* the right moment?"

"When you are a composer," he reminded me, "you will not ask that question. No artist worth his salt writes merely because he wants to. If he does, his music is not worth the paper it is printed on. The only valid reason for composing is compulsion— an impulse to say this or that, impossible to resist. Why and how,

[41]

do you suppose, did Beethoven come to be called the great Liberator of music? By ignoring the established rules he was breaking? No: by first becoming a complete master of them. You cannot make a successful revolution without knowing what you are rebelling against. You *can* perhaps provoke a riot which will end in confusion, and face a firing squad."

Many were the firing squads my attempts at riotous writing had to face in trying to follow that thorny path. For a long time, too, I had to indulge clandestinely my enthusiasm for that strange and dangerous Frenchman, Debussy. The sweetness of forbidden fruit led me far astray from a world whose last word was Wagner. One day I impudently introduced a progression of unprepared ninths—quite inappropriate to the matter in hand, but it gave me a sense of elation. On my way to my lesson, however, I had a sudden mental picture of Scontrino's expression when he came upon this passage. I lost my nerve, consigned the manuscript to the river, and arrived shamefacedly for my lesson with only a stilted and simple four-voiced chorale. I was scornfully reprimanded for my laziness, but it was gentle castigation compared with what I would otherwise have received.

Curiously enough, I remember that fiasco of a lesson as a rather happy accident, for it turned out to be one of the most constructive hours in my student days. In the absence of work to criticize, it was Scontrino's custom to turn with me to the piano, where we would explore some masterpiece of symphonic or chamber music in four-hand arrangement. And it often happened that, if no other pupil was to follow close on my heels, the hour's lesson prolonged itself indefinitely. On this particular occasion he dealt impressively with the alchemy of Beethoven's revolutionary methods in treating a musical idea. I was shown innumerable examples of the progressive stages through which a Beethoven theme might travel before emerging in its final form. It was almost unbelievable to see how, with here an addition and there an omission, rough ore could be transmuted to pure gold. Noteworthy, Scontrino pointed out, was Beethoven's unerring instinct in the use of a rest for inaudible modulations: a sudden and dramatic change of key was masked only by an eloquent silence. No master before him had so successfully used this device, and few have done it since. I have always had a profound respect for rests since that day, and often search in vain for another Beethoven to proclaim them.

I began to look with longing and envious eyes at the prodigious wealth of piano literature compared with the modest portion devoted to the violin. With totally inadequate fingers I spent hours at the keyboard—somewhat to the detriment of my bow arm.

I had been so accustomed to rely on that natural facility which is a kind of birthright of children that in those readjusting years of adolescence and early manhood, when awkwardness replaces a certain unconscious grace and dexterity, I was amazed to find myself unable to execute a passage with the effortless ease that I had been able to depend on a few years before. Staccato bowing—that brilliant phase of the right-arm technique—I had apparently never had to learn as a child. Up bow or down bow, it had rippled off at any speed. All of a sudden it left me; at least, only a shadow of its former self remained, labored and halting. And just as suddenly it became, when missing, a most prized object. I had to devote many hours during my twenties to recapturing that which a prodigal providence had showered on unappreciative childhood. This time facility proved capricious and reluctant, and I had to relearn the staccato from the ground up. It taught me never again to be priggishly disdainful of details that came easily.

CHAPTER SIX

MY début took place in Paris when I was sixteen years old. Lefort, my teacher, led an orchestra composed chiefly of students at the National Conservatory. To my family and friends (and to me) it was an event of gigantic proportions. In two years' time I had shot up from the scraggly little boy of fourteen to some five feet, ten inches, a fact which comforted me tremendously. I had despaired of reaching the noble proportions usually attained by male Spaldings and was deeply ashamed of the constant emphasis on my youth, provoked in part, I thought, by my stunted growth. Clad in long pants, I was relieved to think that most people would believe me to be approaching the mature age of twenty. At least the horror of being classed as a boy prodigy was to be spared me. I nearly ruined my skin as I hacked away with a safety razor at a beard that wasn't there. But it was activity of a reassuring nature.

My chief pieces on the program were the Concerto in B minor by Saint-Saëns and the Bach *Chaconne*. In addition to this there were orchestral excerpts, a group of violin solos including the *Romance in F* of Beethoven, and the *Gipsy Airs* by Sarasate as a display piece. As was customary at such events, a singer—on this occasion a baritone named Charles Clark—had been engaged as assisting artist. Clark had a pleasant voice and I was awed by his calm assurance in approaching public performance as though it were an everyday occurrence. The audience, largely an invited one, seemed prepared to like everything; once on the stage I forgot to be as nervous as, doubtless, I ought to have been. It was pronounced an auspicious début and there was no lack of extravagant praise.

The elation I should have felt was checked to some extent by the realization that the indifferent deliveries were praised with the same fervor that greeted the ones I knew were really good. It was bewildering and tiresome to hear my mother triumphantly quoting extravagant sentences from such and such a critic, musician, or friend—to the effect that I had the *feu sacré,* that my tone spoke straight from the heart, that I was destined to . . . etc., etc. Sweet at first to the taste, it eventually soured on the stomach. More satisfactory was the wholehearted interest and (I believed) genuine approval of many of my colleagues sitting behind me at their orchestral desks. Their enthusiasm was a source of strength and confirmed me in my appraisal of the parts of the concert that had gone well. Best of all was Lefort's verdict. He mixed praise and pleasure in my success with a sober recital of less satisfactory details.

"Do you know," he asked me, "why you stumbled in such and such a passage?" I didn't. "Well, I will tell you," he went on. "Because, depending too much on your natural facility, which in ordinary circumstances is apparently unfailing, you don't take into account the added excitement of public performance. Where is your margin of safety to meet this? Yes, I know! You probably returned home and the next day repeated that passage ten times without turning a hair. But you were alone in your room, undisturbed by the electrical current produced by a thousand pairs of ears, with no hindrance to concentration. The intricate pattern of notes is fixed in your mind rather by ear memory or muscular association than by a clear visual representation of the printed page. Here, just try an experiment. Take this sheet of paper and write out for me from memory the entire passage, together with fingerings and bowing."

I tried and could do so only very haltingly.

"Yes," said Lefort, "but you hesitate. It is fatal to hesitate in a concert hall."

I murmured something to the effect that accidents were known to happen even to famous players, and cited some cases.

"True," said Lefort, "but in the first place you are not a famous player. You are a débutant. In the second place, I am not speaking of an accident; what I am referring to is overconfidence in the infallibility of facile fingers and an inadequate insurance against the perils of public performance. However," he concluded, with an indulgent smile, "on the whole, I was very pleased with your playing. It had depth and meaning and true virtuoso fire. Above all, it sounded like you. You were born to play publicly. Also, what is rare, you have that in your presence which makes an audience want you to succeed. It is like a present from Heaven. Only, be careful never to be satisfied with cheap victories."

Repercussions from the concert were flattering, but hardly profitable from a financial standpoint. For an aspiring virtuoso, the road toward self-support was indeed a long one. There was an occasional concert with a meager fee, and others at which it was an honor to play without pay. Among these latter were charity events. One that I remember with special interest was a gala affair organized at the Châtelet Theater by the renowned actor, Coquelin, for the benefit of dramatic artists. For this concert he had enlisted the services of every musician of note in Paris at that time. Singers included Félia Litvinne, Clément, Renaud, Delmas; pianists, Diémer and Lausnay. To cap all, that mythical bird of song, Adelina Patti, had been lured from her retirement in the fastnesses of Wales to lend the tarnished gold of her voice to the affair. Edouard Colonne's orchestra was to officiate at this Gargantuan affair.

Colonne had heard me play and liked my work enough to ask me to participate in several concerts under his direction. The length of the program planned did not deter him from asking me to take part in it. It was a signal kindness to me, even if not quite that to a patient public already condemned to some four hours of music on behalf of aged and indigent actors. A hastily scribbled note from him scarcely needed the admonition, "Vite, une bonne réponse"; the "réponse" tumbled from pen to paper, for I trembled to think how easily Colonne might change his mind in the meantime.

It was stimulating to a young fiddler to see his name featured on a poster along with so many celebrities. As a sop to the soloists contributing their services, an accompanist was to be provided. Probably French economy in the matter of his fee was a little too stringent, for the one assigned to me never turned up at the concert. We had rehearsed carefully and I was comfortably ignorant of my approaching difficulty. My first piece with orchestral accompaniment under Colonne's direction had gone well, and generous enthusiasm was showered on the almost unknown young violinist. A short group of violin solos with piano was to follow—and it was then that I discovered that my accompanist was nowhere around. Probably he had found more profitable employment elsewhere; or perhaps the hours of *cinq à sept* had lured him to amorous activities. In any case, he wasn't there.

At this juncture it was Madame Patti herself who came to the rescue. Hearing about the missing accompanist, she summoned me to her private loge, and I found myself face to face with the famous lady. Propped against, rather than sitting upon, a chair in a room smothered with floral pieces, she looked like an animated wax figure lent by Madame Tussaud for the afternoon. The heavily enameled face defied time, and I wondered whether she possessed a mechanism that could even produce speech—let alone song. But she could speak, and did. After detailed scrutiny, she asked me kindly enough about my predicament, and generously offered the services of her accompanist. Was I prepared to carry on without benefit of rehearsal? I stammered my thanks, willing to seize any kind of help; the one thing I couldn't face was cancellation of the violin group.

Patti's interest was evidently aroused, for she came and stood in the wings while I performed. Curiously enough, luck was with me and the pieces went quite at their best. Whether word had reached the audience of this incident I am not sure, but the reaction was of exciting proportions, and I had something approaching an ovation. After my numerous recalls, Patti again addressed me, her lorgnon and her face still in action. "Young man," she proclaimed, "you'll do!"

Patti's own performance was something I shall never forget. It was the masterly campaign of a general whose depleted army, ragged in equipment and lacking in munitions, has to be supplemented by the genius of cunning and strategy. Lee in the closing battles before Appomattox, and Napoleon in 1814, must have whispered some of their secrets in her ear. Or perhaps she could have taught them a lesson or two. There she stood, unafraid, relying on that unappraisable power built up by a thousand victories. First she sang Cherubino's tender air to "those who know what love is." Fortunately this song lay in the middle range of her voice, and a crack here and there was almost unnoticeable in the revelation of a tone that had once been precious metal and still shone with a kind of ageless luster. She sang it simply and unaffectedly, and it was deeply moving.

Later on, she was reckless enough to include an old warhorse written especially for her by Arditi, *Il Bacio,* and this was where the old campaigner had to call on all her tricks to mask a totally inadequate battle force. There were high notes that the aging voice simply couldn't reach, scales and roulades that creaked at the hinges. It promised to be lamentable. Standing in the wings, I could see Colonne frowning under his shaggy eyebrows and momentarily expecting the worst. He had, however, reckoned without Patti. When she approached a passage where she apprehended difficulty, or perhaps disaster, she employed her fan with telling results. She would start the scale or arpeggio with aplomb, the fan in her outstretched arm slowly unfolding. This would continue to the register beyond which lay danger. Then, with a sudden gesture, the arm would fly up, the fan snapped shut with a click, the audience would burst into a tumult of applause drowning out both orchestra and voice, and triumph greeted a *fioritura* or a high note that was never heard.

CHAPTER SEVEN

M Y father was a remarkable man. His share in the general rejoicing over what was assumed to be a fine success for his son did not cloud his practical judgment. He it was who insisted that, until I should become self-supporting in my chosen calling, there would be a general tendency to regard me as a dilettante; for I must not forget that I had against me the popular belief that talent must be born in an attic and nourished on poverty.

"With this in mind," Father would say, "there is little to be gained by giving so many concerts in large cities at a loss, when you can be heard elsewhere and be paid for your work—even if only a pittance." He reminded me that he had not in any way opposed my wish to become a musician; in fact, he had welcomed my initiative in choosing a career of my own. But this generosity, which must have hidden some secret disappointment over my not following in his business footsteps, stopped abruptly at any suggestion that I was merely to play at the game of a profession.

This was good judgment, good advice; and so it followed that—sandwiched in with some important appearances, usually on the debit side—I had a long apprenticeship in remote and provincial towns where often one emergency after another had to be met. I remember one experience in a town of southwestern France. Our concert company, haphazardly organized under somewhat doubtful auspices, consisted of a singer, a pianist who consented to play our accompaniments, and myself.

The singer, Mlle. Rozanne, was a soprano who had "THÉÂTRE DE LA MONNAIE" proudly engraved on her card, and she never let you forget that connection. She was an attractive woman with dark hair, and eyes that she knew how to use to advantage, but her voice was less promising. Head tones were produced in a peculiarly pinched fashion that constricted the tone, and there was a tremolo. Tremolo, do I say? It was rather a palsy that defied any approach to definite pitch. However, she used nice perfume and you can forgive a woman almost anything for that.

Madame Moreau, the pianist, was quite another type. Small, demure, and tightly Gallic, she held us (the singer and myself) in constant fear of a nervous crisis on her part. They were formidable, those nerves, and almost anything could animate them to violent action. If the program failed to make plain that she "assisted" (rather than "accompanied") the singer or the violinist, there were palpitations. If the piano was below minimum requirements, there was hysteria. And if the applause proved too feeble to warrant her responding with a carefully prepared encore, she was as likely as not to faint dead away. Mlle. Rozanne had told me that, when this happened, I could revive the lady by stretching her flat on her back and administering aromatic spirits of ammonia; so I provided myself with a small bottle of ammonia which I carried on all occasions.

Our remuneration was a percentage of the net earnings— promised generously but fulfilled meagerly. And when the pickings were poor this, too, meant difficulties with Mme. Moreau, though of a less violent nature. She was an artist, and, as such, above sordid preoccupations.

We set forth bravely one morning from Paris to Bordeaux where the opening concert of a series of twenty was to take place. It was not easy to find room in our second-class compartment for the vast amount of hand luggage that swarmed around these ladies. Besides being the only man of the party, I was young and totally unprepared for the helpless embarrassment that attacks all males under such circumstances. Having filled the available space and found it inadequate, we littered the corridors with an overflow that drew protests from fellow passengers and remonstrances from the conductor. Maritza Rozanne smiled at them all. Knowing she had pretty teeth, she smiled on the slightest provocation. She admitted her desolation, but what would you have? Well, it appeared that nobody would have anything. The protests melted away.

Having arrived at Bordeaux, we lodged at the Chapon Fin. Preceded by reservation orders, we were accommodated at artists' rates: four francs a day for bed and board, including *vin ordinaire*—such a plebeian title for a princely beverage! Wine is never "ordinary" in Bordeaux. Introduced so modestly, it speaks to you with the voice of a nobleman.

It was my duty, on the day before a concert, to seek out the prominent local musicians to whom we had letters, and to call on the mayor and other dignitaries whose patronage it was important to enlist. I performed my appointed calls dutifully, but blanched at the prospect of the mayor of Bordeaux. Later on, as you shall see, I was to become more intrepid. A visit to the hall assured me that everything was in good order; the piano (a concert grand of Pleyel's make) would, I knew, delight Mme. Moreau's heart. Tonight, at least, there would be no need for ammonia.

The program went well. A Bach Sonata that had been eyed askance as heavy fare for the provinces slid by unscathed, and Rozanne's tremolo was not apparent enough to mar the public's pleasure in her excellent diction and striking appearance. There were encores and generous applause for all, including Moreau, who had abandoned somber black for an audacious gray. The total receipts hardly fulfilled our sanguine expectations for, though the hall had been more than half filled, our expenses were considerable—including the special poor tax and the authors' and manager's fees—so that the sum remaining to be divided in three parts would hardly suffice for a diamond tiara.

Still, it was not too bad, we reflected. We had enough money for our hotel bill and for our railway fares to the next town, and even a little something left over. Best of all, we had a delicious evening snack at the Chapon Fin and, relaxed after the excitement of performing, found the world a happy place, especially when touched with the liquid sunshine of Bordeaux. Maritza

Rozanne suddenly found that I was her *chéri,* and Moreau followed suit. This new role both flattered and embarrassed me. Had the stay at the enchanted Chapon Fin continued under such auspices, awkward youth might have shed some of its callowness with unpredictable results. Too often, however, my mission was to be the bearer of unpalatable tidings to these ladies— a kind of weather-breaker, in fact, which is an impossible role for romance to play.

Our array of hand luggage seemed to grow rather than diminish with each stop. My ladies had a passion for acquiring knickknacks—*souvenirs d'une tournée artistique,* they called them. The climax was reached in Carcassonne, where Rozanne became the proud possessor of a bronze Napoleon.

"You will carry him yourself," I warned her, thoroughly exasperated, and at once losing any chance of remaining her chéri. And Napoleon was shipped to Paris—though only after I had been proclaimed a brute and an executioner of all delicate feelings.

We progressed with varying ups and downs through that favored land where every city is so miraculously unlike every other. Rozanne used to keep the greenroom door invitingly ajar so that prospective visitors would not be scared off before voicing their enthusiasm. "There is something about a closed door," she said, "that is definitely forbidding." I didn't press the point, although I felt that the open door was almost demanding in its expectancy. Often her tactics were rewarded. Once, we remembered with satisfaction, an enthusiast pressed upon me two francs as testimony of his esteem. The top price for seats was only three francs, and, deciding that it was too little for the quality of the concert, he was determined to remedy the matter. I demurred, but to no avail. He was aided and abetted by Moreau. "Money talks," she insisted, "with an eloquence unrivaled by words!" She was quoting Montaigne, she said, though I have always doubted it.

Another time we were approached by one of our listeners who was, it seemed, overcome by his emotions. Having been an artist himself, he was in a position to judge merit when he saw or heard it—and he was happy to assure us that rarely had he experienced such an artistic experience. He singled me out for special praise. Rising to the occasion, I said that of course I knew his name (which I didn't), and that I was deeply touched. He then went on to expand. His tours had taken him to the Orient, to America, both North and South, to successes far and wide. "And your instrument?" questioned Moreau, hoping that it was the piano. "The trapeze," he replied. . . .

Moreau was becoming more and more difficult to handle in the matter of pianos. We had to take pot luck with them, and often it was pot without any luck. In time I adopted the plan of writing or telegraphing ahead to ascertain the worst, but Moreau had meanwhile resigned herself to the inevitability of an upright instead of a grand in the smaller towns. "The idea of calling it *droit* when the tone is *gauche!*" she would protest—and I could feel a *crise de nerfs* just around the corner. In the politely formal world of the eighteenth century it would have been called "the vapors." That languid weapon, so delicately and yet so potently employed by many of Mr. Congreve's ladies, was revived two centuries later under less picturesque circumstances. Moreau was acutely conscious of its efficacy. Then, too, she must have argued to herself, Am I not, of these three, the one and only indispensable musician? The singer may be taken ill. Too bad—but the concert can still go on. As for the violinist, his absence may cause regret, but not disaster. The defection of both singer and violinist would still leave the alternative of a piano recital; worse eventualities have been faced. But lacking the pianist, there is nothing to be done: there can be no concert. Moreau never said these things aloud. She was an artist, she was a lady—she would have considered it indelicate. But she implied them with eloquent silences that trumpeted her protests in a way words could never have done.

Madame Moreau longed to play Debussy. Her ambition had been thwarted each time she proposed it. One evening in Toulouse, pleased by the polite reception accorded to her Chopin and Schumann, she returned to the stage with the secret determination that it was now or never. As an encore she played one

of the *Préludes*—the *Dance of Puck*, that gossamer thread of
suggestion that today so delights our metropolitan audiences.
But to the corseted prejudices of provincial France in the early
years of this century it was utterly incomprehensible. When the
piece ended there was a glacial silence. Moreau rose from the
piano, and it seemed to us, waiting anxiously in the wings, that
her pallor suddenly took on a new intensity. She walked steadily
enough to the greenroom door, her retreat not covered by even
the most meager patter of applause. Once she was inside the
artists' room, we knew that a *crise de nerfs* was at hand.
Moreau's eyes flickered. She swayed. Murmuring "the assassins"
(we? the management? the public?) she sank to the floor in
a swoon.

Maritza Rozanne took charge of the situation like a sergeant
major. "You have the ammonia?" she asked me. I had. "Good—
let me have it. Now help me to raise her legs over the seat of
that chair. Don't be afraid of her legs—they won't bite you!
While I work her arms, you let her sniff the ammonia. Not too
close. There, she's coming to. . . ." And then, with extravagant
and consoling terms of endearment (and who shall say they were
insincere?), she persuaded her beloved friend, her delicious cabbage, her ideal artist, back to a kind of tepid consciousness. According to Rozanne, Moreau had played beautifully; she was a
pioneer in the world of art, a soldier on the field of battle!

Meantime, the intermission which had fortunately intervened
to give us a breathing spell was stretching itself to dangerous
limits. Moreau was not yet in a condition to reappear. I had a
group of solos to play, but a pianist was indispensable. "Could
you," asked Rozanne, "play some Bach or Paganini unaccompanied?" Yes, perhaps I could. "You must announce, then," ordered
Rozanne, "that it is in answer to insistent requests."

"But no one will believe that," I protested; "and, furthermore,
I wonder if they'll like Bach unaccompanied any better than they
did Debussy."

"Probably not," agreed Rozanne, rather cruelly, I thought;
"but there is nothing else to be done, and anyway appearances
will be saved."

I was right not to be too sanguine about Bach in Toulouse.

But I salted and peppered the group with some Caprices of Paganini—one of which contained some rather spectacular left-hand pizzicato. I didn't play them too well, but they served their purpose . . . they saved the day. Toulouse applauded Paganini and was polite to Bach. By the time the group was over, the miraculous Rozanne had restored to action our indispensable Moreau.

The little town of Castres was a delightful place. The charming Louis Seize theater was one hundred and twenty years old and had been well kept. The gaily painted boxes of the auditorium shone bravely, with some of the gold leaf still bright, and the brilliantly lighted chandelier gave a gala air to the assembled audience. There was no multitude. Multitudes did not swarm to our halls. It was, as the French would say, discreetly garnished. But we had long ago learned to be satisfied, and even happy, with discreet garnishment. The piano, moreover, although an upright, was a more than respectable instrument. It was a fairly recent Pleyel with a good tone, and had been carefully tuned. All these reassuring facts we had learned on the morning visit to the theater. No need, I thought, to visit the pharmacy for ammonia.

Two days from that time, however, we were scheduled to play in Mazamet. The very name Mazamet had a somewhat forbidding sound. At all events, I was filled with deep distrust. So a wire was dispatched to the agent of the theater asking about the piano. In due time the answer came. It said:

CONDITION OF PIANO EXCELLENT—ONLY
LACKING IVORIES TO SOME OF THE KEYS.

The telegram was hastily hidden away where our weathervane could not see it. This would not be a *crise de nerfs*—nothing short of apoplexy would do justice to the situation.

What was to be done? Twenty years of inexperience made me weak in the knees. I tried to practice for the Castres concert and couldn't concentrate. Then, remembering the call I had still to make on Monsieur le Maire, I invited all the fairies of chance to assist me in a wild scheme to which I was clutching like a drowning man to a fragment of floating wood. The mayor was sympathetic and, so he said, a music-lover. Had he not accorded us his patronage? Was he not to be in the official box that evening? Castres, he assured me, would show how it honored the Lyric Muse that evening. I preserved the amenities, complimented him on the theater, the musical interest of his fine town, and, above all, on the piano.

"But, Monsieur le Maire," I said, "imagine my dismay at hearing from Mazamet this morning that the piano there is in a condition shameful, deplorable. No ivories on the keys. Is it to be believed? What a reflection on its municipal government! What a contrast to Castres!"

It was a wild arrow I had shot, but it found its mark. I saw the magistrate's eyes kindle with the zest of rivalry. I expatiated on the shame, the ignominy of Mazamet—and Monsieur le Maire was a willing listener. He was desolated, his artistic heart felt for me, he was chagrined at the shortcomings of his neighbor, but what would I? This was just the opening I was awaiting. He was soon to learn that I "would" a good many things. But the ground had to be prepared very carefully. I made a trial balloon of the suggestion that now was the moment to teach a lesson to this backward community that hadn't the decency to maintain a playable piano. Imagine the example, if you, Monsieur le Maire, would, in the service of art, lend your excellent piano for that evening! A service to art and a just rebuke to shiftlessness. I held my breath while official gravity considered the question. "But how," he asked, "could it be transported?" Vastly encouraged that there was no categorical denial, I ventured to assume all responsibility. The distance to Mazamet was but eighteen kilometers. A cart drawn by white oxen could be procured. And if Monsieur le Maire thought it opportune, a detail of four soldiers could be begged of the commandant of the small army post there; ample protection as well as sturdy muscles were to be had for the asking.

Decision trembled in the balance during the silence that followed. My trial balloon seemed to be going places; at least it had not collapsed, and I am an optimist by nature. Rivalry with the mayor's neighbor was a strong factor working for me;

little by little, I could see that it was winning. Sober officialdom gave its consent with impressive solemnity. The necessary orders were issued, and the following morning a stately procession was in progress.

In the meantime, we had taken the little branch-line train to Mazamet and awaited the arrival of our precious cargo. It came, finally, a bright pageant in the clear, wintry sunlight. The piano, swathed in gay bunting, looked like a strangely deformed sarcophagus, drawn by the white oxen and flanked by the four soldiers in their flaming red pants and blue coats. The whole town was agog and turned out first to see, then to follow. They crowded the narrow streets on the way to the theater, and there was soon a healthy waiting line at the box office doing the briskest business we had yet seen. By evening the house was completely sold out. That night we had champagne for supper.

CHAPTER EIGHT

Servants make me very nervous. They have a technique for deflating whatever self-assurance I have been able to summon up when knocking at the doors of the illustrious. And French servants are particularly skillful at this art. As I stood at the threshold of an apartment near the Place Victor Hugo, I found myself faced by a valet clad in his working jacket of dull red plaid. He eyed me with deep distrust, and his query, "Monsieur?" with that upward inflection of the voice, seemed to accuse me of outrageous intrusion. I looked around for my own voice, finally found it, and—stifling an apology—asked whether the Master was at home.

"The Master?" he repeated, in a struggle to understand this enormity. "The Master does not receive!"

"But I have an appointment!"

"An appointment? At this hour?"

"At this hour," I insisted, marveling at my boldness.

Reluctantly he consented to accept my card. It was a clean card, but the gingerly way he placed it on the silver tray suggested pollution. While I waited in the antechamber I reassured myself that the appointment was right, that the hour was right; but my reassurances seemed somehow unconvincing. Waiting, hat in one hand and violin case in the other, I felt completely defenseless; I expected the worst, but reminded myself that physical assault is not usual among the French. I could not, however, subdue the attractive idea of a hasty retreat. How easy it would be to slip out and find myself again on the friendly streets below! Before this prudent impulse could be put into effect, the lackey returned. His "Passez, Monsieur," indicated only a slight shift toward unconvinced compliance, but I did get in.

The living-rooms conformed to the usual standards of Paris apartments. A large salon that was not large—it only seemed large by contrast with the small salon that led to it. Both rooms were choked with gilt furniture, the vitrines crowded with bibelots; the walls would have regarded any space between the pictures that elbowed each other as a chink in the armor. The stiff brocade-covered chairs gaped indignantly at you; to sit on them would be an intolerable affront. In this assembled and forbidding array the black piano was a sober intruder. Its ebony nakedness looked like an upstart revolution against the intrenched tradition of a Paris interior.

I had thought myself alone in the room, and I was startled to hear a high-pitched voice with a pronounced lisp address me. When I admitted to my host's query that I was, indeed, the violinist Spalding, I was given a cordial welcome. Would I be seated? I sat, hesitantly. It appeared that pleasant things had been said about my playing of his violin concerto. I was flattered. Would I, perhaps, play something? I was glad to change the perhaps into a certainty.

Camille Saint-Saëns, stunted in height but impressive once you accustomed yourself to looking down on Majesty, could be genial when he wished. This morning it was apparent that he wished. It was one of those happy days when it seemed as if I could do nothing wrong. I had been warned repeatedly of his caustic tongue, but an early breakfast had providentially spread it thick with honey. He sat at the piano playing accompaniments with a marvelous fleetness of fingers that belied his age. He asked me mine.

"Seventeen? That is a coincidence. One-and-seven. And I am just seven-and-one. It is an omen. We must have a concert together. Would you like it?"

Would I like it? Then we played more. His knowledge of the violin and its possibilities was prodigious.

"Sarasate," he suggested, "performs that passage with a kind

[59]

of flying staccato. Try it." I tried it. "Not bad, not bad. But it sounds studied. It should fly out into space the way a dancer defies gravity. Try it again."

This time it pleased him. His eyes sparkled.

"A la bonne heure!" he exclaimed. "That is the way it should sound. Study it to be safe, but play it dangerously. It is, in effect, an audacious passage." Then again: "Why do you play this passage so expressively? You make it sound well tonally, yes—but it has no meaning. Put more gray into your tone here. Save the warmer colors for a more ardent moment. Ysaÿe plays this phrase almost without vibrato.—No, that is dead. I want it quiet, but at the same time alive. Once again.—That is better. You are approaching the suburbs of understanding. Once again. Patience! One-and-seven must have patience! Look at seven-and-one—he has a white beard and still so many things to learn!"

He had an astounding parlor stunt in which he delighted like a child. This was the ability to solfège at an incredible speed. The opening sixteen scales of the closing movement of one of his violin sonatas he lisped out with breath-taking rapidity as accurately as a finished virtuoso could have delivered them. And he seemed to revel in my astonishment over this feat more than in all my homage to his musical literature.

His piano-playing was remarkable: rhythmically incisive, individual, and with a patrician disdain of every obvious effect. It was lacking, however, in tonal beauty and tenderness. These were qualities he was quick to admire and demand in others, but incapable of imparting to his own playing. His rather brittle touch I attributed to the considerable amount of organ-playing he had done. Long hours before the keyboard of this great instrument have a tendency to encase one's hands in gloves of steel.

The invitation was repeated to participate with him in a concert in Florence. He was shortly to make a tour of Italy where, in several towns, festivals were being held in his honor. It seemed too good to be true. Plans for the program were outlined then and there. In addition to the concerto, I was to play his sonata and several other solos. Mme. Lili Braggiotti was to be invited to sing songs—some of his, and some ballads from the pen of her old father, Sebastian Schlesinger. Concerts in those days were not concerts unless, like dinners, the fare was more than ample.

This first interview with Saint-Saëns had lasted well over two hours. I felt that, as with royalty, the signal for my departure would be given by him when he decided the time had come. Nor was I wrong. With a twinkle in those eyes that would never grow old, he said: "That, that is well! Now get along with you. I have writing to do, and you have work to do, and—what is beautiful—a lifetime of youth to lavish on it. Allez, uph!" I went. My exit through the antechamber was attended with warmth, almost with respect. The valet had been impressed. Two hours with the Master! It was a diploma of a kind. Did Monsieur desire a fiacre? No, Monsieur would walk. In any case, he would illumine the dark stairs Monsieur had to descend. Decidedly, Monsieur had gained some prestige.

I returned to my hotel that day treading on air. After such a stimulus you want to stretch the twenty-four-hour day to astronomical lengths in the desire for unlimited practice time, to put into effect one illuminating suggestion after another. Even if you are unsuccessful, there is a light on the horizon, beckoning and inviting. Former results look cheap, indeed, in the light of new vision, and what one can do seems a pale counterfeit of what must be done. One precept I treasured especially. It had to do with the relationship of time and practice. It was not the quantity of work that counted, but the quality. "Never," the Master had said, "practice mechanically, or the mechanism will master you and you will be its servant. The utility of a practice period consists not in its length of days, but in the use you put it to; one may have practiced long and yet understood but little. That," he said, with the ironic and quizzical look that was habitual to him, "is a paraphrase of a great philosopher, but perhaps he will pardon the liberty!"

How strange that after many years it is a rehearsal rather than a concert that stands out vividly. In the intensity of excitement pervading everything you do during the long-awaited evening, events occur too fast for accurate mental photography. I remember a crowded hall, brilliantly lighted. It was the gay Pergola Theater of Florence. Not large compared with the vast auditoriums of recent years, but it looked enormous to me. Interest centered, of course, on the illustrious Frenchman in whose honor this festival concert was being given. However, there was also considerable excited curiosity about the American lad who was making his first appearance in the city that had almost adopted him. I think I played well, but how is one to judge after all these years? Saint-Saëns expressed himself enthusiastically, both in private and in public. He seemed to take a generous pleasure in sharing with me the great success that was his. The last number on the program was a purely orchestral piece, the *Marche héroïque,* and there was a remarkable ovation for the old master. To my surprised delight, he insisted that I accompany him to the stage. Hats were thrown in the air—handkerchiefs were waved—and people shouted themselves hoarse. It was a thrilling, an unexpected, an undeserved, accolade. The Count of Turin represented the King in the royal box. Resplendent in a dazzling uniform, good-looking, vain, and somewhat uncomfortably aware that on occasion even a Royal Highness must occupy second place in public attention, he joined politely, if stiffly, in the applause—careful not to be so vigorous as to risk displacing his monocle. I think the concert must have bored him unutterably. But princes are inured to ennui from an early age. It is part of the price they pay.

During his short stay in Florence, Saint-Saëns lodged at the little Hotel Bonciani, an obscure hostelry "où on mange bien sans peur d'être embêté." He came once to dine with us, however, on the condition that it be a family affair and that we give him chicken. He was denied meat—bladder trouble, he explained, with that disarming Gallic frankness. He enchanted my mother by saying agreeable things about me, and she decided to like his music better than ever.

After dinner, which he appeared to enjoy, he drifted quite naturally to the piano and, to everyone's delight, started to play Bach and Chopin; later he asked me to join him in some Mozart sonatas. "No one was ever like Mozart!" he exclaimed, with childish enthusiasm. "One should really invent a new adjective when speaking of him. Transcending an artificial age, he is nature itself. Master of every form of technique, he is the soul of simplicity. What say you?" turning to me. "No, I suppose one-and-seven prefers Wagner. You have to be seven-and-one to understand and love Mozart!"

Saint-Saëns gave but short shrift to the autograph hounds. There were fewer of them in those days, but their methods of attack were identical "Master, please, just one line," shoving a leather album under his nose. "Impudent woman, take it away!" he would snarl in reply. We had been warned about this, and a long row of books were returned unopened to their importunate owners.

I accompanied him to the train when he left Florence. "Come and see me often," he said. "I shall watch your career with interest. Work!—work hard! Not only at your violin, but at composition. Above all, study counterpoint. Do a lot of fugue. That won't necessarily make a composer of you, but it will improve your playing—give it more character. So! Good luck, and au revoir."

CHAPTER NINE

IN the Edwardian era, London lived a kind of defensive prolongation of the Gay Nineties, impregnable to the assaults of the twentieth century. "So you are going to try your luck in London," an old French musician said, on the eve of my departure for the British capital. "Well, let me give you a word of advice. Don't be disappointed if your first results seem to be tepidly negative. It is the Londoner's habit to chill you with a refrigerating tolerance before admitting you to the warmth of his fireside affections. Remember, too, his prejudice against central heating. . . . I predict that you will freeze in more ways than one. But don't let that disturb you. Playing in London is like taking out an insurance policy against one's declining years."

"But," I objected, with all the tenacious confidence of youth, "see the success that Vecsey has had, that Elman has had. It seems to me that London can like the very young, too."

"Ah, yes," he countered, "but *they* wore short pants. I like you better in your long trousers, but London will like you less. London takes quickly to the very old and the very young. You are neither. You are a callow youth whose talent will be scrutinized through a skeptical microscope. If you are passed upon with tolerant interest, it is enough. It is much more if you are asked to return, even if the invitation is accompanied by patronizing admonitions. You will find it all very disconcerting. Don't let it discourage you."

His predictions were painfully true. I was to remember them ruefully. Every young artist envisages a campaign in a new

[64]

country with a kind of Caesarian anticipation. Perhaps this will be the place where dreams come true; where "I came, I saw, I conquered" is turned from wishful thinking into reality.

Armed with useful letters of introduction and high hopes, I arrived. The Channel crossing had been grim and gray and cold —and rough. "Why is it," I wondered, "that a usually good sailor on the stormiest seas of the Atlantic should find himself so upset by this impudent little arm of the sea?" However, I felt better after a cup of strong tea at the Dover station while I waited for the train. And the excellent manners of custom officials, railroad guards, and station porters further helped my morale.

Just before the departure of the train I discovered, with some dismay, that my compartment was in a car of the old-fashioned, non-corridor type in which the passenger who has imprudently taken tea is painfully reminded of the absence of indispensable conveniences. There was just time—and none to spare—for me to avert this threat to both comfort and dignity. England, like my own country, imposes a rigid censorship on any mention of physical needs, however imperative. The Latins are more frankly and articulately comfortable about these things and, I thought, infinitely more civilized.

The short November afternoon robbed me of any glimpse of the lovely country between Dover and London. On such a journey you press your face to the black windows, you try to picture through the darkness those stretches of smiling landscape you have so often read about. When imagination runs dry, you turn to the bulky newspapers—so unlike ours, and indeed so unlike the Continental dailies. British newspapers carry reticence to the furthest degree. The front page, innocent of any breath of news, is devoted entirely to polite advertisements, and the really important news is hidden away on the inside pages. To find it, you have to go through Court decisions (Smith vs. Smith), the cricket fields (Mr. Brown bowled neatly), and the intricate weather reports (apparently the British Isles were in for an indefinite depression).

I did, however, find my name on the *Daily Telegraph's* front page: among the advertisements there was a notice of my forthcoming début at Queen's Hall. Then I turned to the music page —and there I was again, this time as follows:

We shall likewise during the current week have the opportunity of appraising the gifts of a young American violinist, Albert Spalding, who has been exciting considerable and favourable comment recently on the Continent. He is said to have both neatness and fleetness of fingers, coupled with a correct style rare in one so young.

If this was a translation—or rather a paraphrase—of the extravagant critiques I had forwarded, it was, I thought, a tepid beginning indeed.

During the next few days, I presented some letters and paid some calls; I made a number of new friendships and renewed old ones. The Gordons were a delightful family in whose home I was often to find myself. They were musically minded in the best sense, and their home was a rendezvous for musicians, writers, and painters. Henry Evans Gordon was of that blond English type that is ageless, with a fresh, ruddy skin that could blush like a girl's with the quickening of enthusiasm—and his greatest enthusiasm was music. His wife, May Sartoris Gordon, had been reared among the mighty of musical and dramatic art. Her mother, Adelaide Kemble, was a famous singer; Adelaide's sister, Fanny, enjoyed even greater fame as an actress. And the next generation back recorded the illustrious names of Charles and John Philip Kemble, and of the Tragic Muse in person, Mrs. Siddons. The Gordons had four daughters: Jean, the beauty, was married to Major (afterwards General) Furse; Margaret was soon to marry Arthur Stanley, then to share his successful political career, and eventually to become Lady Stanley of Alderley; Catherine, the eldest, and Molly, the youngest, even then showed the vague but unmistakable signs that point to spinsterhood. I found all of them bewilderingly attractive. My favorite was Margaret, and I remember how I secretly resented her engagement.

Mr. and Mrs. Gordon were the soul of generous hospitality and made me feel at home at once. I was told to come when and as often as I wished. I wished very often. They lived in a comfortable old house in Cadogan Square that had been her mother's.

[66]

Here the lovely Adelaide Kemble Sartoris had revived memories of her too-short career by singing to her friends of the musical world. Here Liszt had often come; here, too, Mendelssohn had brought the young Joachim to play his first soirée for the London audience that was still—at the time of this visit of mine in 1906—faithful and adoring. The red damask on the walls was a little frayed; the strips of needlepoint that bordered it at the ceiling were somewhat worn; the whole room breathed an air of proud and gentle shabbiness. But it had an air—people had been happy and life had been interesting in this room.

Two nights before my concert I played there for a few invited guests. The Henry Woods; the Landon Ronalds; that forbidding and terrifying old wit, Gilbert; the Egerton Castles, and others who contributed to the *Who's Who* effect. I played first some unaccompanied Bach—the Adagio and Fugue from the G minor Sonata. I thought it went uncommonly well and wondered whether my hearers would think my fingers both "neat and fleet." As a matter of fact, they did. My efforts were acclaimed with a very un-British and gratifying warmth. I was pressed to play more and more. I did so, feeling that the world was an enchanting place.

Old Victor Maurel, the renowned French baritone, was there. He liked my playing, and asked whether I had ever heard him sing. Alas, I hadn't, but could assure him that I realized his renown. Though gratifying, this was not enough. He said, "I will sing for you." I was delighted, but didn't see quite how it was to be done. . . . Had he brought any music? He hadn't, but the versatile Landon Ronald was at hand to accompany him from memory.

Maurel then sang the "Credo" from *Otello,* bits of *Falstaff,* and Don Giovanni's Serenade. His voice, like the damask on the wall, had gone threadbare, but the majesty of an undying art was still there. He couldn't possibly have sung a real forte. He had to suggest it, but how he suggested it! After all these years it is Maurel's portrayal of the naked villainy of Iago, the sophistical and Rabelaisian philosophy of Falstaff, the elegant and unscrupulous licentiousness of the Spanish Don that I recall each time that I hear this music. He sang also a little song by Massenet—a rather cheap and sugarcoated morsel in which an old gallant recalls to his Marquise when and where she wore a dress of white satin. Maurel whispered this not-too-distinguished text with a kind of magical subtlety that was transfiguring. One could all but smell the perfume from that white satin dress and hear the swish of its flounces as it rounded a corner.

Forty-eight hours later my concert had been played. There had been applause; there had been encores; there was a crowded greenroom, and some extravagant compliments—but I knew it had not quite clicked. Nor was I to be consoled the following morning by having a "brilliant" press. The press was good, it expressed genuine enthusiasm; there were, so my jubilant manager informed me, many usable lines—excellent, so he said, for the box office. But here, too, I felt a reticence, a qualification. No, the Caesarian dream was not yet to be realized. The French musician had been right in his prophecies. London was not a citadel to be carried by assault. At least, not by me.

Although the front doors to success were not to open wide, there were many side doors, modest but for the time being satisfying, and I did not lack opportunities to be heard. Concerts in many drawing-rooms—sometimes with fees, more often without—and an occasional engagement in the provinces marked the slow progress of the campaign.

My most important London appearance was an engagement by the London Symphony Orchestra to appear on their regular series. The conductor was that renowned, that almost legendary figure, Hans Richter. What a name to conjure with! I felt myself suddenly linked with the illustrious past. Had he not been the friend of Brahms, the friend and apostle of Wagner? The *Meistersinger* had had its first hearing under his baton.

For my appearance he chose the Saint-Saëns concerto. It was, I thought, a very French work for so German a musician to choose. Later on I was to learn that my appearance at this concert and Richter's choice of concertos had been brought about by a brief note to him from Saint-Saëns. The old French master had been as good as his word. "Rest assured," he had told me, "that I shall not forget to spread good news of your playing."

The concerto was comfortably in my fingers, but I nevertheless spent many hours in repolishing. Yesterday's "good enough" would never do for tomorrow's ordeal. That is always the way with a fresh test, a new challenge to endeavor. As the morning rehearsal approaches, you are more easily assailed by doubt than fortified by conviction. Conviction often returns in time for the evening concert, but it is invariably a truant at rehearsal.

Richter proved formidable-looking. He growled rather than spoke his "Good morning" in response to my timid salutation. "He has a head," I thought, "somewhat like Socrates—though probably he hasn't a Xantippe for a wife, or he'd have gentler manners!" His reddish-brown hair and beard, shot with gray, surrounded a face that seemed to have been shoved into slovenly shape by blunt instruments. It had the effect of unfinished masonry. It did not invite assurance.

The opening of the Saint-Saëns concerto is dangerous. Bold strokes of the bow announce a vigorous theme proclaimed dangerously in the high register of the G string. My bow arm felt shaky, and my left hand seemed to have mislaid its security. I felt miserably and woefully inadequate. I fully expected a harsh condemnation to oblivion. However, I kept playing and, after a few unsteady and unpromising phrases, things went better. By the time I reached the sub-theme the violin was singing reassuringly, and as I successfully negotiated the flight to a high harmonic there was an unmistakable grunt of approval to my left. From then on it was smooth sailing, and at the end of the rehearsal Richter was actually jovial.

The concert itself went excellently, and the Queen's Hall audience was prodigal with its applause. The press, too, was quite extravagant in its praise. Best of all, Richter thereupon engaged me to play with him in Manchester. He was at that time conducting the old orchestral society so long associated with Sir Charles Hallé. The Manchester concert was a frosty disappointment. The concerto went less brilliantly than in London, but it had, I thought, its respectable points and hardly deserved the blast of condemnation that greeted it. The shades of Sarasate and Lady Hallé (Norman Neruda) were apparently at the elbow of every scribe reporting the concert, reminding him just how I had failed in this or that phrase to approach their unforgettable performances in this same concerto.

Richter found me the following morning half hiding myself in a dark corner of the hotel lobby, miserably reading and re-reading the uncomforting news. It was a gloomy morning. Richter lost his temper with me. "So," he exclaimed, "I find you wasting your time. The papers they are bad—so you are unhappy. Another time they are good—so you are happy. That is no way for an artist. I thought you were an artist. Have you forgotten that? Perhaps you think newspaper print more important than *my* opinion?" I found his irritation more comforting than a tonic and managed to say so. He went on in a kindlier tone: "Don't read notices! Let your manager do that—it is part of his business. It is not part of the artist's business." I murmured that I realized I had played less well than in London. "Yes," Richter agreed, "it was better in London. It is good that you know it. But it was not bad last night. A musician is not a machine, *Gott sei Dank*. If one were always sure of the same performance, it would lose life, lose interest. Those fools," pointing disdainfully to the mass of strewn papers, "see only the things on the surface. They are superficial. Don't read them."

"But," I dared to point out, "you yourself have read them this morning." He gave me a quick sidelong glance and I wondered if an explosion was coming. Then, with as near an approach to a smile as the old round head could manage: "Yes, *Esel* that I am, I did read them this morning. They spoiled my breakfast. Na, let us have a cup of coffee and forget it. It will be bad English coffee, but perhaps it will be hot."

The coffee they brought us looked like treacle, thick and syrupy, and tasted worse. Richter philosophized on the unmusical nature of those countries that had no proper respect for the coffee bean. Germany, Austria, Holland, the Scandinavian countries, even Russia—all lands of excellent coffee—music flourishes. England, France, Italy, Spain, Belgium—miserable coffee—music languishes. I longed to point out some notable exceptions, but forbore.

We journeyed back to London together. He told me many anecdotes of Olympian figures—Brahms, Wagner, Joachim, Bülow. With a kind of Homeric simplicity he brought these Gods to earth, humanizing them. Little personal details, weaknesses even, rubbing shoulders with unapproachable exploits. "Do you play the Brahms concerto?" he asked. I had studied it but had not yet tried it publicly. "Don't play it too soon," he advised. "Above all, when you do play it don't be too impressed by its reputation of having been written *'gegen die Geige.'* It is written *for,* not against, the violin, and one day—perhaps I shall not live to see it—the Brahms concerto will be as popular as the Mendelssohn." Though I could hardly believe his prophecy, I was not disposed to question it.

The next evening Richter invited me to Covent Garden to hear his performance of *Meistersinger.* Compared with today's smoother, more manicured exposition of this mighty score, there were many rough and uncouth deliveries. It certainly had not been sufficiently rehearsed to have elegance or perfection of detail. Much of it moved at a considerably slower tempo than was to prevail later. I was, however, profoundly moved by this great tapestry of sound. It still remains for me Wagner's uniquely successful opera. For once the imperative and compelling action depicted in the music does not conflict with the inertia of a paralytic stage—that conflict between eye and ear which all but ruins my enjoyment of Wagner's other music dramas.

I went backstage to see and thank Richter for the beautiful evening he had given me. "Na," he said, and he was in a very bad humor, "it was not a good performance. The Overture, yes! The Quintet, yes! The rest, it was bad, very bad. Yet," he added, with a touch of sardonic humor, "look at the reviews in the morning. They will be very fine. That is because I am old, and have a beard." He stroked my chin. "Grow a beard! You will see what an easy way it is to eminence." He was quite right about the press notices. They went into raptures over what they regarded as flawless perfection.

[71]

CHAPTER TEN

THE Gordons passed half their time in London, the other half in their lovely old country house hidden away in Kent. I used often to be invited for the week end. On my first visit I was thoroughly unprepared for the rituals and protocols of an English country house, unprepared to run the gantlet of appraisal which British servants subject you to. I was to be tried, and often, too often, found wanting. In spite of the unfailing warmth of my hosts, it proved a test of my self-confidence.

A good London tailor had provided me with evening clothes of approved cut, as well as day suits. I was, however, not so well equipped when it came to more intimate details. Nightclothes and underwear were things to be worn and not seen, and it troubled me not at all if they failed to match or if they showed a neat patch or mend here and there. Provided they were clean, I gave them not a thought. This serene unawareness of danger had a bad jolt when I found that I was not to be allowed to do my own unpacking. No—my bags were firmly taken in hand by a severe-looking valet called Jenkins. He asked for my keys. I felt foolish as I confessed that I never locked my bags. He let this pass as regrettable, but not highly important.

"Black tie, tonight, sir," he announced. "Dinner is at eight. I shall have your hip-bath ready for you at seven-fifteen." I had had a bath that morning and would have liked to dispense with another one, especially in the chilly atmosphere of my bedroom; but he looked very firm about it, so I decided to say nothing. Meantime he was approaching my bags with a businesslike air.

I recalled the hospitable warmth downstairs and fled, leaving him in full possession of the field.

Tea at the Gordons'—such a little phrase for so important an event. This was no ladies' affair of dangerously tilted teacups and party food. This was a man-sized meal. Everyone sat at a substantial table in the corner of the living-room, a table laden with scones, crumpets, sandwiches, thin slices of bread and butter with jam or marmalade, heavy fruitcake, and tea that had been gathering strength in a cavernous teapot, tea with a kick to it, tea with a loudspeaker—in short, British tea. It fortifies you against fog, it defies the cold without and the not altogether tempered chill within, it speaks with authority. We sat down at the table, sharing an intimacy that is absent from every other meal.

How had it gone with Richter? I must tell them everything. I emphasized the London performance (of which they had heard) and minimized the Manchester; those disapproving Midland ghosts seemed far away from this pleasant interior. Besides Mr. and Mrs. Gordon, three of their daughters, and myself, there were several young men who may have been prospective suitors, and Vivien Scovel, a pretty cousin on the American side of the Sartoris family—her mother had been Nellie Grant. Vivien, before her marriage to Fred Scovel, had with her sister, Rosie, been partly brought up by the Gordons. "But," said Margaret Gordon, "Marmy could do nothing with them—they were always eloping!" Apparently the elopements had not been serious. . . . Marmy—Mrs. Gordon—presided at the tea table. She was tolerant, tender, witty, altogether adorable. Less articulate than her enthusiastic husband, she was nonetheless the pivot on which their household world revolved.

The conversation reflected a rich life of many interests, literary, musical, and political. Musically, the Gordons were pro-German; politically, pro-French. The recent Entente, initiated and promoted by King Edward, had their enthusiastic sanction. Many people in England distrusted this reversal of time-honored traditions and shook their heads as if to say, "This could never have happened under the dear Queen!"

But such doubts had no place in the Gordon house. I was

constantly reminded of their American connections; it seemed very un-British to speak so proudly of them. Did I know their cousin Owen Wister, grandson of Fanny Kemble? I didn't, but was glad to say that I had read and liked his book, *The Virginian*.

Lloyd George was merely a name that one was just beginning to mention—to mention and then peremptorily dismiss, after which he was never again referred to by name, but only spoken of as "that man." For he had, it seemed, been proposing unspeakable things, unheard-of changes in the House of Commons. It was not to be tolerated.

I hated to leave the cheerful tea table to face the ordeal I knew awaited me upstairs. But it was after seven and there was no way to avoid it. Should I, I wondered as I went up, be allowed to bathe and dress in private? It seemed doubtful. My evening clothes had been carefully laid out. Fresh everything, to the last detail. How often, I went on wondering, must one change from top to toe in order to pass muster in an English household? Had I enough spare parts? Still, it was a short week end; if worst came to worst, I could leave on Sunday evening. . . .

A clatter down the hallway announced the arrival of the hip-bath. Innumerable jugs of hot and cold water accompanied the top sergeant of the ménage. Unable to carry them all himself, he had as an auxiliary the "h'under 'ousemaid"—a bright, willing little blonde without whom I am sure the household could not have functioned. Jenkins looked at me with disapproval when he saw that I had not yet undressed. "Your bath will be ready, sir, almost immediately," he announced. "Your shiving things are there, sir"—indicating the washstand. Now I had shaved only the night before, and at eighteen didn't grow enough soft moss in twenty-four hours to command the respect of a razor. I hesitated. Would I have the courage to face him down and descend to dinner unshaven? I observed his resolute expression. No, there was no use—shave I must! So I went through the motions of lathering a stubble that wasn't there, apparently to Jenkins' satisfaction. Would he, I wondered, at least leave me alone for my bath? Naked and doubled ridiculously in that absurdly small bathtub, I should have felt hopelessly at his mercy. I prolonged that unnecessary shave as long as I could and, providentially, Jenkins departed. Then I bathed and dressed at breakneck speed. Privacy was delicious!

Dinner had transformed the household. The sober tweeds of the afternoon had been replaced by the resplendent satins and velvets of the opulent Edwardian age. Ostrich feathers abounded. They were worn around the neck, they bordered the wide flounces of a skirt, they towered in stately dignity above the lofty pompadours then in vogue. They were also the decorative fan of that period. In 1906 and 1907 the ostrich strutted his gay plumage through English drawing-rooms, a symbol of his time. The dining-room was gay, it was decorative, it was cordial; but the intimacy of the tea table had departed. We were the same people we had been two hours before, but I felt we should all have to get acquainted again.

" 'Ock or claret, sir?" asked an unfamiliar voice behind my shoulder. Not knowing for a moment what " 'ock" was, I asked for claret—clearly the wrong thing to do, for we hadn't yet finished with fish. Mr. Gordon repaired the trouble. "Wouldn't you rather, Albert," he said kindly, "have a bit of white wine first with your fish?" I would—of course I would. But why offer a choice? It seemed one of those unanswerable riddles of social usage. After dinner, taking my courage in hand, I asked Mr. Gordon this very question. The tiny lines at the corner of his eyes contracted quizzically. "That," he said, "is a mystery, one of the mysteries we must not attempt to pierce. It is part of a game between masters and servants. The rules are all made by the servants. They enjoy the game. They cannot lose, we cannot win. It is hallowed by tradition, and—it is such a consolation to them. Doubtless the next time you are asked, you will not fall into the trap. Never mind—the butler will be intent on his next victim." It was, I thought, not unlike hazing.

Retiring for the night, I was faced with another ordeal. Jenkins was on hand to ask me, "And what, sir, may I bring to your room tonight?" This was plainly an important question.

Could I answer it correctly? I couldn't. After some hesitation, I vouchsafed tentatively, "Some cold water, please." His respectful acquiescence was tinged with rebuke as he said, "Very good, sir. And what, sir, shall I bring you in the morning?" He waited, sure that no American boy would know about early-morning tea. He was right. After an even longer hesitation, all I was able to murmur was, "A little hot water, please."

Could rout be more complete? But I was to score one decisive win over Jenkins. The following morning he brought me not only the hot water I had asked for, but also the inevitable cup of strong tea. I saw that he was removing my evening clothes. Before leaving the room he had approached the window with them. I suddenly realized that a shock was in store for him. My tailor had persuaded me to accept the new midnight-blue cloth: "It looks blacker than black at night." Truly, it did. But in the cold gray light of a wintry English morning it was unmistakably, it was accusingly, blue—and Jenkins eyed it with deep distrust. I thought quickly. I had slept well and felt intrepid. "Oh, yes," I remarked casually, "my blue evening clothes—very practical. Very black in artificial light. The King"—I paused at the invocation of the all-highest—"the King has just recently set the style." My chance arrow hit its mark. Jenkins was shaken. Some of his confidence evaporated, and in his departing "Quite so, sir" I fancied I detected an unfamiliar note of respect. It was very exhilarating.

English breakfasts are bewildering meals. There is an impressive array of covered silver dishes on the sideboard, flanking the urns of tea, coffee, and hot milk. The element of surprise is the main theme. Only at a village bazaar can you find a display of more things you are sure *not* to want. The saving grace is that you are free from scornful surveillance. The servants are absent at the breakfast hour, and your host and fellow guests are too sleepy, too busy, or too tolerant to notice what you choose. As I gingerly lifted the silver covers, I discovered one affront after another to the delicate morning appetite. I did not want kippers, nor sardines, nor mushrooms—were they, I wondered, left over from last night's hors d'oeuvres? My search continued.

Kidneys in brown sauce. Liver and bacon. At last, some eggs. Was I to be the only one with so little imagination? I watched with curiosity and to my amused satisfaction, everyone else took eggs. More and more had to be brought while the other dishes were left untouched. Apparently they were stage props to undefeated tradition.

Breakfast is disjointed into friendly segments. One member of the household after another wanders in. You must mention how fine the weather is, no matter how gray or threatening the sky, how gloomy the atmosphere—it is a matter of general agreement that in the absence of positive storm the weather is fine. The bashful streaks of morning light that timidly brighten the room need all the encouragement they can get. Desultory plans are made for walks in the morning, possibly a game of croquet. After lunch, a visit and tea at Knole, the show place of the vicinity.

Mr. Gordon had a pleasant surprise for me. He had just recently heard from Joachim. The venerable master was, it appeared, to be in Berlin during my visit there.

"I had thought," said Mr. Gordon, "to give you a letter of introduction to him. But I am tempted to go along with you for your concert in Berlin. Perhaps a personal introduction would be better. Should you like that?" No need to answer; my delight was evident. "Very well, then. It is settled. When do we start?" It was to be the following week.

Joachim did not attend my Berlin concert, but he arranged an appointment at his house, where I was to play for him. It was an exciting moment. I had hopes of taking a few lessons from the master. Mr. Gordon and I arrived punctually at the appointed hour. Joachim received us with great kindness; he evidently had a deep and devoted affection for Mr. Gordon. We spoke in English, which was fortunate for me, for my German was lame and halting. Joachim's command of English was perfect. He asked questions about all the Gordon family.

"They are more than friends," said Joachim, turning to me, "and have been since I was younger than you are now." He recalled Mr. Gordon's mother with admiration—"such a woman!"

[77]

"And what," he asked, "will you play?" I had a number of things for him to choose from—the Bruch G-minor Concerto, the Bach *Chaconne, The Devil's Trill* by Tartini. "In fact, an entire recital," smiled Joachim. "Play them well, and we shall listen to a recital."

I had only seen Joachim on the stage and was surprised at how short he was. The stage has a deceptive way of adding stature to those who tread its boards. Joachim was short and stocky. A leonine head and shoulders seemed to have mislaid its own figure and to have appropriated, for the time being, a totally inadequate one. It seemed utterly wrong to be looking down, rather than up, to so much greatness.

"You have recently played with Richter," he remarked. "How did it go?" I was happy to give him a glowing account of the London concert.

"Did the old bear growl at you? He generally does."

"Only with the greatest kindness," I hastened to reply.

"That means he liked it," pronounced Joachim. "Richter is not famed for kindness. Nor does he put any brakes on his displeasure; he lets it run downhill. Now, play me some of the Bruch concerto."

I played all of it. Joachim listened intently. He was pleased and enthusiastic; but he could be critical, too.

"The opening martial passage of the finale is too tame. There must be a quick, full sweep of the bow arm for that tonic chord —the whole arm. From hilt to tip the bow must fly with an irresistible rush. Here—give me your violin." Impetuously he attacked the passage. The result was not impeccable. His tired arms, racked with rheumatism, were rebels to his intention. The bow rushed in a bold sweep, but it slipped from the strait and narrow path. My Montagnana violin snarled in return. Joachim immediately repeated the phrase—this time, I noted, with a little more deliberation, and this time with thrilling effect.

"Now," he said, "you do it." I did. I was never afterward to play it otherwise. He had me play on and on; in fact, it was a full recital. He would not listen, however, to the Bach air which Wilhelmj had transcribed for the G string. Wilhelmj was obviously one of his pet dislikes. "He has an immense tone," said

Joachim, "which he misuses with a disgusting effect. His violin-playing amazes but tires me. It is never natural. It is like some orators who know only how to shout or to sob. One can bear to hear them only if the locale is as large as the Colosseum."

But, for all his generous praise of me, he was deaf to my plea that I might study with him. "No," he said, "the only way you could do that would be to enter the Hochschule in the regular way. I no longer give private instruction. If you entered the Hochschule, I should, of course, have you in my class. But I do not advise it. Your course is already charted and your career begun. It is a good course, stick to it. Above all, you have character in your playing; it sounds like you, and that is rare. I do not mean that you have not much to learn. But from this time on, it is your developing in yourself that is to be of value. Please, please, keep that simplicity of approach. It is really the shortest cut from mind to mind, from heart to heart. I like it."

It was time for us to be going. Joachim bowed us out. He was standing close to the admirable portrait that Sargent had recently painted of him. The room was furnished with the type of garish French furniture that must have been dear to the heart of Frederick the Great. A profusion of the most useless bibelots littered every table and crowded every cabinet that flanked the walls. Such artificiality to house so direct and simple a soul. . . . Only the realistic and lifelike portrait seemed really related to the man standing beneath it. It was the last time I was to see, and the only time I was to meet, Joachim. His death was announced a few months later.

CHAPTER ELEVEN

BESIDES the Gordons, there were many other English homes to which I was to be warmly welcomed, but in which I was to feel less at home. Part of the campaign was an occasional soirée played at discreetly modest fees. Once, I was noticed by representatives of our own diplomatic corps. An impressive note on Embassy paper informed me that Mrs. —— desired her secretary to ascertain my availability and my fee for such and such an evening. She was anxious to have me perform for her guests provided my terms were not prohibitive. I asked for ten guineas, having learned better than to speak of pounds on such occasions—in professional circles that odd shilling seems to lend dignity to the lowly pound. I thought ten guineas a very modest fee, but I did not want to lose the engagement. I did lose it, though; apparently my ambition had flown too high.

A few days later an inquiry arrived from a less impressive source. This time I asked for twenty-five guineas; at least, I thought, there will be a certain satisfaction in losing a more substantial fee. But that engagement went through without further discussion! It suggested a chapter from *Alice Through the Looking-Glass*.

From an economic standpoint this procession from drawing-room to drawing-room was hardly a royal road to riches. Furthermore, it was a severe tax on one's repertoire of short pieces. To introduce a long piece would have been to affront my clients' patience and was not to be thought of. However, it was progress of a sort: if you played enough ear-ticklers in enough drawing-rooms you could count on a respectable number of followers who might then attend your recitals even when a sonata or a concerto threatened to usurp time that might have been more profitably employed. It was a negative but time-honored strategy.

Once in a while I was vouchsafed the fleeting attention of royalty. There was the Royal Amateur Orchestra, formed by one of Queen Victoria's numerous sons, the Duke of Edinburgh. He was said to be a violinist of sorts and until recently had played regularly at their concerts—called "smokers." It was customary for the King to attend one of these "smokers" annually. My manager informed me with breathless excitement that I had been chosen as instrumental soloist at this year's smoker. There were, in addition, two singers, one of them the charming Suzanne Adams, of waning voice but winning personality. "In addition," do I say? That is ostentatious on my part. In vocally-minded Britain, it is the violinist, not the singer, who is the addition, usually considered superfluous.

I was pleased, but not enough to satisfy my elated agent. "Do you understand," he said, "that this is the one concert His Majesty attends? The Prince of Wales also will be there, with many representatives of Court circles and of the Diplomatic Corps." Whereupon—though none of this excited me half so much as a Richter concert had—I tried to appear properly impressed.

The evening came. I was coached in how I was to bow: first to Royalty, then to the general audience. The Queen's Hall had been quite transformed. The first few rows of orchestra stalls had been removed to allow a semicircular line of gilt fauteuils to be installed. In the very center sat Edward VII, and at his side the Prince of Wales who was later to have the distinction of being the first monarch to make the name George palatable to the British. It had been until then too gloomily associated with Hanoverian heaviness or a Regent's profligacy. The dazzling costumes of members of the Diplomatic Corps mingled with bright uniforms; it was an impressive sight. To be in a plain dress suit unadorned by decorations seemed downright nudity.

I played part of the Bruch concerto; the whole of it would have tried royal patience too far. It was not an impressive performance. The orchestral background was ragged and rough, and at many points I had to try to decide whether to press on with the strings or to lag back with the winds. Often there was a discrepancy of a beat or more between these two unneighborly groups which I tried unsuccessfully to bridge, with a foot now in one camp, now in another. The Adagio seemed interminable. I was playing, I thought, not too badly, but the ensemble could only be noted by its absence.

The King, sitting directly under me, not ten paces away, bore up regally. He was a sovereign figure. Clad in resplendent knee breeches of black satin, the bright ribbon of the Order of the Garter all but hiding his shirt front, he patiently endured such boredom as kings are heir to. Once or twice the heavy eyelids were raised expectantly. Did that last cadence promise the end? It didn't. The eyelids settled again. Next to him the Prince of Wales likewise fortified himself with a cigar—shorter, less regally handled. The sailor prince seemed far from that type of kingship patterned by his father.

The concerto finally ended. The last movement had gone with considerable zest and ragged brio and the applause was generous. The King and the Prince politely joined in. It must have been a comfort to have it over. Songs were providentially much shorter; and the group of violin solos with piano that was to come in the second half of the program promised by their titles to be engagingly brief. There was Schumann's *Melody in the Garden,* and that whimsical trifle by François (not to be confused with Franz) Schubert, called *The Bee.* This fleeting bit of fingerwork, which lasted but a minute, I had recently heard Fritz Kreisler play as an encore with his customary and bewitching effect. I used it on all dangerous occasions. But it was not to reach real fame until some thirty years later, when recognition by the unique Jack Benny canonized it. I speak of those more modest days when it was played by mere violinists.

The two small pieces did their work with gratifying results. Suzanne Adams, however, had the real success of the evening. She sang not wisely, but she looked too well not to provide the major enjoyment of the royal party. After the concert there was a brief ceremony of presentation in a special room flanking the foyer, set aside for just such occasions. Miss Adams dropped into the deepest and most graceful curtsy I had ever seen. "How *do* ladies contrive it?" I thought, and wondered if she could rise again without disaster. She could! I bowed as low as I could while shaking hands, but it was not so deep, and certainly not so graceful. The King murmured something—I never knew what it was; but I thanked His Majesty just the same. The evening was over. It had, I reflected, been a very dull one, but it was recorded in detail and at a length denied to many better events, for it commandeered the cables of the Associated Press. Clearly, in the Edwardian age it was important to pass a dull evening in the company of a king.

CHAPTER TWELVE

THE London season of 1906-1907 had interludes—some brief, some considerable—of visits to Florence. On each of these visits I resumed my studies in counterpoint and composition with Scontrino. They became absorbingly and increasingly interesting, often usurping the hours that should have been devoted to the violin. But I was recklessly unaware that there was any limit to the spontaneous facility which had, oftener than not, pulled me out of tight places.

Scontrino, too, was an unconscious agent in promoting this recklessness. He welcomed me each time as if I were returning to my real destiny, that of composer; and was, I think, not a little jealous of the increasing number of concerts that claimed my attention. Rather less success in performance would have pleased him better, although he professed great enthusiasm for my playing. Careful not to irritate him, I concealed as long as possible the date of my next departure. In the meantime, we plunged into a huge program of work: fugue, orchestration, chorales.

At home I was frequently called upon to play at social gatherings in the large, square music room of my father and mother's house. It was a noble room for sound and I always enjoyed playing there. Its acoustics were miraculously flattering. They persuaded you to your best efforts with the beguiling tact with which an adroit woman can make any man believe that his conversation is interesting.

Sometimes I played well, sometimes not so well, but the reactions were always vociferously satisfying to my parents. Less so, perhaps, to my mother, who was a good critic and would often take me to task after a sloppy performance, though she was careful to do this when we were alone.

The friends and acquaintances who assembled for these evenings were a strange mixture. They made up a pattern of society peculiar to Florence. British, Americans, Germans, Austrians, Russians, and some French (not many of these) formed the fringe around a carpet of native Florentines. At times it seemed as if the fringe dominated the central substance. It was indeed the city of clans and cliques. It was also a city of derelicts. Good living was incredibly cheap, and to this city repaired the victims of financial, and sometimes social, disasters. Did they hope to find refuge from gossip? If they did they were disappointed, for gossip flourished abundantly. If the gossip was at times vicious, however, it was rarely vindictive. I think that perhaps the Florentines were grateful for an addition to their rather limited conversational subjects, so that, though the newcomer might find his character darkened by scandal, yet his welcome remained undimmed.

My mother had a rare talent for assembling many of these groups harmoniously. She often succeeded in promoting, if not peace, at least a comfortable armistice, when they came together under her roof. Perhaps it was her abiding faith in the soothing properties of good food and good music that led her to attempt combinations which had daunted many another hostess. I can remember the astonishment that prevailed when the Florentines beheld Janet Ross and Lady Paget crossing the same threshold. It's true they didn't cross it together; it's also true that they rigidly maintained their distance from each other, moored to opposite sides of the large room. For years they had prudently avoided residential proximity; Lady Paget's villa on Bello Sguardo hill was safely distant from Mrs. Ross's villa at Settignano. A city and a river intervened—necessary buffer states.

I never knew the original source of the friction between these two great ladies. Certainly it was not scandal. It was, I believe, the conflict of ideas—something far less reconcilable. Lady Walburga Paget was a mystic, a vegetarian, a theosophist, and a dreamer. She was also something of an artist, without the energy to persevere with stark details when the delightful mirage of a new and less exacting activity lay just ahead. She was beautiful with the beauty that does not fade or disintegrate with age. It had, doubtless, changed from what must once have been a dazzling radiance to a sort of mirrored distinction.

Everyone knew and cherished Lady Paget—everyone, that is, except Janet Ross. Lady Paget's world had been the glittering diplomatic pageantry of the late nineteenth century. An intimate friend of Queen Alexandra, whose marriage to Edward VII she had done so much to promote, she could easily have preserved the contacts with front-page personages of every capital in Europe which life had abundantly afforded her. They were there for the asking, and often without the asking. A chance visit would sometimes bring you face to face with peripatetic Royalty enjoying the intimacy and cordiality of a casual visit that would have been all but impossible elsewhere. She never exploited these intimacies into anything approaching social tender, and her door was equally open and welcoming to others of less exalted status. Indeed, her interest in the mystic, in the occult, in the mysterious, sometimes betrayed her into downright gullibility.

Of sterner stuff was Janet Ross. She was not beautiful. No trace of her former comeliness remained except the fine, flashing, black eyes. As squarely built as the turrets of her medieval villa, she wore square-cut, boxlike coats and skirts, and square-toed boots meant for trudging through her *podere*. She had been the friend of poets and painters and of her own devoted peasants. She had not forgotten, nor did she let you forget, that she had been the Janet Ilchester of George Meredith's *Harry Richmond* —that Janet of the fine eyes and just a trace of down on the upper lip. The trace had deepened with advancing years. Mrs. Ross would have disdained any effort to obliterate what was now a quite pronounced mustache.

With her, often, came the Bernhard Berensons. They were neighbors and great friends. Mary Berenson was a lovely, gracious, intelligent woman. Taller than the average, she towered over her husband, around whose occasional and sometimes irritating cleverness she managed to throw a cloak of the most disarming tact. B.B., as his friends called him, had already achieved an august reputation. His books on the painters of the Italian Renaissance were quoted as gospel. It was, I thought, very frightening and not altogether human to be so infallibly accurate. His attitude toward music was, I had heard, distressingly intransigent. Had he not said: "No painter since Giotto, no composer since Bach"? When I knew him better I learned that this attitude had been grossly exaggerated—that he had a real affection for Mozart, and could even tolerate Beethoven at times. I felt vastly relieved.

There were, of course, many others who used to come to these musical evenings, but it is curious how memory focuses on certain salient personalities, and is blind to all others.

I used often to go to the Berensons'. She had, I think, taken a real fancy to me, and I was devoted to her. It was a rare privilege when I was invited to go with them to a gallery, church, or museum of sculpture in the role of a disciple. It was at first a bit bewildering to learn how much I had enjoyed paintings for the wrong reasons, but I was soon to find compensation in a new short cut to beauty and in certain definite standards by which to appraise it. Pictures, sculpture, and architecture took on a new meaning for me.

Sometimes I would be put through a regular catechism. Once, as we paused before a vitrine in one of the rooms of the Bargello where a great number of ivory figurines of the French Gothic period were exposed, Mary Berenson asked me, "Which of these do you like better?"

I was puzzled and embarrassed. I didn't know, but I felt I must make a stab at it. "This one," I said, pointing to a particularly benign and serene Madonna and Child.

Mary Berenson looked both surprised and pleased. "Why?" she asked.

I hastened to give my reasons. She looked less pleased.

"You have," she said, "given the wrong reasons for liking the right thing." I felt apologetic and murmured some of the studied values I had been diligently absorbing of late. It must have had

[87]

the dead quality of a recitation by rote, for I was given a disappointed though indulgent look.

"Oh, Alberto," she said, "you don't feel or believe a word that you're saying. I think I liked your wrong reasons better!" I did, too, but how was one to please the lady?

Near the Berensons in Settignano there was a fine artificial lake on the estate belonging to the Vincigliata Castle. It was an emerald-green pool, incredibly deep, its waters incredibly cold. I was frequently invited there to swim when the spring sun had become temptingly warm. In the spring, too, came Mary Berenson's two daughters by a previous marriage. Ray and Karin Costello had a wild Irish loveliness; there were apparently good looks on both sides of the family. They were older than I was—not much, but a year or two of seniority at that age counts painfully. They were both in college, I was not. They could both swim, easily outdistancing my best efforts. They were abominably superior to me in every way. Ray was particularly disdainful of the young fiddler her mother seemed to like. Karin, the younger, was more tolerant. She was nearer my own age and even, in time, got to like me. I admired them both prodigiously but was careful to keep my distance.

It troubled Mary Berenson not a little that I was not going to a university. She frequently urged me to consider a sabbatical year from music in which to take an academic course at Oxford or Cambridge. "Musicians, Albert," she would say in support of her argument, "are for the most part awful bores!" I was far from agreeing with her, but the rebuttal was a purely mental one on my part. While I seemed to toy with the fascinating notion of a year or two at Oxford, I knew absolutely that it was not my cup of tea.

For musical companionship and collaboration I had a new friend. Alfredo Oswald, a young pianist three years my senior, had recently developed the most promising powers as an interpreter. With a Brazilian father and a Tuscan mother, he combined some of the best talents of both nationalities. When we met there was an immediate sympathy, both musical and personal. We often played sonatas together, racing avidly through the entire literature. He appeared to like my playing as much as I admired his, and that intimacy so often promoted by a common love of music found us suddenly and spontaneously using the pronoun "thou" without preamble or invitation. The association was profitable to us both, I think, for our criticisms and suggestions were as free as only such a contact can comfortably sustain without friction.

After work with and for Scontrino, Alfredo and I used to meet, sometimes at my house but more often at his apartment in the Via dei Robbia in the "new center" of Florence. It was a modest apartment, too small for the good-sized family. There never seemed to be enough chairs, but I loved going there. There was an older brother, Carlo, who painted; and two sisters, one of them quite pretty, obviously in quest of husbands. The family was dominated by Signora Oswald, an ample Florentine matron who had an indulgent proverb for every difficult occasion.

She presided at the immense bowl of *spaghetti al sugo*. I cannot remember ever eating anything else when we sat at table there. There was other fare from time to time, but that alone would have sufficed. I had had enough training in spaghetti-eating to use the correct technique, carefully coiling the limp strands around my fork until a sizable and not too fringed croquette was poised, waiting consumption. But compared with the Oswalds I was a novice. They all talked at once, gesticulated violently, and ate all the while with prodigious speed. Emily Post would hardly have approved, but this was hospitality I heartily enjoyed. It was also rewarding on the musical side.

Henri Oswald, Alfredo's father, was a composer of distinction, and a pianist of the most fastidious taste. He had been director at one time of the conservatory in Rio de Janeiro. He would sit patiently by the hour while Alfredo and I made pilgrimages from one musical shrine to another. For so quiet a man he could be surprisingly articulate and convincing in focusing critically on one weakness after another. His help was particularly valuable in matters of phrasing.

In the spring of 1908, Alfredo and I were hard at work preparing for the American tour I was to make the following autumn.

Although it was his ambition to become a soloist, Alfredo had consented to play my accompaniments during the season of 1908-1909. The terms I could offer him were necessarily modest, but there was the opportunity to gain experience both in ensemble and in solo work, as I was glad to propose that he play a group of piano pieces at each recital. He had a touch that sounded as if, during its infancy, it had been cradled in Genoese velvet; and, considering his small hands, his agility and accuracy were amazing. You wondered how he could encompass an octave stretch, let alone a tenth. Indeed, his bravura playing was on rather a miniature scale. He could be bewitching in a performance of Scarlatti, seductive in the Chopin of the pale, nostalgic phase; but when it came to pieces of massive or epic structure he was likely to speak in falsetto when he should have thundered like a basso cantante.

Padre Oswald would say, "Coraggio! Stir up the embers. Give it more fire, more freedom, more stancio! This is Beethoven you are playing, Beethoven with the claw of a lion—you scratch like a kitten. Beethoven with thunderbolts—you are setting off a toy popgun. Beethoven, the revolutionary, the emancipator—and you hardly incite a street riot!"

We would return to attack the *Kreutzer* Sonata again. This time, perhaps, it went too explosively, for again he would shake his head. "Nah, I didn't mean hysteria. You must shake the rafters, but don't let the building crumble. It was the rhythm that went wrong this time." At it again and again, until he would say indulgently, "Basta. That's enough for today. Now you've taken the right turning. . . . Your road lies ahead!"

Alfredo adored his father, and I could well understand why. In this quiet Brazilian there was a happy balance of well-poised judgment and deep feeling that was impressive.

We spent hours, days, and weeks preparing program upon program. I have never enjoyed work more.

CHAPTER THIRTEEN

SUMMERS, as I have said, we customarily spent at Monmouth Beach, on the Jersey coast, and the end of June, 1908, found us there. The little frame house of 1880, originally two stories high, had swelled to two or three times its initial size. An extra floor, a tower here, an ell there, an extension on each side, had made it an unrecognizable but still lovable monstrosity. The rooms were spacious and cool even on a blindingly hot summer day. We were never anything but a crowded household, yet there appeared to be no congestion. Mental and physical ventilation abounded.

My brother, Boardman, had graduated from Yale in June, and was to enter the Harvard Law School in the autumn. He had fallen in love with a young lady, pretty as a *Munsey's Magazine* cover. They were not officially engaged, but there was a subtle flow of post-adolescent romanticism between them. We all attended the Yale commencement exercises and Prom. I was a poor dancer, knew it, and felt nervous about it. I danced, badly but indefatigably, until four A.M., and thought I had never seen such a fleet of pretty girls assembled in one place. I was abashed, too, to meet so many superior young men about to take ship from the port of a university. Mere fiddling seemed suddenly a most frivolous pursuit.

Hadley was president of Yale then. He looked like a college president, just as Boardman already looked like a lawyer. At the Hadleys' home we met the new Republican candidate for President. Teddy Roosevelt had willed it so—the Republicans then were not a party, they were a dynasty. William Howard

Taft was a giant. His dimensions spread more generously in the horizontal than the vertical, but, all in all, his capacity for displacement was fabulous. He had a winning smile and a genial manner. He had always wanted, so it was said, to be Chief Justice rather than President of the United States; it was his wife who had the latter ambition. Both hopes were realized— hers first, that being the general rule in these United States.

The Hadleys entertained simply but charmingly. Mrs. Hadley had an easy manner that I suspect made an undergraduate feel his oats before his time. That same talent could evidently make a prospective President of the United States feel his youth again. In any case, the Taft smile stretched from ear to ear.

"How do you do it?" my mother asked our hostess.

"Oh, this is the least of it," returned Mrs. Hadley. "A politician is sometimes easier to handle than a freshman. Just this year, at the first reception of the season, I had a rather novel experience. The cards I had sent out read 'from four to seven o'clock.' To my astonishment and dismay, one tow-headed young man arrived at three, because, as he nervously explained, he could only stay until six!"

"What did you do?" my mother asked again.

"Do? What could I do? I entertained him—he was a nice lad!"

In August I had an invitation to visit Walter Damrosch at York Harbor. I had never met him. But my American début the following November was to be with the New York Symphony Orchestra, of which he was for many years the permanent conductor. In fact, permanency in the tenure of this distinguished office seemed to come as naturally to Walter Damrosch as an unlimited Congressional career did to "Uncle Joe" Cannon.

Damrosch himself met me at the station. It was early morning and I was groggy with sleep, having allowed only a quarter of an hour for the transition from sleeping berth to station platform. But the welcome was cordial and heart-warming and I was soon to know all the Damrosches: Walter, Margaret and four daughters sat around the breakfast table. Walter, at that time in his mellow forties, was remarkably handsome, with the kind of handsomeness that would, I thought, mature like Lady Paget's. He had the vigor and fluidity of youth, coupled with an irresistible geniality of manner. He made me feel at home at once. Mrs. Damrosch was not less cordial, though she was somewhat reserved at first—not for nothing was she James G. Blaine's daughter. I recognized at once a genius for hospitality, but close intimacy was a jealously guarded treasure not given easily or immediately. I liked her at once; and she, in turn, grew to like me. Alice, the senior daughter, was at the critical age of seventeen. There was more appraisal than approval in her dark gypsy eyes that had a trace of satirical smile lurking in their corners. I felt suddenly and justly ashamed of a purple shirt, and after breakfast I hastily changed it for a white one.

We talked of my début numbers. At the first concert it was to be the Saint-Saëns B-minor Concerto, followed two days later by the Tchaikovsky.

Damrosch had heard directly from Saint-Saëns about me. He told me many anecdotes of the composer, and I was able to respond with some, though not so many, of my own.

"A wonderful old man," he commented. "A great wit, a caustic critic, an astute politician (without portfolio, it's true), an admirable organist, and an amazing pianist. His main job, composing, would almost be forgotten amid this catholic array of talents were it not that he is so good at it. He has admirers and acquaintances all over the world, but very few real friends. Tell me, how did you come to gain his interest?"

I explained how we had met and played together on more than one occasion.

"He apparently liked your playing. Saint-Saëns doesn't write enthusiastically unless he means it."

This was all very cheering; but I can remember glancing apprehensively out of the window at the grim Maine fog that was rising from the sea. That stealthy enemy of fiddle strings paralyzes one's best efforts. It is as menacing to the violinist as an attack of laryngitis to the singer. "It's no use," I thought somewhat desperately. "He's sure to ask me to play, once breakfast is over. Why did I come today? Why did I come at all? And, above all, why must there be *fog?*"

[93]

Damrosch, however, had heart and understanding. He did not propose music, bless him! Instead we went for a drive with the whole family in the newly acquired car. There were several miles of firmly packed sand on the level beaches where you could speed (Was it at the incredible rate of forty miles an hour?) to the accompanying rhythm of the waves. We rode in an open car, and—since this was long before the days of windshields—we met, face on, the rush of wind seasoned with an occasional spray of sand and salt water. The younger girls, Gretchen, Polly, and Anita, who was then little more than a baby, crowed with delight. We were seven or eight in the car; but in those days cars were built for capacity and disdained streamlining.

Back home again, Damrosch went to the piano. It was an upright and not a very good one at that, but the amazing man contrived to make it sound well. He had some manuscript scores that had recently been sent him. I have always had an admiration mixed with awe for the musician who can read with facility from an orchestral score. With Damrosch it seemed to be second nature; I have rarely seen his equal in this field. He observed—he could hardly have missed—the admiration that his performance evoked, and he was pleased.

"Can you read from score?" he asked me.

I was ashamed to admit that I couldn't, or, at least, only lamely.

"Don't be ashamed," he consoled me. "But it's a good habit to get into. It's a matter of habit, of practice. You can, of course, play the piano?"

I could strum after a fashion, but what of that?

"You can, certainly you can," he persisted. "All violinists can—or should—play the piano. Be sure that you make yours 'can,' and not 'should'!"

The fog had lifted by this time. The atmosphere was still heavy with moisture, but the sun was breaking through. Perhaps the violin strings would not be so bad after all. As though reading my thoughts, Damrosch proposed some music for us both.

"Get your violin," he said, "and let's hear how Old Man Saint-Saëns sounds."

I opened my case and found two broken strings on the Montagnana; I strung it up with new ones. I put extra resin on the bow.

"May I," I asked, "prelude a little to warm up?"

"Do so by all means."

I warmed the fiddle as best I could with some unaccompanied Bach. It was not too bad, but not too good. Suddenly I had another thought.

"Do you mind? I have another fiddle; it's only a cheap modern one that I use for practicing purposes, but maybe it will stand up better in this dampness. This old Italian seems to have lost his voice in the dampness of Maine."

"Mind?" asked Damrosch. "Why should I mind?"

I got out my Paul Blanchard of Lyons. It had cost fifty dollars and was a serviceable working machine with a clear, rather blatant tone. It defied the elements more successfully than did the distilled mellowness of two-centuries-old wood. With the Blanchard tucked firmly under my chin I played more boldly. I attacked the Bach fugue in G minor. Damrosch was delighted, and showed it.

"And now the concerto," he said.

Full of confidence by now, I played it well. Half of the time I could see the fine aquiline head pivoting around to watch me. How he could continue to play, I don't know, for the upright piano faced the wall, so that while he was watching me his hands stretched in the opposite direction. But they found the correct keys with uncanny precision. I wondered if he knew the whole score by heart. Apparently not, for there was an occasional wrong turning. The head swung back—an instantaneous recovery, and the error was gracefully camouflaged by an approving smile and a murmured "Bravo!" It was apparent that I was making a fast and faithful friend.

The next day a few people were invited to hear me play. Among them were Mrs. Bryan Lathrop, one of the pillars of the Chicago Orchestra, with which I was to make my first appearance in that city; and the Peter Dunnes, she tall, willowy,

good to look at—altogether too patrician, I thought, to be partnered to the comical "Mr. Dooley," whose political quips in
broad Irish brogue were then being quoted in every household.

We played a Brahms sonata, the one in G major, and some
bravura pieces. Damrosch expected, and exacted, extravagant
reactions. Under these benign auspices it would have been difficult to fail. Furthermore, although I did not know this until
later, my generous host had busied himself writing letters for
publication which contained the warmest praise. "Spalding," he
wrote, "is the first great instrumentalist this country has produced." He was willing to stake his reputation on my fulfilling
every high expectation, though a long time was to pass before
there was any general acceptance of this heart-warming accolade.
In one's own homeland, public favor does not come at first
bidding.

Damrosch had set the stage for a triumphal New York début.
The reality was to fall far short of that.

November 8 came. It was a Sunday afternoon. Carnegie Hall
was filled. Excitement mixed with skepticism ran like an electric
current through the audience. It can be felt more easily than
described. I was nervous; more nervous, perhaps, than I had
ever been, or was ever to be again. Under such circumstances
no artist is likely to be a good judge of his own performance.
But I shall venture the judgment that it had quality, marred
here and there by outward blemishes. It was neither my best
nor my worst performance. The dangerous opening of the concerto, punctuated by daring shifts of position on the G string,
suffered from overattack and doubtful intonation. After the first
page or so, things went better and my confidence returned. Results were no longer halting. The hazardous harmonics at the
close of the second movement were successfully negotiated; the
finale went brilliantly. Most of the audience, after preliminary
hesitation, took heart at these latter proceedings, and the spontaneous burst of applause which continued through many recalls would have satisfied any artist. My friends and well-wishers
were elated. It was, they pronounced, a highly successful début.

[96]

Damrosch said: "You are now a ship in full sail. You will travel far and wide!"

The sailing, however, was not to be so free and easy as all that. Damrosch and the others had reckoned without the morrow's press—and some of it was bad. Few débuts evoking such enthusiastic applause can have elicited such blasts of scornful rejection as mine received from the dean of New York music critics—Henry E. Krehbiel of the *Tribune*. He had a powerful pen and he used it pungently on this occasion. Of all the "rasping, raucous, snarling, unmusical sounds" he had ever been subjected to, mine apparently figured as "tops"—or "bottoms," if you like to put it that way. He recalled that another American violinist had recently sought publicity by implying that he had been lost in the Alps, only to be miraculously rescued. What connection this item had with me I am not sure. But the authoritative arbiter of musical opinion was clearly suggesting that my future be consigned to oblivion—a permanent, not temporary, disappearance in the Alps. I still have Krehbiel's initial estimate of me; it is a treasured document.

What about the rest of the press? That was a completely different story. The reviews ranged from paeans of praise to more moderate estimates of my talent. But they were unanimous in acclaiming what they felt to be genuine talent. If some of them tempered admiration with qualifying criticism, all reflected the enthusiasm that had pervaded Carnegie Hall the day before. It was evident, however, that Krehbiel's notice constituted news, and that the others didn't. His vituperations seemed to spread like poison gas. A rival agency circulated throughout the country numerous copies of that issue of the *Tribune*. What they expected to gain by this questionable procedure I am not certain; perhaps they figured that, if my contracts should be abandoned, there might be some new engagements for their own candidate. I had no way of judging the success of this campaign, but I doubt its efficacy. The wide broadcasting of Krehbiel's condemnation drew upon me the full glare of public notice, and eventually won me as many friends as it did opponents. My adherents became as violently enthusiastic as my detractors were

[97]

damning. This was not quite the oblivion to which Krehbiel thought he had consigned me.

Damrosch called me on the phone that depressing Monday morning. He wished to console me. Had I read Krehbiel's notice? I hadn't, but I knew about it.

"I am glad to hear it," said Damrosch. "Don't read it. It's vindictive, it's vicious, and it's untrue. I meant what I said yesterday—you are a ship in full sail! Maybe you'll have to take a reef here and there, to tack before this or that unruly wind. But you'll be a great navigator for all that. And Master Krehbiel will eat his own words."

I told Damrosch the advice old Hans Richter had given me about criticism. He was amused and delighted.

"I wish," he remarked, "that more artists did the same. Krehbiel is an old friend of mine. He is an ardent lover and student of music. He writes well. And he is uncompromisingly sincere. But where you are concerned he is prejudiced, mistaken, and all-fired wrong. Keep on playing and you will prove him so."

The musical season of 1908-09 was a brilliant one. It was the year of Toscanini's first appearance at the Metropolitan Opera House. His conducting of *Aïda* ushered in the glittering array of performances with which he was to dazzle New York. The principal singers were Destinn and Caruso. Other Metropolitan stars were Sembrich, Eames, Farrar, Fremstad, Gadski, Homer, Scotti, Amato, Didur, and Witherspoon. Gustav Mahler held sway as chief conductor of the German operas. I remember particularly a performance of Mozart's *Marriage of Figaro*. I thought I had never in my life heard anything quite so entrancing. The title role was sung by Adamo Didur. Scotti was the Count Almaviva; Eames was the Countess; Geraldine Farrar made a captivating Cherubino; and Sembrich, perhaps the greatest artist of them all, sang her way into everyone's heart in the part of Susanna. Mahler presided at the harpsichord for each and every recitative, and conducted the matchless score with infinite and profound understanding. It was a performance and a cast difficult to duplicate, impossible to surpass. I have never heard its like to this day.

Mischa Elman made a spectacularly successful début that year. He played the Tchaikovsky concerto with such sweeping dash and brilliance that he was greeted with cheers. I heard him, and cheered with all the rest. His success was not to be wondered at. It was such a success as I hoped for, would work for.

I was by no means idle during that season. I played fifty or sixty concerts, thirty of them with orchestras. The reception was often enthusiastic, often critical, but rarely, if ever, indifferent. I was discussed up hill and down dale, pro and con. Inevitably there were comparisons with the new Russian luminary, generally in Elman's favor. Though this taxed my patience, the resulting réclame was not without its advantages; at least, it helped to postpone that predicted oblivion.

Lovely Lillian Nordica was still singing, though she now appeared oftener in concert than in opera, for the opulent voice was beginning to show the wear and tear of too many Brünhildes and Isoldes. Her immense technical equipment and long experience were great strategical allies, however, and she was still queenly. No majesty born to the purple could have competed with her royal entrances and exits. The audience was spellbound before she sang a single note.

Her accompanist was the same André Benoist who was afterwards my faithful friend and collaborator for so many years. Through him I met Nordica. She liked my playing and immediately took a fancy to me. At her request, in fact, I played as assisting artist at several of her concerts that season. I was flattered at the great lady's interest, but one thing made me extremely unhappy. Nordica would insist that the piano be tuned to the old (low) international pitch. It might otherwise have been difficult for her to negotiate the high B's and C's for which she had, in her prime, been so justly famous. But a low pitch is one of the things to which most violinists are allergic. They need high pitch, for the sharpened strings and the greater tension it produces, increasing the fiddle's speaking power, the brilliance of its tone. This is especially true in large halls, and, of course, the diva sang only in such.

Nordica and I had the same manager, R. E. Johnston. Minus

one leg, bereft of teeth, and with a high, cracked voice, he was hardly an attractive person. Nor was his reputation altogether enviable: irresponsibility and unsound business practices were imputed to him. It was whispered—no, actually shouted from the housetops—that he had taken on my management only because of immense sums of money paid him by my father. In justice to Johnston's memory and, incidentally, to my father's good sense, let me say that this was absolutely untrue. Johnston took me under his management on a regular commission basis; he undertook to get me profitable concerts; his share was fifteen per cent of the gross fee for each concert, no more, no less.

Johnston sincerely believed in my talent. He was a genuine music-lover, and I suspect that he risked his shirt many a time on a musical venture that caught his fancy. His particular star in the instrumental field was Ysaÿe, whose name he pronounced "Yeesahyee"—and with such warmth in his cracked voice and such enthusiasm in his tired eyes that he at once became lovable.

Johnston had counted a great deal on my first New York appearance. Perhaps he overshot the mark in his preliminary advertising campaign of me; at any rate he was deeply chagrined by Krehbiel's attack, bitterly resentful. But he refused to be disheartened, and redoubled his efforts on my behalf. To anyone who suggested that I had not "arrived," he would stoutly reply that I was on my way. "Not arrived?" he would croak. "Of course he hasn't arrived. But that's only because he's going to go so far that none of you'll be able to see him. Pull up your jeans, and wait and see!"

The Metropolitan was not without competition that season. At the Manhattan Opera House, opened in 1906, Oscar Hammerstein was making history with his performances of *Salomé, Pelléas et Mélisande, Louise,* and *Carmen.* At his Sunday night concerts he repeatedly had Elman as the instrumental star. If, by ill luck, I was slated to appear on the same evening at the Metropolitan, you could bet that his would be the full and mine the lean house.

Mary Garden was amazing and bewitching the multitudes with the force of her dramatic impersonations. Her French accent had been born in Scotland and unashamedly wore kilts. "It is," said one wag, "a Kiltic pronunciation." But no matter, she strode the stage like a conqueror. Musically, her results were sometimes doubtful, and her voice always had more brass than gold to it, but for Mary we were ready to go off the gold standard any time she would sing.

It was the period during which the "horseless carriage" was growing into familiarity and popularity. So, too, with the voiceless singer. Dr. Ludwig Wüllner made, in 1908, the first of his successful American tours. No longer young, gaunt, gray-haired, and with but the shell of what had never been a remarkable voice, he declaimed so musically and eloquently that people thronged to hear him. His devotees were wont to ask, "What price Caruso?" He was accompanied at the piano by Coenraad Bos, that prince of lieutenants from the Low Countries, and it was an irresistible combination. Wüllner was past master of the art of suggestion. I shall never forget the matchless way he could deliver Schubert's *Wanderer*. He breathed the chill air of poignant loneliness into every phrase. Nor the drama projected into the *Erl-King*. Nor the stirring impulse of *The Two Grenadiers*. *The Witch's Song* by Max Schillings was a feature of almost every Wüllner recital. Today we can still hear his unique rendering of it; a treasured recording echoes from time to time his compelling mastery of the art of declamation.

Bos and I were to become warm friends later on. At that time he wore a Napoleon III beard which made him appear older than he was. I have always suspected that this was done out of consideration for the much older artist he was then accompanying. Bos is, and always has been, more than an accompanying artist: he is a staunch ally. Julia Culp used to tell me: "Coentjie gives me courage when most I need it, scolds me when most I need it, and consoles me when most I need it. Na, often I need all three at once!"

CHAPTER FOURTEEN

THREE years after this, I played a whole series of concerts with Bos, on my first trip to Holland. We had, it's true, met in London a year or so before and played together—one or two recitals in Aeolian and Wigmore Halls, and the usual round of private engagements. It was heartening to know that this admirable musician enjoyed playing with me as much as I with him. "Lowk 'ere," he would say, "you mawst play in de Nederland, Awlbert—you vill lak it. De peoble, dey vill lak it—very mawch. You cawm to Holland vid me some day, no?" And who could say "No"?

So there I was, arriving one damp December day at The Hague. Coenraad and I were to meet the following day for rehearsal at the Hôtel des Deux Villes. He had programs carefully selected and revised. "De Hollanders are very musicaal, very criticaal. Dey lak loong pieces. Doon't play too many shoort ones. Dey voon't lak it." I took him at his word, and we had chosen substantial musical fare.

Bos warned me about the reserved manners of the Dutch public. They have not the habit, he explained, of expending much energy on applause at the beginning of, or even during, a concert. They sit stolidly in their seats not lifting a hand until an entire concerted number or a mixed group is finished. However, if they are pleased, they make up for it by an unusual demonstration at the end of the concert. The greatest accolade they can give, Bos added, is to rise en masse after the closing number and do their hand-clapping and bravo-shouting while standing. One must be careful, he enjoined, not to shorten the intermission period. It is during this time that the hungry Hollander fortifies himself for the second half of the program. There is a concession to sell food at intermissions; to disturb it might cause a serious upset of the Dutch economic system.

I fell in love with Holland at first sight. In those northern stretches of unpromising marshland, nature has done so little, and man so much. Neat little fields face the menace of an avaricious sea. Tulips and hyacinths surround the friendly windmills like bright moats. The subtle play of clouds, over a country half land, half sea, teaches that where nature is less opulent she need not be less expressive.

It is a land where strength of mind is honored above strength of arm. There, freedom of speech and freedom of religion have been coupled with the necessary courage to maintain them against all odds. It could not have surprised the Dutch when far away across the Atlantic many of the same principles were embodied in the Declaration of Independence. They had known and cherished them for many generations. Such a people can be temporarily subdued, perhaps, but never conquered.

Unconquerable, too, is their love of beauty. To illustrate this it is not necessary to dwell exclusively on their masterpieces of painting. Turn away from those dazzling highlights, and what do you find? Shadow, perhaps, but no real darkness; poverty you may see, but never squalor. Even in the most congested districts of Rotterdam and Amsterdam poverty is not abject nor sordid. It presents rather a picture of modest and neat frugality. Observe those slow-moving barges that inch their snaillike way through the dark canals. See the touches of color at the windows of the small living quarters. Spotlessly scrubbed sheets and towels and garishly patched underwear are strung like banners of cleanliness across the broad decks. This is a poor life, a hard life, but it is a life which yet proclaims the dignity of man.

In the small towns you find the best, the essence, of Holland. Pause at any street corner, and you will think that a Pieter de Hoogh picture has come to life. Good food abounds, and a meal is an elaborate ritual. But an invitation to dine is rarely repeated if you commit the crime of tardiness. At The Hague, one may often see an entire dinner party assembled in front of the house one or two minutes before the appointed time. A few guttural greetings are exchanged while the men consult their massive gold watches—those watches that are as broad of beam as the women. (The Hollander disdains the knifeblade discs made fashionable by Cartier of Paris.) The women are sometimes richly, but rarely fashionably, dressed. The materials are reminiscent of portraits by Ter Borch, Hals, and Van Dyck in the same way that their figures are derived from Rubens.

As the clock strikes, they go in, Mijnheer and Mevrouw entering side by side if the doorway is accommodating. Salaams are made to host and hostess; then everyone shakes hands with everyone else. The guttural sounds multiply until they sound like a Frogs' Fugue. No cocktails are served; the serious business of eating is to begin at once.

The dining-room is the most important room in the house. The sideboards and the serving tables that hug the walls are generally of marqueterie, that heavy type which William and Mary insisted on taking with them to England when they were called to occupy the shaky Stuart throne. A typical dinner is as follows:

1. Soup—clear or thick, generally thick—it is more substantial.
2. Fish—and potatoes; in fact, you have those heavy, mealy potatoes served with every course.
3. Entrée No. 1—sometimes sweetbreads, sometimes mushrooms with a vegetable. More potatoes.
4. Roast No. 1—beef, mutton, lamb, or veal. Encore potatoes!
5. Entrée No. 2—perhaps a mousse of ham or some pâté de foie gras.
6. Roast No 2—game or poultry, with salad. Once more, potatoes.
7. Dessert—on rare occasions an ice, more often a combination of cake and fruit. Sometimes Bavarian Cream, or an omelette confiture.
8. Fruit—Nuts—Coffee.

This formidable meal is accompanied by an unending procession of wines—Rhine, Moselle, Bordeaux, Burgundy, Champagne, and, when very swanky, a choice Sauterne with the sweet. Since eating and drinking are an engrossing occupation, one wonders where to find the time for conversation. But conversation there is, nonetheless. Mevrouw de V., my dinner partner at one of these meals, asked me, after some polite remarks about my playing, whether I had heard the Concertgebouw Orchestra headed by their beloved Willem Mengelberg. I had.—And was I to play with it?—I hoped so, of course; but no date had been set.—How many Dutch towns had I already visited?—Amsterdam, The Hague, Rotterdam.—I mentioned a score of others.

A concert trip in Holland is not really touring, it is commuting. When you visit Leeuwarden or Groningen on the far side of the Zuyder Zee, it seems like a major undertaking. This great journey is the equivalent of a trip from New York to Boston.

"And do you like Holland?" Mevrouw de V. went on.

My reactions were apparently appropriate and satisfactory.

"So," she croaked, after absorbing with relish the last of many potatoes on her plate, "eet eeze a nize goundry, niet waar? Goed things do eat, goed things do zee, goed moozick do 'ear. De peoble dey lak dat very mooch."

I looked across the table at Coenraad Bos to see how close the blood relationship was. She spoke just the way he did. No kinship was necessary. The English of all Hollanders sounds very much the same.

"But," protested my hostess, "you are eating nothing, absolutely nothing, Mr. Spalding."

I thought that I had struggled manfully with both food and wine, and said as much.

"Nah," she went on, "you will lose your strength if you do not eat!"

I pretended to interest myself in the now unwanted victuals.

"Do they then," asked my hostess, "eat so much less in America?"

I said that we did, explaining that we were a feebler race than the Hollanders. She looked very sympathetic.

It would be helpful, I reflected, if there were some invisible receptacle where guests with less vigorous stomachs could dispose of surplus food without giving offense. I had eaten too much; I had drunk too much. Everything suddenly became heavy, alien, oppressive. Before my next dinner, I decided, I should go on a twenty-four-hour fast.

An important factor in the success of my first trip to Holland was the enthusiasm of my friend Bos. He was indefatigable in spreading his good opinion of me. One evening, after a concert in one of the provincial towns, we waited for the little commuting train that was to return us to Amsterdam. At the station restaurant there was good coffee, and those inviting tartines of Dutch bread, thick with sweet butter. But Bos was paying no attention to his food—not even to his coffee. He was busy writing letters, one after the other.

"Who are you writing to?" I asked.

"Vait." He paused, pen in hand. "I vos not going do dell you, Awlbert. Doze letters, dey are all about you. I wrote one each to all pabers in Holland. Dey are good letters," he admitted, smiling.

When I tried to thank him properly he would have none of it; in fact, he seemed annoyed that I had discovered him in this activity.

The morning after an important concert in The Hague or in Amsterdam he would wake me early and insist on reading in full his rather grotesque translations of the lengthy criticisms in the *Handelsblad,* or the *Telegraaf,* or the *Vaderland.* This was generally over the phone. I hated leaving my warm bed and standing on the icy tile floors, first on one bare foot and then on the other. Still too sleepy to understand his excited voice, I was half irritated, half amused, and altogether grateful! There was no stopping Coentjie once he got started. I had explained to him my lesson from Richter on the subject of criticism.

"Nah," he said. "Dot iz fine for rrotten notices! But deeze! Deeze are splendid vons!"

Christmas Day approached. I had looked forward to a respite from playing, but I had reckoned without the Dutch. When I approached our manager about it he said: "On the contrary, Christmas is an excellent date for Holland concerts. You will play not once, but twice. In Amsterdam in the afternoon, and in Deventer in the evening." Observing my hesitant expression, he went on: "You want to make some money, no?" Of course I did. *"So was!* You will see—splendid houses!"

I fully expected Bos to protest, for he had his wife, Elsa, and two small daughters, Yolanda and Erika, with him for the holiday. But Bos, too, was a Hollander. He found this arrangement quite natural. He even approved of it.

But we were not deprived of a celebration after all. We caught a late train into Amsterdam from Deventer, and went for a midnight supper to a restaurant famous for fish.

"Do you like our Zeeland oysters?" asked Bos. They have a coppery flavor quite unlike American oysters, but who would have had the courage to say "No"? I must confess that they later acquired a permanent hold upon my affections.

We had oysters, dozens upon dozens of them. You never do anything by half-measures in Holland. Empty bottles of a noble Moselle marked the milestones of this Lucullan feast.

Elsa brought news from Berlin. Julia Culp had just sung there.

"Did she sing well?" asked Bos. Yes, she had sung well.

"Not too many slowings down, too many retards?" insisted Bos.

"Ach, die Julia," sighed Elsa. "She has so much breath she is like a violinist whose bow is a mile long. Naturally, she sing too many retards, especially when my Coentjie he not play for her. My Coentjie, he smack her hard when she not rytmik!"

"Elsa means I smack vit de vords, not de hands," explained Bos, somewhat unnecessarily. "Julia, she komm here for vun concert next veek. You and I, vee haf vree day—so I play vit her. You komm hear her, no?"

Indeed I would.

"Fine! You not hear die Julia before?"

No, I hadn't.

"So! You will hear. She sing beautiful—Schubert, Brahms, Hugo Wolf. Loafely voice. She go this year to America. I go vit her. She haf much success, no?"

I hadn't heard her but I agreed, of course, that she would.

When I did hear her, Culp's singing delighted me. A mezzo-contralto of medium range, she had equalized and perfected the limited scale within that range. She possessed a rare command of legato, and had excellent diction. Some very effective and expressive portamentos she was likely to abuse whenever Bos' back was turned; and, as Elsa had remarked, she had an almost irresistible inclination to retard the end of every phrase. You could hear Bos pulling lightly but firmly at the rhythmical curb; it was, I suspect, his method of spanking, and it did the trick.

Her success in America was everything, and more than everything, that Coentjie had predicted.

CHAPTER FIFTEEN

IN later years my wife thoroughly approved of the yearly pilgrimages to Holland. For a month or more each season we stayed at the Hôtel des Indes at The Hague. This was headquarters, although we usually spent the night in Amsterdam if I happened to be playing an engagement there with the Gebouw Orchestra or appearing in a recital of my own. Mengelberg was still, as he had been in 1912, musical dictator. His every appearance evoked a demonstration. I recall some remarkable performances: Mahler's *Lied von der Erde,* indescribably poetic; Beethoven's earliest symphony, the one in C major; and, of course, Mengelberg's famous exposition of the *St. Matthew Passion* by Bach. His performance of the *Matthew* always took on something of the air of a religious rite—received not so much with enthusiasm as with awe; one instinctively made one's comments sotto voce.

Mengelberg took a great fancy to Mevrouw Spalding. Mary has many different methods of approach to her prospective conquests. She had seen his tired smile in response to fulsome compliments, and had planned her line of attack quite differently. Men, she reflected, are more vulnerable when flattered in their individual tastes. What then, she asked, are Mengelberg's tastes? Why, his cigars of course, his little light-colored cigars manufactured especially for him in Java. They were, I am persuaded, of the vilest and rankest tobacco, but that would hardly discourage Mary.

"You do not smoke, Mevrouw?" asked Mengelberg, her dinner partner.

"No," sighed Mary wistfully, "I have never liked cigarettes. If I smoked at all, it would be something more ambitious. Now, that cigar of yours . . ." There was a hesitating *rallentando,* but the implied compliment was quite apparent.

"Ah, Mevrouw," exclaimed Mengelberg delightedly, "you shall smoke one, here and now!"

Nothing daunted, Mary accepted in turn a cigar, a light, and the astonished gaze of the entire table. Out of the corner of her eye she was watching for my reaction. Would I be shocked? To her great satisfaction I was. I thought she might be suddenly sick. It would serve the imp right—had she not repeatedly claimed a most delicate stomach? But Mary was not sick, she was triumphant. She had achieved a dual victory: the conquest of Mengelberg was complete, and her husband was flabbergasted.

On our next visit to Amsterdam the major-domo (one hesitates to call him a porter) who presided at the stage entrance of the Concertgebouw was obsequious. "I have," he announced, "a package for Mevrouw Spalding, a package from Mijnheer Kapellmeister Mengelberg." You would have thought he was presenting the crown jewels.

I had forgotten the incident, but not so Mary. She controlled her laughter out of consideration for the major-domo. "It is," she explained as we moved on, "Mengelberg's cigars, of course. He promised me some, and here they are!"

"Mengelberg's cigars?" I repeated. "What on earth do you intend to do with them?"

"I shall accept them, naturally. It is most kind of him to have remembered."

"And will you smoke them?" I persisted.

"What I do in private is nobody's business. In my letter of thanks I shall point out that I will be careful not to enjoy them in public places. The Dutch are punctilious. They are conservative. But he will be delighted with my pleasure none the less. You will see."

Mengelberg particularly liked my performance the next night. I told Mary that her cigar strategy had done the trick.

"But no, darling," she protested, almost maternally, "only your playing could have evoked that enthusiasm."

Mary is certainly wasted as a fiddler's wife. Her talents invite the widest competition—the arena of politics or diplomacy. I don't know what ultimate plans Mary may have had for the cigars. They were, I know, preciously guarded as souvenirs, and accompanied us on our travels across frontier after frontier. Till then we had gone through the customs with nothing but personal effects to declare. Now the presence of an unopened box of a hundred cigars had to be disclosed, and there was always a negligible but irritating duty to be paid.

"Let's get rid of the damn things," I proposed.

"You would be quite content," said Mary with devastating logic, "to put up with a little fuss if you enjoyed smoking them."

"But I don't. Nor do you, for that matter."

"I may; indeed, I may. And anyway they are souvenirs of a delightful incident."

"I suppose," I remarked, "that when we get back to New York you will deposit them in the Lincoln Storage vaults for safekeeping."

"Why not?" said Mary. "They will be delightful heirlooms for our grandchildren."

To speak of our grandchildren is one of Mary's favorite ways to conclude an argument. We have no children of our own, but she blandly assumes ultimate, if not immediate, posterity.

I do not remember what eventually became of the cigars. Perhaps, unknown to me, they actually are in a safe-deposit box. Meantime, Mengelberg still believes that Mevrouw Spalding is one woman who appreciates his Javanese cigars.

We used often to visit the picture galleries in Holland. One day we had paused before a large canvas by Hals—a group of portraits of burghermasters and other notables of the painter's time. "Look!" exclaimed Mary. "What a likeness of Uncle Harm." Moving closer, we found at the bottom of the picture, in gold lettering, the names of the various sitters. And what was our astonishment, on identifying the man in question, to find that his name was "Harmon Van der Hoef"—and my mother-in-law's older brother was Harmon Vanderhoef! Mary's "Uncle Harm" had been painted with photographic accuracy, several centuries before he was born.

Mary is a keen art critic. Her brother, Scott, was a painter of unusual talent. She affectionately differed with him in most things, but about pictorial art they agreed completely. Scott Pyle was one of the handsomest young men of his time. He inherited good looks from both sides of his family, and bore them easily and unself-consciously. Scott had an uncanny sense of draughts-manship. It was one of those untaught facilities which, though they can be greatly developed by study, are innate from the beginning. The family used to say of him that he could draw accurately long before his spelling was correct. In him, Mary's "gambling sense of time" was accentuated a hundredfold.

"Invite Scott to dinner," sighed one hostess, "and he arrives, breathlessly, an hour and a half late. Not only is the soup cold, but also the last of the ice has melted. The worst of it, with those Pyles, is that you are so pleased to see them that you forget your just indignation. They are so consciencelessly disarming!"

In contrast to the disorderly sense of time of these two young-sters was the uncompromising punctuality of their majestic mother. Everything seemed to exist in verticals in Mrs. Pyle. Her carriage, her virtues, even her vulnerabilities, were all erect. The phrase "a pillar of the church" must have been originated to describe someone like her.

She overawed me till I discovered what a sense of humor she had. Beneath the façade of a patrician dignity there was, I found, something vastly more attractive—a healthy plebeian humanity. I always felt sure of finding the way to her heart through the plebeian.

We used often to see members of our own diplomatic corps while staying at The Hague. The William Phillipses had leased the beautiful old house of Count Bentinck, just a stone's throw from our hotel. It was perhaps the most elaborate house in the city with the exception of the Royal residences. Even these were ultra-modest for a Queen whose private fortune was larger than that of almost any other monarch in Europe.

The fine Dutch residences of The Hague, more noted for dignity than for splendor, reminded me of many New York houses. You usually entered a rather narrow hallway; the staircase to the upper floors rose abruptly from the front door. It would have been against the dictates of Dutch frugality to waste space on a vestibule. The rooms were spacious, high-ceilinged, with generous doorways. They disdained excessive ornamentation. The windows were heavily and somewhat gloomily hung with textiles loomed in Utrecht, the town famous for velvets.

Entertaining was done on a smaller scale than in other capitals. It was unostentatious, comfortable, and lavish only in regard to food.

Before William Phillips officiated at The Hague, we had known his predecessor, Henry Van Dyke. He was one of Wilson's appointees to ministerial duty, chosen, like others, from literary ranks. I had called on him to pay my respects. I was kindly received and invited to stay to tea. Mary, and Mary's family, he had known. It must have been with deep distrust that he learned of her marriage to an itinerant fiddler; she would doubtless have chosen more prudently from the field of literature. However—let us see what this strange young man is like. . . .

Mrs. Van Dyke officiated at the tea table. She was extremely hard of hearing. Without aid of ear trumpet or other device our efforts at conversation never synchronized, and were seldom coherent.

"Mr. Spalding, my dear, is a violinist," shouted Dr. Van Dyke.

"Indeed? How interesting!" Then, scrutinizing me more closely: "But I fear that there are no churches of your sect to attend at The Hague."

I was bewildered and said nothing, but Dr. Van Dyke went on more loudly, *"Violinist—violinist,* my love," gesticulating to suggest the sweep of a fiddler's bow arm.

"I heard you the first time," said Mrs. Van Dyke coldly. "I am," she went on to me, "particularly interested in the Waldensians. Are you studying for the ministry?"

By this time Dr. Van Dyke's impatience to establish my identity had reached a frenzy. He got as close to his wife's ear as the tea table and decorum would allow, and roared three times: *"Violinist,* VIOLINIST, VIOLINIST—do you hear? He plays the VIOLIN!"* Again the sweeping gesture, even more graphic.

Mrs. Van Dyke's interest then dropped instantly. She nodded. "Ah, yes, violinist," she murmured, in pale diminuendo. She did not add what a pity she thought it; nor was this necessary—her tone implied it. However, as the wife of our plenipotentiary to Holland she remembered her diplomatic manners and inquired whether I was to give a concert in The Hague. I replied that I had already played there, not once but twice.

"Not recently, though!" said Dr. Van Dyke.

"As recently as last night."

"Why was it not advertised? I have heard nothing of it."

"It was advertised in the usual manner," I said somewhat stiffly; "in newspapers, on bill-posters—"

"Dr. Van Dyke and I must certainly go," announced his unpredictable lady. "When did you say it was to be?"

But by this time I was quite weary, and handed over to the indefatigable Doctor the task of enlightening his wife. The news, when it finally penetrated, must have been a considerable relief to her—one fewer of those onerous duties to perform—but she masked it by polite regrets. I made my adieux shortly afterwards. The call and the tea had not, I thought, been a conspicuous success.

Later, I learned Dr. Van Dyke's opinion of me. He closely questioned one of Mary's intimate friends, Peggy Sloan. What did she think of me? How had Mary's family regarded this doubtful alliance? Were they not opposed to it, unhappy about it? Peggy spoke stoutly on my behalf. "Well, well," said Dr. Van Dyke, apparently unconvinced, "I cannot help having misgivings. He impressed me as a singularly choleric young man."

I did not fare so lamely with all our diplomats. But I did learn very early in the game not to count on patronage from the official representatives of my own country. The welcome exceptions to this rule were a few career diplomats like William

Phillips. For the most part, our amateur Ambassadors were tired business men who had contributed substantial sums to a successful presidential campaign, and were rewarded with these coveted posts. Their chief motive appeared to be the fulfillment of their wives' social ambitions. Business was perfunctorily performed and was often reduced to a minimum to make way for brilliant entertainments, at which few Americans were to be seen. There were, of course, certain official receptions—as on Independence and Thanksgiving Days—to which their unwanted compatriots had to be invited *en masse*. But these tiresome events did not occur very often. Mme. l'Ambassadrice could soon forget that she owed her position to an accident of birth that linked her to a people of whom she was apparently ashamed.

In Berlin, once, my manager suggested that I call at our Embassy and invite the entire staff to attend the important orchestral concert at which I was to be soloist. He seemed astonished that I should be so little sanguine about the results.

"But," he protested, "you are already well known in your own country. You are even known here. Of course they will come. Have you not also a personal letter to the Ambassador?"

I had, but what of that? I called, and was received by one of the numerous secretaries. I told him my object in calling. Tiresome fellow, tiresome business, thought the elegant young man as he listened with slightly elevated eyebrows. He accepted the letter, which he would transmit to His Excellency. He would also deliver my kind invitation to the concert, although, of course, I would understand that it was improbable . . . I did understand. I had expected neither more nor less; I had been unhappily misled too many times in the past.

The concert took place and was quite a brilliant affair. It was attended by many notables, among them the French Ambassador, the venerable Jules Cambon, and his family. Were not French composers' works included on the program, the Saint-Saëns concerto being one of them? The Cambons singled me out for special attention and honor. I was invited to a reception at the beautiful Embassy on Pariser Platz and introduced to everyone. Cambon could use grandiloquent phrases on occasion. I was, he declared, *une des gloires de l'art musicale en Amérique.* Here I met for the first time the Mr. and Mrs. of our own Embassy. It appeared that I was actually worthy of notice. Even the eyebrows of the secretaries seemed to be less arched than usual. Would I not come to dinner one night during the next week? Was I to have another appearance soon in Berlin? It was clear that the plain dish of Americanism had suddenly been rendered more palatable by passing through the practical hands of a French chef. I had an almost malicious satisfaction in my inability to take advantage of their cordiality because of concert dates elsewhere. . . .

CHAPTER SIXTEEN

ARLY in 1910, I made my first trip to Russia. A free-lance manager named Magnus, half German, half American, had heard me in Paris, liked my playing, and thought that a good field for exploitation was to be found in this largest of European countries. He had had some managerial experience there, his most recent success having been the tour of Isadora Duncan. She had danced to crowded houses in St. Petersburg and Moscow and had aroused great enthusiasm. Discriminating critics were quick to note her many technical deficiencies, but just as quick to applaud her imaginative and original ideas, which contributed toward producing a minor revolution in the world's greatest ballet school. As a well-known paraphrase put it: "She came, she faltered, but she conquered."

Magnus had never managed a fiddler before. But he was not unmusical, and he had a number of good contacts in Russia. He offered me a contract that was modest from a financial viewpoint: I was to be paid two hundred rubles per concert, with a minimum guarantee of twelve concerts; all traveling expenses and the cost of an accompanist to be met by him. It was not a contract to make one rich overnight but, at twenty-one, I was dazzled by the mere prospect of spreading my wings in that land of fable and fancy.

Magnus had arranged for an orchestral appearance in Warsaw as a prelude to my introduction to Russia proper, and was at the Warsaw station to meet me when I arrived. It was early in the morning, but there were enough streaks of gray light filtering through a dirty glass roof to show a depressing scene. Herded together in the overcrowded station were huddled scores of squalid human beings—standing, sitting, and lying in sprawled confusion. They were, for the most part, unmistakably Hebraic; it was as if all the ghettos of the world had disgorged themselves, with the Warsaw station as the appointed place for the next trial of Jewish patience and fortitude. The bitter cold neutralized what would have been, in a more temperate climate, an unendurable stench. But though it was a picture of abasement, the abasement was not without a certain dignity and courage. There was something deeply poignant about these unfortunate people. I stood watching them while my luggage was collected.

"Let's get out of here," said Magnus impatiently, when the last bag had been found. "You must be longing for bath and breakfast after your long trip." Quite true, I was; but curiosity is perhaps a stronger human impulse.

"Tell me," I asked, "is the Warsaw station always as crowded as this?"

"You mean the Jews," said Magnus with a slight Teutonic curl to his lips. "Yes, it is typical. They crowd in here, coming from heaven knows where, and going—I sometimes suspect that they are neither coming nor going: merely staying. They do not trouble one much, for in this country they are taught to know their place. Did you ever," he added with an unpleasant laugh, "see so many dirty beards in your life?"

I glanced quickly at him. Decidedly, I thought, I do not like nor trust you. Was there not more than a suspicion of Semitic blood in this anti-Semite?

"It seems to me, nevertheless," I replied slowly, "that there is tragedy in this sight."

This time it was Magnus who glanced sharply at me.

"You are not Jewish." It was not quite an assertion, nor quite a question. I settled the matter to his satisfaction, conscious, however, that had my answer been "yes" it would have been said with pride, not with an apology.

We rode in horse-drawn droshkies to the Hôtel Metropole. In the cold gray light of a January morning Warsaw was not an attractive city. A few fine buildings could be singled out, but most were nondescript. Can there be, I wondered, a special quality in a people that gives homogeneity and character to its cities? If so, it is a quality utterly lacking in the Poles. Their peculiar and impatient genius runs in other channels.

The hotel was large and opulent. Not many of the personnel were yet awake; I had come to a land where late hours were kept. However, Magnus gave orders in a Prussian way, and it was not long before I was luxuriating in a steaming hot bath, followed by delicious coffee and crescents. My room was comfortable—extravagantly so, as I learned when I asked the price. I decided on more modest quarters, in keeping with the fees I was to receive. Magnus applauded my prudence, and gave me further tips on economy. "Did you notice," he asked, "that when I ordered our breakfast I asked for two glasses, not two pots, of coffee?"

"But they brought us pots—"

"Yes; that's just the point. Their esthetic sense will not allow them to serve coffee in a glass. But when the bill comes it will be quite a different matter."

"How so?"

"If I had ordered pots of coffee, we should have been charged one ruble apiece for them. By ordering glasses of coffee we get the pots but we pay only twenty kopecks apiece—a net saving of one ruble and sixty kopecks on the deal."

"I can't see any sense in that."

"My dear fellow," laughed Magnus, "no one comes to Russia to see the sense in things. Unless you enjoy being bewildered, you have certainly come to the wrong corner of the earth. Above all, do not try to make two and two add up to four; your calculation will be wrong. Guess at five or seven or some other indivisible number. The Slavs are a mystic people." He paused a moment, then suddenly, "What month and year is it?"

I spoke too quickly. "January, 1910."

"Wrong. *Here* it is still December, 1909."

Of course, I thought, I would stumble into that trap. The old Julian calendar—thirteen days behind ours!

Magnus triumphant could be magnanimous. "That was," he agreed, "a mean trick. I always use it when I can. And I can promise you many other similar upsets. Be prepared to enjoy the element of surprise!"

The Warsaw concert went well. With the orchestra I played two concertos, the one by Beethoven and the Tchaikovsky. As encores I played some unaccompanied Bach and, with piano, an interminable series of shorter numbers. I had planned a maximum of three or four encores, but at the rehearsal the pianist protested. "Not enough, not enough!" I had learned not to question advice from that quarter, so we arrived at the hall with a sheaf of short pieces. To my astonishment I played them all—a dozen or more.

Two days later we took the night train for St. Petersburg.

"Do you notice," asked Magnus, "that the sleepers—in fact, all the cars—are somewhat wider than in Western Europe?"

I asked why.

"They claim," said Magnus, "that it is for strategic reasons. They are obsessed by the fear of a sudden attack from their powerful neighbor to the West."

"How well grounded is that fear, do you think?"

"Nothing to it," was the emphatic reply. "Kaiser Wilhelm is really the man of peace in Europe. Oh, he does a bit of swash-buckling now and then; he likes to appear, he says, in shining armor whenever there is a crisis. He has built up the most per-fect war-machine in the world, but in reality his ambition is to be the arbiter of pacification—the mailed fist, perhaps, but gloved in velvet. Wilhelm will never make war, and he is too strong to have it forced upon him."

I hoped it was true, but couldn't help pointing out that the rest of Europe seemed to have only one fear: the military ex-pansion of Germany.

Magnus brushed this aside.

"It is," he said, "less fear than jealousy—jealousy of Germany's peaceful penetration into the world's markets. What will give Germany economic mastery is not military power, but the genius for work, for organization. You will see!"

I remarked that America knew something about industry and organization, too.

"Yes," agreed Magnus, rather grudgingly, "but America's prosperity is due rather to unexampled opportunity than to an aptitude for work and organization. Give those two countries equal access to raw materials, and Uncle Sam will be left far in the rear, utterly unable to understand how it happened."

Clearly, Magnus took more pride in his Teutonic than in his American blood. I changed the conversation: When and where was my first appearance to take place?

"The first date," announced Magnus, looking at me somewhat quizzically, "is the day after tomorrow; hour, one o'clock."

"One o'clock?" I repeated. "So early in the day?"

"On the contrary, so late. I mean one o'clock after midnight. No one would be awake, much less come to a performance, at one in the afternoon."

I said nothing, but wondered how I was to keep my enthusiasm and co-ordination alive so late into the night as that.

"This first appearance," said Magnus, "is for a private club, one of many such organizations. You will accept a number of these engagements before appearing in your own recital."

"You mean that they serve as an effective build-up?"

"Yes, largely that. But they are something more than a means to an end; they can be very delightful events in themselves."

It was not late, but we decided to turn in. "It's only on trains," remarked Magnus, "that one has the chance to go to bed early. We may as well make the most of it."

The car was overheated, and the windows tightly sealed. One had to choose between the precious warmth and ventilation. I stifled a protest—when in Russia, do as the Russians do. I resigned myself to insomnia or suffocation . . . and went promptly to sleep.

In the morning we arrived at the St. Petersburg station. The city seemed to be an assortment of hastily assembled sheds. It looked more like a railroad junction in a remote province than the famed capital of the Tsar of all the Russias.

This is, I thought, much the same as your first sight of Venice.

You cannot believe that it is Venice; by mistake you have been put off the train too soon. Your *facchino* reassures you, but you look in disappointment down the dark and murky platforms. The wily Venetians are master artists in the drama of contrast. They steadfastly refuse to decorate or even to clean that first view of their lovely city. Is the surprise, I wondered, to be repeated here?

Outside the station was a city of broad streets carpeted with snow. It was late in the morning but there was little traffic. A few sleds were moored to the station in a field of snow and ice. The drivers were asleep, sitting up. They looked like bearded bears, trained to an uncongenial task. Two of them woke up reluctantly after much prodding.

"Yes," said Magnus in answer to my unspoken question, "these are our conveyances. Luggage will go in one, we in the other. And they are not," he added, "from the circus. All the drivers look like that."

"How do they get such figures?"

"They sit, they eat, they sleep. In their youth, I am told, they procreate. I doubt it; that takes too much energy."

"But even so—"

"And besides, it is a matter of clothing. Over their regular clothes they wrap a sort of thick quilting until they approximate a sphere from which, unrealistically, a pair of arms and a head protrude."

The little sleds traveled rapidly down the deserted streets. The horses, at least, seemed to be thoroughly alive and awake. So was I. It was, after all, a city of splendor, a city of color, even though its inhabitants were not yet stirring. Vivid blue, red, and green domes rose like intrepid bubbles above the ocher-colored buildings. The streets were wide and empty, our sleighs seeming absurdly small and alone in them. It was as if spacious rooms awaited the delivery of appropriate furniture. The atmosphere had a crystalline transparency; the sharp northern sky seemed farther from the earth. I felt no sense of cold.

We arrived at the hotel where the welcoming "glasses" of coffee were soon served. The coffee, too, seemed to have a special flavor. The Hôtel de l'Europe did not disappoint us. It was a combination of European comfort and Asiatic ostentation. It was subtly implied that you were a guest there not because of rubles and kopecks, but because of influential friends. What friends? That question was never explored, but the sense of your heightened importance was inescapable.

The food was marvelous. I shall never forget the array of hors d'oeuvres on the serving tables in the room next to the dining-hall. It was a meal, several meals, in itself.

"Another timely tip of economic importance," admonished Magnus. "If you wish to enjoy a good meal and spend kopecks instead of rubles, follow me; do as I do."

He ordered a vodka.

"But I don't like vodka, especially at noon."

"Patience, you idiot! You don't have to drink it. Watch me, and follow suit!"

I followed suit and furnished myself with a generous plate of smoked fish, vegetable salad, cold game, mushroom and cèpes in cream. It was delicious—and economical: all we paid for was the vodka, forty kopecks apiece. If you wanted more food, you ordered a second vodka; for which the price was reduced to thirty kopecks.

"What capacity for drinking do you have to have," I asked, "to bring the price down to zero—or even to end up with the hotel in your debt?"

"I don't know," said Magnus. "Shall we try it?"

"Not with work to do, and a concert tomorrow night."

As a matter of fact, I had emptied my vodka into my finger bowl when the waiter's back was turned.

We went that night to the Théâtre Michel, the French repertory theater. Its excellent stock company was frequently augmented by guest artists from the Comédie Française and the Odéon in Paris. You could go every night in the week and see a different play. I enjoyed these performances immensely.

"They've got to be good," asserted Magnus. "The Russian public is used to the finest acting in the world. Wait until you see the Moscow Art Theater. They have a perfected technique that makes life itself seem artificial."

The next morning I wanted a cold bath and rang for the chambermaid. She spoke no French and but little German. She would get the valet. I explained my wish to him. He gazed at me stupefied. *"Un bain froid?"* he repeated, utterly incredulous. He disappeared. A few minutes later he came back with the clerk from downstairs. I was thoroughly embarrassed, but Yankee determination made me persist. "Have I, then, asked for something impossible?"

"But a cold bath!" said the astonished clerk. "A really cold bath?"

"Utterly, completely cold. May I have it?"

"But certainly, most certainly. At once. Please excuse."

A few minutes later the valet announced that my bath was ready. Would I accompany him? There followed a trek down the hallway. The bathroom door was flung open. It was a spacious apartment, and it contained an audience. There, in breathless expectation, stood the waiter of the floor, his bus-boy, the chambermaid, the boots. Did they, I wondered, expect to remain? *"Sortez,"* I commanded, borrowing for the moment Magnus' Prussian tone. They reluctantly filed out. I wanted to lock the door but there was neither lock nor bolt; apparently baths in Russia are not private affairs.

I stuck one foot into the tub. An icy, numbing pain shot up my leg. Evidently I was to pay handsomely for my extraordinary demand! I could not, however, face the humilation of asking for some hot water to take the chill off. Never was a tub entered or vacated more rapidly. While I was gasping for breath and toweling myself vigorously, there came a knock on the door. No need to say "come in" or "stay out"; the coming-in occurred simultaneously with the knock. The valet entered. He gazed at me with astonishment not unmixed with awe.

"I have brought you," he explained, "some hot coffee."

Bless him! I drank it with profound gratitude.

I spent an endless day waiting for the one A.M. concert. I had a rehearsal with my accompanist, an excellent musician by the name of Dulov. I took a walk, and got lost. Fortunately, all sled drivers knew the name and the location of the Hôtel de l'Europe.

To my relief I found that there was no ban on after-dinner practicing in my room. No one had gone to bed as early as that; no one would. I shaved and dressed for the concert about midnight.

On my arrival at the club I found the medium-sized concert room already thronged to capacity. The audience were all in evening dress, and everyone was talking animatedly. Some had come from late dinners, some from the theater or ballet, explained Dulov.

"Is there," I asked, "no end to their appetite for entertainment?"

"On the contrary," he assured me, "the Russian appetite grows by what it feeds upon."

The square hall, paneled with dark wood, promised good acoustics. An improvised platform perhaps a foot high served as stage for the piano and the solo performers. Several other artists had been engaged to perform. One was the opera singer Marya Kussnetzov, tall, dark, with a brittle kind of beauty. She sang with great ease, sometimes masking the natural hardness of her tones with a sudden shift of voice production, adopting a husky throatiness to soften a tone that otherwise was blatantly clear and on the verge of harshness. I have heard many Russian singers and some Negro singers use this same device.

As my turn to play approached I felt a nervous excitement that was not exactly fear and yet threatened the control and steadiness of my bow arm. It seemed impossible that much notice would be taken of an unknown fiddler following a favorite prima-donna.

Magnus had wanted me to start with some brilliant pyrotechnics—Wieniawski or Sarasate. At the last moment I changed my plans and began on sober, low-in-key material: some Corelli, and a simple little sonata by Handel. It was a wise choice; I felt sure of this from the first austere phrase. Kussnetzov had ended her group with the most spectacular roulades and fireworks in the coloratura arsenal, and the audience was ready for something simple. And who is more serene than Corelli or Handel?

Even before I finished my first piece I could feel that wave of sympathy from the audience which is such an extraordinary source of strength to the performer. You cannot see it, you cannot easily describe it—but its presence often makes the difference between defeat and victory. There were no set programs. The artists announced their numbers *a piacere*. I had not expected to play for more than fifteen or twenty minutes: I played for an hour. Several members of the audience left their seats and stood around the piano, some of them following the pianist's score, others looking through the extra music I had brought with me. At the end of each piece there would be a vociferous shout for more, with specific requests. I glanced several times at Magnus; he nodded back, urging me to continue. It was evident that he was more than satisfied.

I had never known such spontaneous enthusiasm. All at once everyone there had become a personal friend. I played well; who does not play well under such conditions? Introduction followed introduction; I received extravagant compliments. Could it all be true? But at three A.M., I reflected: For once in a lifetime, let's be recklessly self-indulgent and believe it—it fits so perfectly into the picture.

That evening I met for the first time Prince Serge Wolkonsky. I had noticed him sitting near the front of the audience, utterly absorbed in the music. He had a fine philosophic head whose aquiline features were accentuated by a dark, pointed beard. He was not among the first who rushed forward to express their enthusiasm, and his terms of praise were measured, but they carried a note of deep feeling. He said: "Your music moves me strangely. I would like to know you—to talk with you. Will you dine with me tomorrow? Oh, no, you cannot, for you are to play again, Magnus has told me. The next evening, then?"

"He is a good friend to have made," Magnus whispered to me after the Prince had moved off. "I will tell you more about him later on. In the meantime, you must play some more."

"Serious or gay?" I asked.

"Well," said one, "it is rather late. Let us be gay with a polonaise!"

The polonaise having been received with gusto, somebody suddenly suggested that we should all move along to the Islands.

The Islands? What Islands, I wondered, and wondered also how far into the morning we had to go before the evening could be thought of as ended.

It proved that the "Islands" were in the Neva, now frozen over; you reached them by driving across the ice. And the restaurants there were popular night resorts. We arrived some time before four A.M. when the night life was at its height. We were royally entertained: we had caviar, buckets of it, like gleaming gray pearls; champagne in magnums (mere quarts would have been disdained on the Islands); and such playing, such singing, such dancing! Six o'clock and the return to our hotel came all too soon. I was much too exhilarated to feel tired. None the less, I slept soundly until two o'clock the following afternoon.

CHAPTER SEVENTEEN

THE next day I reminded Magnus that he was going to tell me about Prince Wolkonsky.

"In Wolkonsky," said Magnus, "you have met one of the great gentlemen, one of the unique figures of Europe. He is something of a student, a philosopher, a poet, a musician. Until recently he has been Intendant at the Marinsky Theater. His title and his wealth are the least of his attractions. He is, indeed, that vanishing type—an important amateur and patron of the arts. In reality he belongs to the sixteenth century rather than to ours."

It was quite true, I thought, even of his appearance: as though a portrait by Sebastiano del Piombo had suddenly come to life in the masquerade of modern dress.

"This evening at the Agricultural Club," continued Magnus, "you will meet some of your 'old' friends of last night, but for the most part it will be a totally different group."

"Shall I play the same pieces?"

"Yes. By all means begin with your old Italians. I wondered at first if you were not knocking too modestly at the door of recognition, but it seemed to swing wide open. You can't do better than repeat the process."

"Will Wolkonsky be there?"

"Perhaps. He was not sure. But in any case you will meet Alexander Stolypin and his sister Madame Ovrossimov."

"Stolypin? Isn't that the Prime Minister's name?"

"Yes—it is Alexander's brother Peter Stolypin who is Prime Minister. Alexander is editor of the *New Times,* 'the most important daily.' "

"Stolypin is regarded as reactionary?"

"Ultra-reactionary," said Magnus. "He is very much hated by the radical elements, and distrusted by the intelligentsia. I should feel more than uneasy in his boots. Although he edits a conservative paper which supports Government policies, Alexander is rather liberal. His sister, Mme. Ovrossimov, is completely liberal. It is said that when she and her elder brother Peter meet, which is not often, there is a tacit understanding not to mention politics. She is interested in agricultural progress and reforms, lives simply, and adores music. So does Alexander, for that matter. Peter rarely attends concerts—*he* says because he has no time, but I suspect it is due to lack of inclination."

"It would be interesting to speculate on the liberalizing influence of music. You can't very well love Beethoven and not be something of a revolutionary at heart."

Magnus agreed with this and advised me to use it in some future interview—not, however, in Russia!

The concert that evening was just like the first one, except that it began at ten-thirty and the atmosphere was more sober. The interest and enthusiasm were just as heartening, and again I played more than I had expected to. The inevitable group again circled round the piano; the semi-formal, semi-intimate atmosphere was established, and introductions followed.

Alexander Stolypin proved to be a ponderous, florid, expansive man, of slow gestures. His speech was more like gargling than like articulation; his deep laughter was a kind of cavernous rumble; his dark and luxuriant beard attested to untamed vigor. It was a massive personality.

In sharp contrast was Constantin Skirmunt, a Pole of crisp, staccato speech and ascetic appearance, whose clean-shaven face looked like naked marble alongside the hirsute fringes of the Russians. He was at this time a member of the Imperial Council. But he was ardently and unmistakably Polish, and I rather think that he paid only lip service to Imperial business, much as the Irish members of Parliament did in the case of British business. Polish patriotism was not unlike Irish in pattern.

Skirmunt had an enigmatic personality. Under a patina of

exquisite manners there was an icy aloofness. His nearest approach to warmth appeared when he talked about music, for which he had a passion. He asked me whether I knew Paderewski. I did, and I must have said the proper things, for the glacier melted a trifle.

"Yes, indeed—he is a great pianist! But he is far more than that: the inarticulate soul of Poland expresses itself through Paderewski. Some day, some day, perhaps. . . ." Then, as if checking something he should not say, "Will you not dine with me? When and where?"

I couldn't say without consulting Magnus and his little agenda. One evening next week perhaps. Slavic hospitality was prodigal. From the invitations of that evening alone I could have dined out every night for the next two weeks.

"I should have liked to talk more with Stolypin's sister," I said to Magnus later. "I was drawn to her in spite of the fact that we exchanged no more than a few words."

"You will, you will," he promised. "She, too, has asked you for dinner. It will not be a social affair, but it will be interesting."

He also told me that Stolypin was going to write an article for the *New Times* about my playing. He was enthusiastic, it seemed. Yes, I said—I had gathered that. "I thought, at one time, that he was going to embrace me!"

"He thought so too," replied Magnus. "But then, perhaps remembering your Anglo-Saxon blood, he restrained himself."

"It must be a Gargantuan accolade," I commented, "and I am just as glad I escaped it."

"You must get used to the masculine embrace here in Russia. It is an expression of natural expansiveness and means nothing more to them than a cordial handshake does to us. If you get self-conscious about it, you may not give offense, but you will feel uncomfortable and make them feel uncomfortable."

The next evening I dined with Prince Wolkonsky. He took me to a famous restaurant—Donon's. Something like the Voisin in Paris, it had doubtless been started by a French chef. There were no gaudy trappings about Donon's, no music, no entertain-

ment. It was an eating place par excellence, and its almost sepul-
chral quiet encouraged conversation.

Wolkonsky was a delightful conversationalist. I found that he
knew my country, having represented Russia in the Congress
of Religions at the Chicago World's Fair of 1893. I asked him
whether by any chance he had met the Swami Vivekananda
there. Oh, yes, he had, and for some time afterward the two had
maintained an active correspondence. But how was it that I came
to speak of him? I was, after all, much too young to have remembered. . . . I explained that my family had been acquainted
with the Swami and had often talked about him.

"He made a—what do you call it?—a sensational 'hit' in your
country," said Wolkonsky, "especially with the Chicago ladies.
Ah, those Chicago ladies! They seemed to take life—and incidentally themselves—very seriously."

"I have no doubt that you came in for a great deal of lionizing
when you were there?"

"I was no lion," this with a twinkle. "I was a Daniel in the
lions' den, but without Daniel's wisdom or his initiative. Even
my feeble attempts at humor, tried only once or twice, came to
abortive ends. Here is an example: I turned to my hostess at
dinner one evening, somewhat, I confess, with my tongue in my
cheek. 'They tell me,' I said, 'that New York society numbers
precisely four hundred. How many, in your estimation, are the
socially élite of Chicago?' She paused a moment—the matter required deep thought. Then said slowly, 'I *think,* Prince, that We
are eighty.' I wondered," added Wolkonsky, "how much farther
west I must travel before reaching a city where I'd be told that
'We, Prince, are seven'!"

Wolkonsky asked many questions about where I had played,
where I had studied, what books I read. Was I fond of pictures?
Had I been to The Hermitage yet?

"There is in your playing," he said, "a distinctive quality that
makes it quite different from any I have previously enjoyed. You
know the refreshing sensation you get from a new author whose
originality of style impresses you. It is like the promise of a new
land you have not yet visited. I knew from your first phrase that
I should want to visit the country peopled by your thoughts."

[131]

Suddenly, then, I wished myself at home, and alone, with twenty-four hours a day for work. Wolkonsky was offering me a vista of the future rather than a true picture of the present. As though reading my thoughts, he went on: "You are modest, and that is right. There is a reserve, a reticence, a modesty in your playing. It is part of your character; do not lose it!"

I do not remember what we had for dinner; it was probably excellent, but memory was busy with other things.

Day by day I was accustoming myself to a new tempo of life. In Russia you resign yourself to an inertia that dims the urgency of practical matters. On the other hand, there is a vigorous reaction to things of an abstract or imaginative nature. The Russian is an escapist from the routine and necessary, but is prodigal with his time and energy when a new idea awakens him. I found myself succumbing to this different rhythm. I remembered Magnus' warning: It does not always make sense, but who comes to Russia for such a purpose?

A few evenings later I dined at Madame Ovrossimov's. Her home was somberly furnished, and as plain as she. She was tall and gaunt; the leathery skin stretched taut over high cheek bones; the chin was square and determined; her angular figure was material for a cubist painter. What humanized her was a pair of keen, intelligent eyes—eyes tired by tragedy, but with an abiding faith in goodness, eyes that you knew instinctively would never say "no" to any appeal. I was glad to find myself seated next to her at the dinner table. We talked some about music, but she wanted most of all to question me about American agriculture. Alas! I knew little or nothing about that subject. As a matter of fact, she—who had never been within three thousand miles of America—told me many things I should have known and been proud of. She herself was both interested and active in the efforts being made to improve Russian agriculture. I asked about the reforms she was so ardently advocating.

"It is the slowest kind of work," she complained. "We progress by inches, and there are limitless miles to cover. And there is still the serf problem."

While she spoke I found myself noticing her hands. The large

[132]

and generous palm had sensitive, tapering fingers which nervously punctuated her speech as she tapped the tablecloth. It was a minute gesture, the only release of nervous energy in an otherwise immobile figure.

But was it not true, I inquired, that serfdom had been abolished by Alexander II even before our Civil War had ended slavery in my own country?

"Yes—in 1861. But in spite of legal emancipation we still have serfdom. The peasant will never be a free man until the soil he works on is his own. We do have some small land-owners, but they are too few—there should be millions of them. There *shall* be millions of them."

At this point the lady on my right sighed—an immense and Slavic sigh. I remembered my manners and turned to her. We went through the initial amenities, and then I discovered that she wanted to talk about her health—or rather lack of it. This species, I reflected, is to be found in all lands.

"I suffer abominably," she mourned. "Maladie de cœur. There is nothing to be done for it." She lighted another cigarette. "I smoke too many of these—sixty a day. They are very bad for my heart."

"Then why do you smoke so much?"

"Did you not know? All Russians are impractical. It is their destiny. I shall, perhaps, die very soon."

This prediction seemed to comfort her, so I made no comment.

"You are a musician," went on this despondent voice. "If I am well enough, I shall come to hear you. Do you not play soon at the Salle de la Noblesse?"

Yes, the following week.

"Well, I shall try to come. I shall not enjoy it as I should. The lights are too bright; they hurt my eyes. And if you play well, I shall not sleep that night. I often have insomnia. Please, you do not smoke? Ever?"

No, I had not yet started; in fact, I was rather appalled by the prospect.

"But you will, in time. And you will smoke too much—all musicians do. It is very bad for them."

I said I should put it off as long as possible.

[133]

"I see," she went on, "that you are not a fatalist. But I do not think that you can escape your destiny. I understand you perfectly. We meet for the first time—perhaps we shall never meet again; but what does it matter? If we do meet again, I know that you will be less cheerful than you are now." Then, suddenly, "Are you a virgin?"

I decided not to answer this, but soon I found that no answer was necessary. Clairvoyantly, she proceeded to describe incidents in my life of which I had never heard.

"But in fact," she ended, "men remain in their hearts strangely more virginal than women."

I was grateful for this back-handed compliment.

"You must come and see me. Perhaps I shall not receive you. I may not feel well. But come, nevertheless."

Mme. Ovrossimov overheard part of this conversation and decided it was time to rescue me.

Had I called yet on the Rockhills? Everyone, it seemed, liked our Ambassador and his family. Did I have a card of introduction to them? Good, I must present it at once.

I called on the Rockhills the day after the Ovrossimov dinner, and found my letter of introduction unnecessary: the Rockhills had heard of me from Wolkonsky and were expecting me. Besides Mr. and Mrs. Rockhill, there were two charming daughters—ages uncertain and unascertainable. When you are twenty-one, a few years' difference in age appears enormous.

The William Rockhills were in every way fitted to represent a new world in a very old, and in some ways backward, one. You knew instinctively that, wherever they went to live, you would find in their home a corner of the United States. They entertained richly but with perfect tact and without ostentation. If there was any sense of privilege, you felt that it was the privilege of bearing an American passport.

I was made to feel at home at once. Where and when was I to play next? They knew about the concert at the Salle de la Noblesse and were going; but was I not to give a recital of my own? Good; would I ask my agent to send them tickets as soon as they were issued?

I was pressed to stay for tea. There is nothing more friendly than the sound and the smell of a samovar. A large one, standing on a corner table, added a whispered orchestration to the pleasant voices.

"This copper friend," said Mrs. Rockhill, "is not an innovation. We brought our own coals to Newcastle. It had served us for many years at home. Some of our new acquaintances here accuse me of diplomatic cajolery, but it's not true: before I had ever set foot on Russian soil I believed their proverb that tea without a samovar is like bread without salt, like a flower without perfume."

The steaming cup of tea she offered me was no longer a mere drink, it was an image and a symbol.

"And," continued my hostess, "are you free next Thursday evening? And will you come? There will be dancing." I thought quickly—yes, Thursday was still unmortgaged.

"A card will be sent to remind you."

Apparently it was to be a very formal affair. (I remembered with dismay the left lapel of my dress coat, shiny from the friction of the violin. Could the valet of the Hôtel de l'Europe . . . ?)

"My daughters will see that you are partnered with pretty girls. I hope you like to dance?" Without waiting for my enthusiastic assent she went on: "Dancing will be in the two large front rooms. Even so, the floor will be crowded. Be sure," she pressed me, "to come early and stay late."

I assured her that I needed no urging.

Mr. Rockhill reminded me in some indefinable way of my father—of somewhat the same build and carriage, though unlike in features. I found myself watching the small, expressive lines at the corner of his eyes that wrinkled in the same endearing way. His contributions to the conversation were brief. He was amused at his wife's preoccupation with the numbers that threatened to invade their home next Thursday.

"You are always worrying," he said, "that there will be too many. In Russia that is a mistake. You ought to worry over the opposite possibility. The people here adore overheated rooms, overcrowded with furniture, and thronged with humanity. If the dancers can only progress by inches, it is all to the good.

They prefer bruised feet to the chill of a vacant space. Invite more, and multiply your order for refreshments." Turning to me with a chuckle, he slapped a chubby hand against his thigh (which again recalled my father) and said, "Eating and drinking are serious affairs here."

A caller was announced—Mme. Nameiev. I recognized my dinner partner of the night before. It was a relief to know that she had not died yet. The Rockhills greeted her warmly, and were about to introduce me when she forestalled them.

"We met last night at Mme. Ovrossimov's," she explained, her voice still gloomy. "We had an interesting talk. I should not have gone—my heart, you know."

Mrs. Rockhill nodded sympathetically.

"But it did me less harm than I expected. May I smoke? Of course, you are always so kind! No, I will not take tea, I will smoke instead. It is a vicious habit. And it is killing me."

Mr. Rockhill, kindly but unalarmed, suggested that the milder stimulation of tea might act as an antidote to her lethal habit.

"How clever of you!" exclaimed Mme. Nameiev. "Perhaps you are right. You are a diplomat and should know. Well then, if it is not too much trouble, I will take a cup of tea—strong, and with five lumps of sugar."

The Rockhill girls exchanged amused glances with me as Mme. Nameiev inhaled a puff from her cigarette.

"I wish," said Mrs. Rockhill, "that Lena had come with you today." She turned to me. "Mme. Nameiev's lovely daughter. You will meet her at the dance."

"Yes," agreed her mother, despondently, "she is young; she is beautiful. It is a misfortune. She is so romantic, so reckless— she will make a bad marriage. It is inescapable."

"How unfortunate for you," commiserated Mr. Rockhill, "that Lena's excess of good looks should so endanger her future." The wrinkles at the corner of his eyes betrayed the irony absent from his tone.

"How understanding you are!" Her gratitude was pathetic. "Yes, Lena and I are coming on Thursday, if my heart permits. In any case, Lena will come. My cousin can chaperone her. Next week perhaps I shall not feel so well."

Mrs. Rockhill was glad that her health was, this week at least, fairly satisfactory. But Mme. Nameiev was quick to qualify the admission.

"I have come to recognize the peril of these respites," she pronounced. "Lena does not suspect the danger I am in. This morning she said to me quite cheerfully, 'Mamma, you *are* looking well!' Poor child, she does not know; I should not want her to know. I withheld my tears and smiled. Soon—all too soon—she will know unhappiness herself. You will enjoy meeting her, Mr. Spalding; you will be attracted to her. All men feel her attraction. Perhaps you will want to marry her. You would not object to a Russian wife?"

I assured her I had no nationalistic prejudices.

"That is imprudent of you, and you should not admit it. But—I forget: you are an American, and Americans are not superstitious. And you are so young. Lena, too, is imprudent. It would be as well, after all, if you did not fall in love, did not marry."

"Lena," observed Mrs. Rockhill, "has a mind of her own. She will, unless I am greatly mistaken, decide her future very much in the modern way."

"Alas! So much the worse for her," assented her mother. "I have given it so much thought, this matter of her marriage—and I grieve to think of the unhappiness in store for her."

"Come, come, Mme. Nameiev," said Mr. Rockhill, "you must not be so gloomy about it. Even *you* may be mistaken."

She looked at him, utterly discouraged.

"That is what tortures me so," admitted this unpredictable lady. "My judgment is often wrong. Poor Lena! If even her mother cannot decide what is right, what, indeed, is to become of her?"

This conclusion appeared to comfort her, for she was almost cheerful when she said good-by. I, too, left shortly afterward, but not before joining in the chorus of laughter which had been politely restrained while she was there.

"Isn't she marvelous?" asked Mrs. Rockhill. "No one would believe it," she predicted, "but you will really like Lena Nameiev."

[137]

CHAPTER EIGHTEEN

ON my return to the hotel I promptly summoned the valet for first-aid treatment of my battle-scarred dress coat. The left lapel was even shinier than I had feared. The valet shook his head doubtfully when I insisted that the grosgrain silk facing must be replaced by Thursday night. He would try, was his unhopeful promise. Unsatisfied, I decided to fire his imagination by explaining the importance of the event. It worked at once; there are few snobs to match a valet.

"The Embassy ball!" he exclaimed. "All Petersburg will be there. But of course your coat will be ready—I guarantee it!" And with my coat on his arm, he bowed himself out of the room. My prestige had grown several inches in the last few seconds.

The following Thursday, resplendent with new lapels, I drove to the Embassy in an open sled, the cold night air whipping my cheeks. Gliding silently and swiftly over the snow were hundreds of these conveyances, all bound for the same destination. Long before reaching the Embassy door they slowed to a walk punctuated by frequent stops, gradually forming an endless queue awaiting entry. A canopy had been erected and a carpet stretched, and numerous flunkeys with lighted flambeaux assisted the guests. It was like a stage setting.

The house was built around an open rectangular courtyard, thus taking advantage of every ray of the Russian winter's penurious daylight. The building was something more than a house, something less than a palace. It was what in the St. Germain quarter of Paris would have been called an *hôtel*. This evening its customary sobriety had been transformed. Thousands of candles were added to the usual lighting. Festoons of roses hung gracefully around the high-ceilinged hall and serpentined in and out of the stair balustrade. The staircase was so broad that eight might have gone up it abreast, but—whether by protocol or by sheer instinct—the guests waited in a crowd below, enhancing the solitary splendor of each single ascent.

Mr. and Mrs. Rockhill received their guests at the head of the stairs where one of the secretaries announced their names. While waiting my turn I listened to the roll-call of princely titles and the inevitable "Excellency" of governmental or diplomatic notables. More than once the title "Highness" announced Imperial blood. But both my host and hostess unmistakably conveyed to me their partiality for a compatriot.

In the apartments above, an orchestra was playing. The two front salons devoted to dancing were not yet so crowded as Mrs. Rockhill had predicted, but the hour was still early—not yet midnight. I was glad of this, for it made easier my appraisal of the necromancer's wand that had so magically transformed the Embassy. Where, I wondered, had all the flowers come from?

Wolkonsky's voice at my shoulder asked: "Is it not lovely? But you must not be too surprised. In your country, or mine, it hardly needs a miracle to turn winter into summer—a hand can stretch from New York, or from Chicago, a thousand miles or more, to pick a flower in Florida. Why should we in St. Petersburg not do the same with our own Crimea? Yes," he smiled, "it does sound like a Monte Cristo exploit—Monte Cristo with his tanks of living sterlet from the Volga—but eighty years have made a difference in Russian transportation."

"It is none the less unreal and dazzling," I said.

"And wantonly wasteful, you are thinking," smiled Wolkonsky. "Yes," with a wave of the hand, "this is indeed a *'Prelude to The Deluge.'* History repeats itself over and over again, but human nature refuses to learn from it. This earth could be so bountiful if it were intelligently and equitably exploited. At present, however, the rich grow increasingly richer and the poor increasingly poorer.

"I have a nightmare picture of my country with the rivers

[139]

dried up, their tributaries imprisoned in man-made reservoirs high in the mountains. The parched earth of the valleys cries out, but the mountains are deaf and unheeding. Nature herself revolts, and there is a cataclysm. The reservoirs are smashed and the torrent pours downward, spreading death and destruction in its furious path—" He broke off apologetically. "You must excuse my inopportune ramblings. Your music makes me forget how young you are. You must dance and forget, for this evening at least, my pessimistic philosophy."

One of the Miss Rockhills approached. "Come with me," she said. "Mme. Nameiev is asking for you."

"Her heart permitted her to come, then?"

"Yes, she decided to postpone her death for this event."

"And shall I meet the attractive Lena?" I asked.

"Attractive is a tepid term. You will be something less than human if on sight of her your heart does not double its normal rate."

"I'll take my pulse and tell you what happens!"

Near the doorway of the first salon they stood, mother and daughter. Lena Nameiev was indeed ravishing. Her white skin was set off by the blackest hair I had ever seen. The features were not faultlessly regular, but there was a witchery in their slight dissonance. The eyes were somewhat too wide apart, the red lips stretched overgenerously. These might have reduced her score in a beauty contest, but they were no brakes on the stirring pulse. She smiled as we met. So perhaps smiled Herrick's Julia when he wrote to her of the "rock of rubies" and the "quarelets of pearl."

"My mother has been telling me about you," said Lena Nameiev, "and we are coming to your concert."

I mumbled my thanks, and asked for the next dance. She was desolated—the next one was taken, but the one after. . . . I would not forget, no? I assured her that this was impossible. At that moment a young officer, resplendent in white uniform and gold braid, claimed her attention. Away they whirled in the glittering throng.

I stood for a while watching the dancing with Mme. Nameiev. For this evening she had assumed the alien aspect of cheerfulness. Even her daughter's beauty failed to depress her. And the kaleidoscopic pageant absorbed and animated her. Light, color, and rhythmic movement in prismatic array were

> "All intervolved and spreading wide,
> Like water-dimples down a tide."

The chandeliers seemed to reflect fire from the diamond necklaces and tiaras swirling below them. The few stray individuals —among them our own Ambassador—who wore the chaste black-and-white of dress clothes looked alien on that ballroom floor.

Que diable allait-il faire dans cette galère, I wondered ruefully of the young fiddler who was finding himself somewhat lonely in these surroundings. But I soon spied friends—Alexander Stolypin, Skirmunt, and old Count Benckendorff whose globular torso swayed like an unsteady balloon on the two insecure stilts that were his legs. He, too, had attended the Agricultural Club concert the week before. I hadn't had much conversation with him on that occasion, but this evening he singled me out, having been deputized by the Grand Duchess Oldenburg to ask me to play at a charity concert she was sponsoring. The renowned French pianist Raoul Pugno, due shortly in St. Petersburg, had already been engaged. Would I play? And what was my fee? (Apparently, I thought, artists in Russia are not expected to be the chief donors at charity affairs.)

Magnus was not at hand to consult. I thought quickly, multiplied his guarantee by three, and said, "Six hundred rubles." Benckendorff did not seem startled by the amount. However, he had not been a diplomat for nothing, and he knew how to bargain. His response was that there might be a decoration from grateful Royalty if I were to reduce my fee somewhat.

Again, I thought quickly. (Certainly, at such a function as this one, for instance, a Royal medal *would* relieve the expanse of black dress coat, but . . .) I decided to keep the transaction strictly monetary, and conveyed this politely. Benckendorff looked neither surprised nor disappointed; indeed, I detected tacit approval. He would see Magnus the next day and arrange details.

We went on talking, half in English, half in French. Like so many cultivated Russians, Benckendorff shifted effortlessly from the one language to the other. What interested me most, however, was the odd vocal apparatus back of his speech. Each sentence was punctuated by a kind of asthmatic sigh, issuing, it would seem, not from the throat, but from a leaky valve elsewhere. My curiosity almost overcame my manners; such a shape and such sounds, I was convinced, bore no relation to the human body. In place of the usual coil of intestines, these must be a set of inner-tire tubes, and one of these must have had a puncture. Really, he should go to a doctor at once—or a garage. . . .

Meanwhile, our conversation went on. Did I know Pugno? My affirmative response appeared to be most satisfactory.

Quel artiste, quelle sensibilité! Had I ever played with him? Yes, as a matter of fact, I had.

A la bonne heure! And was it not a delight?

I said it was.

The *Kreutzer* Sonata—we had played that together?

We had.

"Ah," he wheezed, "the Grand Duchess will be so happy—she longs to hear it." (How easy it is, I thought, to make a Grand Duchess happy!) "You know—you have read—our Tolstoy?"

I was puzzled for a moment till I recalled Tolstoy's well-known but foolish novel entitled *The Kreutzer Sonata.* I knew that Pugno and I would lend no neurotic flavor to that massive torrent of Beethoven's. All musicians resent the sentimental implication attached to it by that powerful but distinctly unmusical novelist.

Our conversation was interrupted by one of the Miss Rockhills. Why was I not dancing? I explained that I was about to repair that omission—that I was to have the next dance with Miss Nameiev.

"Then go and claim it at once," Miss Rockhill advised. "See —she has just rejoined her mother." I bowed my excuses to her and Benckendorff and lost no time in taking up my option. It was clear enough that being a few seconds late would surely mean a lost opportunity, for already Lena Nameiev was besieged by fresh suppliants. She smiled her acknowledgment of my priority, and took my arm. But as the music started, she paused.

"It is a mazurka," she said. "Do you know that Polish dance?"

Alas, I didn't.

"Never mind. Let us sit in the conservatory and talk for a while—the heat here is stifling. You are not disappointed, no? There will at most surely be an extra—a waltz, perhaps. We will dance that."

I was not disappointed. Indeed, I was relieved not to expose my ignorance of that intricate dance, and I relished the prospect of conversation with this delightful girl.

Lena Nameiev's education had been unusually complete, even by Russian standards. She had fluent command of several languages, her knowledge of literature was wide, her reactions to music showed more than surface acquaintance. I was struck by the penetration of many of her remarks. We talked about books. She was surprised and pleased to learn that I knew some Russian authors: Tolstoy, Turgenev, and Dostoevsky.

"But why should you be astonished?" I protested. "You who know our literature so well."

"How gauche of me!" she laughed. "I did not really mean that. It is our unconscious habit of thought—not that we underrate education elsewhere, but rather that we overrate our own remoteness. We seem so incredibly far away from everything. It is we who visit many lands, but few people visit us. Our alphabet and language are impossible, our manner of life is a century behind, our very Christianity is of the most Eastern brand, so we are childishly pleased by any sign that the Western world knows of us."

We were sitting on a marble bench in the relatively cool conservatory. Palms and evergreens rose from floor to ceiling.

"You have traveled a great deal?" I asked.

"Every year—extensively."

"But perhaps not now so much? Your mother's health . . ."

"Ah, Mamma! I see you have not escaped her lamentations. They are so painfully sweet to her! Please believe me, I am not being cruel or heartless. Mamma is a darling, and I adore her, but she is a direct descendant of Molière's *malade imaginaire*."

"You mean in all seriousness that there is nothing the matter with her?"

"I mean," said Lena, "that Mamma has lived so long under the shadow of a comfortable infirmity that it is perhaps, next to me, her dearest companion. Like Othello, she would be without an occupation if the insecure span of her life were stretched from days to weeks, weeks to months, and months to years. The doctors all recognize her condition, and humor her whim, while they assure me that she is in no danger. Indeed, they tell me that it might be a risk to undeceive her."

"When did it start?" I asked.

"Who can tell? A long time ago, certainly. Failure, perhaps, on her wedding day."

"Her wedding day?" I echoed, mystified.

"It is part of a superstition. I do not, I suppose, have to tell you that Mamma is superstitious? Well, there is a tradition that whichever one—bride or bridegroom—first sets foot on the raised dais at the marriage ceremony is the one who will rule the family. Between every engaged couple there is a good-humored race for this advantage—within, of course, the prescribed rules of decorum. Mamma has often confessed to me that when her marriage-day was coming, she slept not a wink, planning how to win. Then, when the day arrived, the absurd fashions of 1890 were her undoing: she tripped on her voluminous skirt and all but fell."

"And your father—"

"Papa, of course, caught her; but he was careful to carry her to the dais, so that it was he who first actually stepped onto it."

"But that— But that—" I ejaculated.

"But that— A trifle light as air, if you like! But Mamma found it very depressing. Papa tried to humor her out of it, but she let it prey on her mind as an omen of ill luck."

"But you—you surely do not believe such superstitions?"

Lena paused a moment, reflecting.

"No," she said slowly, "but it is curious how many traditional idiocies habit urges you to observe, even though you reject them intellectually. But listen—the orchestra is beginning a waltz. Shall we dance?"

It was not easy to weave one's way through the crowded ballroom. But Lena Nameiev was incredibly light on her feet and followed my steps with flattering facility. I found myself perspiring with exhilaration at negotiating the turns without mishap. The waltz ended; Lena was besieged by eager partners, but I was consoled by the promise of another dance later on.

I was joined by Constantin Skirmunt. "You have not," he observed, "been losing any time. She is one of the loveliest girls on the floor."

I assured him that I fully recognized my good fortune. Then I asked about old Count Benckendorff.

"Oh, Benckendorff," he said. "Yes, I saw that you had a long conversation with him."

I told him of its subject.

"That should be a great affair," said Skirmunt. "But I am glad you held out for your fee and were not tempted by Benckendorff's system of barter. He is a wily fox, for all his smooth manners."

I could not resist commenting on the Count's peculiar voice.

"How right you are," agreed Skirmunt. "He is a natural comic. But he takes himself very seriously. His world is a world of detail, of privilege, of custom. He is aware of large events only in a subconscious way. He resents their intrusion on the well-combed, exquisitely manicured life he leads. But in an event of this kind he is indispensable. Shall we go for some refreshments?"

In the dining-room we were joined at a small table by the younger Miss Rockhill and her dancing companion, an officer of the Imperial Guard. The champagne appeared to flow, not from bottles, but from some vast reservoir. Imaginative chefs had prepared a pageant of dishes that tempted the eye as well as the palate. Glacéed game wore the borrowed plumage of peacock feathers; vegetable salads pyramided to extraordinary heights. Who, I thought, will venture to desecrate these laborious achievements?

After supper dancing continued. The hours passed unnoticed. When I returned to my hotel I couldn't quite believe the clock that told me it was after seven in the morning.

[145]

CHAPTER NINETEEN

A NIGHT train took us over the Karelian isthmus to the capital of Finland. It was a welcome diversion from the fascinating but unreal splendors of Imperial Russia. The morning arrival in Helsingfors itself typified the contrast. Politically, Finland was, and had been for a hundred years, a province of Russia. Since, up to that time, she had been under Swedish rule, she had never enjoyed autonomy. But freedom is a mental concept, and you could not visit this land, even in 1910, without feeling the spirit of freedom.

The people attracted me at once. I liked the clean, cold-cut look of them, the high cheekbones, the wide, deep-set eyes that look straight through you; the well-co-ordinated bodies, sparing of gesture; and the proud carriage which commands immediate respect. Even the porter who carried our bags from train to droshky exemplified this. His act was one of service, not of servitude.

It is something of a paradox to leave the land that has the greatest potential wealth in the world, and to find across the border, in a conquered province (and an unpromisingly poor one at that), a greater richness of life.

We were lodged at the Societetshuset—comfortable, neat, and unpretentious. I did not miss the Asiatic splendors of the Hôtel de l'Europe. After breakfast we walked to the University Hall, where concerts were usually held and where I was due for rehearsal with the orchestra. To take a cab would have seemed ostentatious. The question was settled by the hotel porter when I tried to order a droshky.

"To the University Hall?" he said with polite surprise. "It is only a matter of a few blocks. Look, I will show you on the map."

The hall was entirely original in shape: a semicircle in which the audience faced the flat wall. What had been planned as a circular auditorium had been cut in two by an uncompromising wall. The stage was at one corner where the straight line met the curved one. Apparently the musical attack was not to be a frontal one, but entirely on the bias.

I was cordially greeted by Kajanus, the conductor of the orchestra. To my unspoken question about the hall, he said: "You are curious about this rather peculiar architectural arrangement. When the building first went up about a century ago, it was by order of the Tsar Alexander I that this wall sliced away half of our theater. Was it just a foolish, arbitrary act, or had it some special significance? I do not know. We resented it, of course; but we have accepted it. And it does not prevent our enjoyment of music. Shall we rehearse?"

The Beethoven concerto had been chosen for my first appearance. It was to be followed, two days later, by a second performance at which I would play the Mendelssohn concerto.

It was not a truly good orchestra. It lacked precision of attack, and among the brass and wood-wind sections there was often doubtful quality and intonation. The strings were, for the most part, good; and I was grateful when the musical score used them generously. But there was an unfailing enthusiasm and *élan* that was heartening. You could feel, in the whole orchestra, a deep and abiding love of music that compensated for the lack of polish. We rehearsed for two hours or more, and I thoroughly enjoyed myself although the results at the end were still too ragged to be thoroughly satisfying.

From the corner of my eye I noticed, seated in the almost empty hall, a large man with a massive head. After listening attentively to the rehearsal he came to the stage to congratulate me. It was my first meeting with Jean Sibelius. He was so big that he dwarfed those around him. His manners were simple but impressive; when he spoke to me I felt, even before I knew who he was, that here was Someone, indeed!

He had liked my playing. He had liked my Beethoven. The compliments were Finnish, frugal, clean-cut—and stimulating. Beside them, more opulent phrases would have felt counterfeit.

"I have written a violin concerto," he said. "Do you know it?"

I was sorry to confess that I didn't.

"It is very rarely played," he went on. "It is difficult, perhaps too difficult—but," with unconscious candor, "it is good music. I hope you will like it."

I was sure I would. I immediately resolved to get it and study it. The resolve was, to my loss, not put into action for many years.

The music of Sibelius is aloof and baffling at first hearing; it eludes easy acquaintanceship. Its surface is not soft; you have to hew your way through hard granite before approaching an understanding of it. One of the most searching appraisals of it that I have heard came to me recently from Fritz Kreisler. He and I were having tea after he had attended a New York Philharmonic performance at which I played the Sibelius concerto.

"One of the most significant and original qualities of Sibelius' music," he said, "is its rather irregular use of rhythmical patterns, like different planes of perspective slightly out of focus. They make their entrances and exits at totally unexpected moments. The harmonic structure is simple, sometimes even conventional; but these architectural innovations produce an altogether new picture."

"El Greco achieves the same effect in painting—the distortion that is so fascinating," I suggested.

"Exactly," agreed Kreisler. "Before you is an altered world—a world with an added dimension."

That new dimension was there for me to find, at the time when I was at Helsingfors in 1910, but I was blind to it for two decades longer. Now, after Sibelius had talked to me a little further, he left abruptly, saying, "I will see and hear you again to-night."

Kajanus was very much excited about it; he had rarely seen the great man so interested. Did I realize, he asked, that in Finland a sign of approval from Sibelius was like a musical Victoria Cross? Had I heard his symphonies? Of the three then composed, I had heard one, the first. Kajanus became positively lyrical in discussing the work, and fortunately there was no need for me to express myself about it, for at that time I had only a rather negative reaction to it and would have been hard pressed to satisfy him.

"Sibelius," said Kajanus, "is Finland itself. He is our musician, our tonal poet, the historian of the world deep within us, and the prophet of the world that is to come to us. He serves as a much-needed outlet for that patriotism which we may not now voice in words!"

Magnus joined us at this point, bringing an Oriental-looking little man with him. His name was Fazer and he was the principal musical agent in Helsingfors. Evidently he, too, had been impressed by the interest Sibelius had taken in my playing, for he was proposing, even before the concert, a return two weeks later for another pair of recitals.

"And who on earth is Jean Sibelius?" asked Magnus of me as we walked back to the hotel. "Of course, I pretended to Fazer that I knew all about him, but until this morning I had never even heard his name."

I explained as best I could.

"Perhaps a big frog in a little puddle," was his verdict. I said nothing, but my uncontrollable dislike of the ready and flippant man who walked beside me increased.

The concert hall was filled to overflowing that evening. It was not my unknown name that had drawn them. They were faithful subscribers to their own symphony concerts—*Mon verre n'est pas grand, mais je bois dans mon verre.* The audience was prompt, and soberly dressed. An occasional evening dress and dinner jacket were conspicuous—a rare accident, evidently, rather than a custom. There was, however, a strongly defined character to this audience that sent some of its strength, some of its aspirations to me, waiting to perform on the stage. After the wave of sympathy that came so generously at the close of the first movement, I stood there aware of the sturdy values of this unique people. I suddenly felt capable of better things, had a desire to prove myself worthy, if for no other reason than that these people believed in me. It was a graduation from triviality, from cheap success.

Each subsequent visit to Finland served to renew this feeling. On my last trip there, in 1927, Mary was with me. She had never been to Finland before, and I was eager to see whether her reaction would be the same as mine. It was.

"They are," she said, "totally unlike any other people I have ever come in contact with—such directness, such simplicity. Life is lived as if it were a straight line; it makes one conscious of the ridiculous serpentining most of us do.

"I had a conversation this morning with the little chambermaid who does our rooms. She was telling me about some relatives of hers who had emigrated to America—to Minnesota, I believe. I asked her if they had done well. Oh, yes, they had. And was she not tempted to follow in their footsteps? She paused a moment; then hesitatingly admitted that she had several times considered it. 'But,' she said, 'I found I could not face the black nights there.' 'Black nights?' I echoed. And then I realized: Patiently she would wait through the long, dark winter, when daylight is so brief, for those white nights of summer when the sun hardly sets before it rises again. Yes, our chambermaid is a poet; she made me feel quite prosaic!"

The Beethoven performance gained me many friends. Though here there were no glamorous "Islands" to visit—no gypsy singers, no caviar, no champagne—the greenroom was filled afterward with people toward whom I was strongly attracted and with whom I at once felt comfortably at home. Sibelius, too, had come as promised, and everyone made way for him as if for visiting royalty. He came, and departed, with that singular abruptness which is so much part of him. Apparently I had not disappointed him. He gripped my hand—crushed it. Next time, I thought, I must be careful to shoot my hand all the way into his to avoid maimed fingers. For once, though, it was not too high a price to pay.

Fazer was there, to press his point about the return concerts. Magnus temporized. "The papers," he said.

"The papers?" repeated Fazer. "But they will be brilliant. I have spoken with the critics— *Sie sind begeistert*. But, more than that, the public is *begeistert*. Wait and see!"

We did see. That very evening when we left the hall it seemed as if half the audience had waited on the broad steps to give a good-night accolade of applause.

The next morning I went for a long walk on the frozen stretches of the harbor. The shipping was solidly encased in ice that would not break up for many months. Some Russian gunboats were unpleasant reminders of absentee ownership; more sympathetic were the squadrons of merchant shipping, barges, and small sailing craft, which would come to life once the long winter was over. I could picture the great stacks of lumber, pine, and spruce, piled high on the barges ready for shipment abroad. This, the greatest natural wealth of Finland, is its chief medium of exchange for much-needed imports. The pine and spruce forests that cover more than half the country are husbanded with care, and the timbering of the land is rigidly regulated.

On my return to the hotel, I found Magnus busy with half-finished translations of the morning reviews. They were, it appeared, everything that Fazer had prophesied. Magnus was not, however, too enthusiastic about the return engagements. He was practical. My fee was paid in rubles, two hundred of them at a throw. Though this was not a great deal in Russia, it did give a comfortable margin of profit. Finland, however, was a different matter, for the Finnish mark was worth only twenty— not fifty-three—American cents. The hall capacity was modest, and even a sold-out house, played on a percentage basis, would not realize more than . . . In short, if I wanted to come back to Finland for the two recitals, would I consider playing them both for the price of one Russian concert? I was twenty-one, and I wanted very much to return; so I accepted the revised fee without question. You cannot be twenty-four hours in Finland and remain rigidly practical.

That afternoon I met another delightful musician, a composer and pianist named Oskar Merikanto who was to play my accompaniments at the recitals ten days or two weeks hence. We did some preliminary rehearsing, four hours of it; in fact, we traveled through quite an extensive repertoire. With his help two programs were chosen, including—over Magnus' protest—some unaccompanied Bach. Magnus was allergic to Bach.

The following evening I played the Mendelssohn concerto with the orchestra. It went less well than the Beethoven had. I was not in bad form, but the spirit of that first evening was missing. The Finale had no sparkle and glow; the flute and the clarinet, which are meant to dance a trio with the violin, were not so lively as they should have been. I found myself repeatedly a half-beat ahead and had to slow down. The dancing bow suddenly turned lethargic and heavy; the spirit of Puck, of Oberon and Titania, faded away and the midsummer night's dream lacked fairies. True, the end brought plenty of cordial applause— but it was not the same, and I knew it. In the greenroom there was more talk of the first concert than of the second one. How friendly, I thought, how Finnish of them, to be so honest!

CHAPTER TWENTY

Back in St. Petersburg, we found that Raoul Pugno had arrived. He was, I could see at once, out of sorts with himself, with Russia, and with life in general. I suspected that this was largely the result of over-indulgence the night before. The spread of tempting food and the choice of any kind of wine, combined with a Gargantuan capacity, presented a temptation which Pugno could not resist. His great torso bulged and heaved in an armchair. His eyes were bloodshot. But not even at this uncomfortable moment did Pugno forget to declaim. He never talked; he orated. The records show that he was born in Paris, but his speech persuaded you that he had grown up in the Loire Valley, which is to the French tongue what Tuscany is to the Italian, and his phrases were well-rounded, literary, polished. But you did not often share a conversation with Pugno—you merely punctuated, by assents, denials, or exclamations, an imperturbable monologue.

"Ah, *mon cher*," he greeted me, "what a misery, this life! See the state to which I am reduced—desperate! And to think that this should happen to me, the most prudent of men. Do not speak! I know what you are thinking, but it is not true. I arrive, I unpack, I am hungry, I eat sparingly—but, oh, so sparingly. You cannot imagine how I deny myself. One, but only one small glass—*un tout petit verre, tout petit, tout petit*. Not more, I assure you, and, nevertheless, see for yourself what it has made of me."

I murmured something unintelligible; there was no need to say more, for he went on:

"Now if it had been Eugène—" (Apparently it comforted him to indict Ysaÿe on such occasions.) "He can indulge with the most reckless impunity, the animal, and feel none the worse. It is not logical; it is not right."

What a pity, I thought, that the other giant is not here to speak for himself. It would be a debate worth hearing. Ysaÿe, though less vociferous, was something of an orator himself and superbly skilled in dialectic. He would have known how to defend himself, how to counterattack. Pugno, however, was thoroughly satisfied with his audience of one.

"I had the most abominable trip. The food was ill prepared. It was not to be eaten—inexcusable. Added to that, the criminal guard of my sleeping car plotted against me. Bribed by I cannot imagine what amount of money, he was ready to pretend that my ticket called for—you will not believe it—an *upper,* instead of the lower I had carefully secured for myself. Imagine me, Pugno, yes, me, sleeping in an upper! Can you conceive such a thing?"

I couldn't.

"I protested; I established my identity. I showed him my passport. The animal was not deterred. There is no hope for him, executioner of his mother!"

"What did you do?" I asked.

"Do? I am not without resource. I cut short my dinner—it was not worth eating—and I went early and hungry to bed, in my own proper berth, of course."

"And were you allowed to remain there quietly?"

"But no! That is the worst of it. No sense of consideration, no shame. There were storms of protest, threats, prayers. I paid no attention to them: I lay without moving. Your person, Pugno, I said to myself, is inviolate; no one will touch you. *Et puis,*" he added, "one must admit, I am weighty!"

"And what happened to the other passenger?" I asked.

"Oh, *quant à lui,*" the pudgy hands waved, indicating indifference, "I know nothing. It was, after all, his affair. Doubtless the guard placed him in another compartment; perhaps—who knows?—in a lower. Not that he deserved one!"

I did not, of course, voice the sympathy I felt for this unknown

[154]

traveler whose distressing misfortune it had been to hold a conflicting reservation. Pugno's good humor was by now restored. He asked me about my concerts in St. Petersburg and Helsingfors. Had I played in Moscow? No? That would come. In the meantime, we must rehearse. Not today—tomorrow would do. Had we not played the *Kreutzer* together, not once, but several times? Should we dine together? Good, and where? I suggested Donon's. His eyes lit up. Donon's, of course, *à la bonne heure!* Had I already dined there? And with Wolkonsky, Serge Wolkonsky? "But, of course, I know him well. *Quel Grand Seigneur!* What a coincidence. We must phone him at once, and find out if he is free. We will invite him to join us. If he can accept," said Pugno, reflectively, "he will pay for the dinner. He always does."

I demurred at such backhanded hospitality. Pugno was not pleased with me, and decided to telephone Wolkonsky himself. "It is foolish of you to feel that way," he went on. "We are in Russia—all Russians are hospitable. They would feel offended if we did not accept their bounty with good grace."

Wolkonsky was not, however, free for the evening. I felt relieved. We should dine alone, after all. But Russian hospitality is apparently inexhaustible; at least, Pugno counted on its being so, for when I left him he was still telephoning, first one acquaintance, then another. When we met again in the lobby at eight o'clock he was triumphant. We were to dine, he said, at Donon's, with Alexander Stolypin.

"As his guests?" I asked, astonished.

"*Mais, bien entendu!* He was enchanted to hear from us. He likes you, too," he added. "Come, we must leave at once. *En avant l'appétit!*"

Stolypin was already at the restaurant waiting for us. The dinner had been ordered. There was no suggestion of improvisation; I felt that it had been planned for weeks. Stolypin was no stranger to Pugno's capacity, and had provided accordingly. He himself was a seasoned veteran in the campaign of consumption. I felt absurdly anemic in my efforts to keep pace, gave it up as a bad job, and remained a fascinated spectator. I was also a fascinated listener. Pugno and Stolypin were talking politics. They spoke of approaching war clouds. I couldn't believe my ears. This, I thought, is the twentieth century—war is a matter of history, a matter of the past. To talk of it as a present or future possibility is unthinkable. But talk of it they did, and as calmly as if it were a game of chess. The Austrian annexation of Bosnia and Herzegovina, less than two years before, was still fresh in their minds, and it rankled.

"We should have called Germany's bluff at that time," he-marked Stolypin. "The Kaiser was really quaking in his boots. But our Emperor is a man of peace. He actually believes in the Hague Tribunal. He is weak. But the next time . . . the next time . . ."

Pugno's eyes flashed. Perhaps he remembered his Corsican blood.

"La France was ready to march," he declared. "General mobilization was on the verge of being ordered."

"And England, what of England?"

"Ah, England, one must not count on her. Anyway, what one calls the Entente Cordiale is only an 'Attente Cordiale' which, above all, lacks cordiality. *Il faut s'en méfier.*"

Stolypin heartily agreed, then turned to me. "I suppose," he went on, "that in your far-off, happy country these matters were only of slight and academic interest."

I admitted as much.

"Yes, you are the one country that can dream of, believe in, peace as a reality. Isolated by two oceans, neighbored by comfortable weakness, you have a cloudless horizon to look out upon. *Le bon Dieu vous a été généreux, tandis que nous . . .*"

"For us," chimed in Pugno, "the cessation of hostilities is nothing but an interlude—a beneficent one when a *point d'orgue* figures above it. And, alas, the present *point d'orgue* is fast coming to its end. There is thunder in the air; when will lightning strike? Who knows? But soon, soon."

"How soon?" I asked Stolypin.

He paused for a moment, stroking his beard. Not this year, perhaps not next. But in two years' time. Trouble was brewing in the Balkans. It sounded like opera bouffe, I thought. Romantic adventure tales and operettas were always laid in the remote

[156]

and quarrelsome Balkans. But why, in the name of all that spells good sense, should this affect the world of reality—our world, and the lives of millions of unoffending people whose only wish was to be let alone? I gave it up!

"What do you think of this young man?" said Stolypin, changing the conversation. "He has pleased us all very much here in Petersburg."

And for the next embarrassed ten minutes, I heard myself calmly discussed, appraised, and in general approved, quite as though I were not there. Pugno orated on, dissected, my qualities as if he had invented them. It sounded as unreal as the political discussion had.

The eating went on with no apparent signs of abatement. If, I thought, the prudence of last night produced today's discomfort, what will tonight's orgy do? I feared nothing less than apoplexy; but it was not for me to speak. And, after all, I was pleasantly deceived. The morrow found Pugno chipper and refreshed, his eyes clear, his spirits resilient. He was ready and waiting for rehearsal. No doubt of it, I reflected—ascetic restraint is what he must shun. Intemperance appears to be his tonic.

It was inspiring to play with him. He was an astonishing pianist. The liquid limpidity of his touch was something quite personal, and in a legato passage he could caress the keys till you looked to see whether it was a percussion instrument and not a stringed one he was playing. In fiery passages he could summon Jovian thunderbolts fit to storm the gates of Heaven, and then, in sudden contrast, display an unexpected delicacy. He seemed to delight in passage work requiring crossed hands. You wondered how he was going to manage it, his arms were so grotesquely short for the length and expanse of his elephantine torso. To heighten the mystery, the long curly beard of which he was inordinately proud would dip toward the keyboard and brush against the racing fingers.

Ysaÿe used to tease Pugno about his beard, pretending that he relied on its undoubted dramatic effect. *"Ce n'est que pour épater le bourgeois, Raoul, et personne ne le sait mieux que toi!"* Raoul would parry with a reference to the lock of Eugène's hair which, after a bravura passage, would swoop its way from pate

[157]

to chin—*"et ce n'est pas moi qui jette la première pierre,"* he would roar. They were an unforgettable pair, prying and prodding each other with barbed quips that only the utmost intimacy and mutual affection could have inspired. It was the jocose raillery of two gods from Olympus taking turns at clowning.

When, as often happened, they played together in a sonata recital, the effect was electrifying. I remember attending a series of all the Beethoven violin sonatas in three sessions in London. Ysaÿe was at his leonine best. His tone was not large, but it had an expressive quality impossible to describe. His famous Guarnerius tucked under his chin looked like a half-sized fiddle, too small for the great gamut of emotions it was to run. How well I remember the tremendous drama of the C minor Sonata (the one dedicated to that same Tsar Alexander who had been so despotic about the Helsingfors hall). The eight-bar exposition of the theme by the solo piano paves the way for its still more telling repetition by the violin. Ysaÿe used to hold that G— sustained through three-quarters of a bar—a fraction of a second over time so that the figure of four sixteenth-notes precipitated themselves with extra speed, resolving the phrase with an explosive quality. It gave you goose flesh! Against this the piano described a rumbling orchestration like the muttering of distant thunder. It was the dialogue of Titans. Then, all at once, the clouds parted, and a ray of Beethoven's tender sunshine projected its shaft of celestial light with the entrance of the ineffable subtheme in E-flat. The piano still thundered, but it seemed more remote as the violin sang this phrase. And who else, I thought, can sing it like that? This mood of serenity and hope lasts only for a brief interval. It is to be repeated once more, and that is a consolation, for the main material of the piece is stormy, revolutionary, a world at war with itself.

These two artists seemed inexhaustible in their supply of dynamic contrasts. Later, when I mentioned this performance to Pugno, he was as naïvely pleased as a child. *"En effet,"* he agreed, *"nous avons rudement bien joué ce jour-là."*

The following day Pugno and I visited The Hermitage together. He had several favorites there that he wanted to point out to me: the famous Van Eyck, now a treasured American possession; the long-limbed beguiling Giorgione, which Berenson declared to be spurious, but which we enjoyed none the less for that; and the long series of masterpieces collected by an acquisitive Empress of wealth and wisdom. Pugno had a keen eye. He made shrewd observations, pointing out a quality here, an effect of light there. He puffed and blew his way through the gallery. "Ah, my legs," he complained, "they protest. *Mais, taisez-vous!*" he would chide them. "If all is not well on the ground floor, have patience for a moment and permit the *mansarde,* at least, to enjoy a bit of heaven."

I brought him a chair whenever I could, and he would sink gratefully into it. Even when the support was solid, his weight was a menace, and I was careful to avoid any fragile-looking chairs.

Did I know, he asked me, some of the notable private collections in the city? Certain of them contained priceless examples of the nineteenth-century French School—such Manets, such Renoirs, such Dégas! He would take me to some of these homes. Observing my eagerness, he at once began laying out plans for several days. Though for various reasons these plans were never to materialize, it was plain that Pugno's name was an Open Sesame to all doors in Petersburg.

Our concert, a gala affair, took place the following night. The price of tickets was, it seemed to me, fantastically high—twenty rubles a seat. Obviously the charity was going to do well, even after paying the performers. In addition to two instrumentalists, Marya Kussnetzov was to sing. She was daringly and exotically dressed. Her costume seemed to consist solely of jeweled beads hanging in loose festoons over a well-formed, naked body. I couldn't at first believe it. Her husband (was he really her husband, I wondered) made everyone verify this startling fact. He looked like a dark South American, and perhaps he was; the type was becoming increasingly prevalent though the term gigolo was not yet in use.

"See for yourself," he insisted, parting the strands of beads and disclosing a marble-white abdomen. "And feel with your hand how firm Marya's flesh is!"

I glanced quickly at the lady. She did not demur. Was it an invitation, or a command? Apparently people are made of asbestos in this country, I thought. I thrust my hand inside. Yes, the flesh was firm, it was cold, it was hard. I tried to look impressed and at the same time unconcerned. I failed. It was an unprecedented experience; I felt very callow, very young. And it was not a good prelude to public performance.

However, the *Kreutzer* went well; indeed, with quite a swagger. My own solos, which came later on the program, received as favorable a response from the audience as though I had been an old favorite.

After the concert we were Benckendorff's guests at the famous "Islands" restaurant. Again we came under the spell of those throaty gypsy singers who, with rhythm and their unorthodox but effective use of chest tones, carried far up into the medium register, can make you forget the passing of time. Here and now is the moment, you think. Nothing else counts. The singers and the dancers circulated from table to table, shrewdly concentrating on the people from whom, in addition to applause, substantial largess might be expected. They singled out our table as a likely prospect, and were not disappointed. Benckendorff had provided himself with what seemed to be an inexhaustible supply of ten-ruble notes. As for Pugno, he contemplated his bulk, and the gravity of his years, and sighed.

"*Ah, d'être jeune et mince de nouveau!* It is a tragedy for imaginative desire to live in a tomb of old age."

Benckendorff nodded appreciatively. He ordered more food, more wine; the age of discretion was not to be without its sensuous comforts.

Pugno was telling us of two great talents, both feminine, whose development interested him greatly. They were two sisters, with a French father, a Russian mother. Nadia Boulanger and her younger sister, Lili, would, he declared, be talked of long after he, Pugno, had shuffled off this mortal coil. He planned to bring Nadia with him soon to introduce her to the Russian audience.

A year or so later, he did. It was to be his swan song, for he did not survive the visit. He died in Moscow on the eve of the joint recital which so brilliantly launched his beloved protégée. There were drama and poignancy in the circumstances of his death—but that is another story which has been told and retold. It does not find legitimate place here.

I was listening attentively. Some time previous to this I had met the Boulangers at Pugno's house at Gargenville outside Paris. The mother, sturdily and substantially built, had a deep voice of unexpected baritone timbre. Although the girls were fatherless, you felt no lack of masculine authority in the family. Mme. Boulanger's French was fluent and expressive, blanketed with the rich sauce of a Slavic accent which is unmistakable once you get to know it. The rolling r's overflowed the river banks of her conversation, and many of the words were spoken (I have never known exactly how!) with the tip of her tongue glued to the roof of the mouth.

The daughters were both comely: Nadia, tall and dark, with hair that you knew was eventually to be "a sable silvered," and large, penetrating eyes illuminated by a finely disciplined intelligence; Lili, slight, fair, and frail, looked like the lost princess of a Maeterlinck play next to Nadia's healthy vitality. It was evident even then that the flame of Lili's talent was likely to overtax her meager physical resources. The coveted Prix de Rome was yet to be hers, in 1913—she was the first woman to receive this honor, and she was but nineteen at the time; and death drew the curtains on her rare and delicate talent only five years after that.

In 1920, I was in Europe with the New York Symphony Orchestra, and one of our concerts took place in the theater of the Monte Carlo Casino. After the concert I returned to the hotel to pack. I had to hurry to catch my train. In the lobby a young girl, dressed in deep mourning, accosted me. She had with her two pieces for the violin composed by her best friend, who had recently died. When I got to my room I found that they were by Lili Boulanger, a *Nocturne* and *Cortège,* both tone poems. I have played them publicly hundreds of times since.

CHAPTER TWENTY-ONE

BEFORE going to Moscow we visited the provincial town of Vitebsk—a large, overgrown village rather than a city. A number of municipal buildings flanked the large, snow-covered square, which served as general meeting place and market—the chief scene of activity. Here I found a poster announcing the concert. I had always to look twice to assure myself that this alien-looking name in Russian lettering was in reality my own. The Russian C (their equivalent of our S) so altered my name that it seemed to announce an important and unfamiliar person. The strange-sounding name of Spalding, I was informed, was a definite asset here; it was so different. How refreshing, I thought, that a name that provokes skepticism in Anglo-Saxon lands should turn out to be an advantage elsewhere!

We went to the municipal hall to rehearse and to exchange amenities with some of the musical potentates of the town. Two members of the musical society which had engaged me met us at the entrance. One of them, the President, whose name was Andreiev, had heard me play in Petersburg. He was cordiality itself. Had we made a good trip? Were we comfortable? Would we have lunch with him at his club? To all of these questions we responded in the affirmative, though candor would have dictated negatives to the first two. The trip had not been comfortable, and the hostelry was both primitive and dirty. But why upset the gentleman?

The room in which we were to play was a fine one in double-cube shape, its white paneled walls hung with large portraits of bygone monarchs and other notables. Facing the stage and dominating the room was a huge likeness of Tsar Peter the Great—no work of art certainly, but the picture of a forceful and powerful man who fused tribal life into national unity, erected a modern city on reclaimed marshland, and eventually crushed the menacing military genius of Europe's greatest contemporary general.

It chanced that at this time I was reading Voltaire's fascinating biography of Charles XII of Sweden, Peter's archenemy; Wolkonsky had recommended it to me as "everything history should be and seldom is." In a bookstore carrying French literature I had found a paper-backed copy, and it was with me on this trip. And now I thought of Charles as Andreiev and I stood looking at the portrait of Peter.

More than life-size, it dwarfed the other canvases. The Tsar wore military uniform, the flaring skirts of his bright red tunic folded back to disclose white buckram breeches. Whether by accident or design, the tailor had so cut the latter garment as to reveal unmistakably what trousers are supposed to conceal, and the artist had obviously accentuated this detail. Was this, I wondered, an eighteenth-century implication of virility? I glanced at the other portraits of military figures. Yes, the custom prevailed, although somewhat less conspicuously than in the picture of the "Little Father"—that term affectionately bestowed by his subjects on the Tsar of all the Russias.

The Russians are mind-readers. I had said nothing, but Andreiev proceeded to answer my speculation. "I can see," he commented, "that details do not escape you. He would have been an unlucky artist, indeed, if he had failed to emphasize

> 'Ce qui servit au premier homme
> A conservé le genre humain.'"

I told him how interesting I had found the Voltaire book. "Yes," Andreiev went on, "here is that shrewd, violent compound of energy and patience that thwarted Charles' brilliance. This portrait was painted shortly after he had disposed of that danger. Something of his triumph is exemplified here—the defiant pose, the assurance of unlimited strength and resistance, the absence of any reflective intelligence. It is the cunning of a trained brute rather than the measured cleverness of man; see the clenched fist, the wide-spread legs. The artist has caught his ruthless vitality, though the painting itself has no artistic merit, of course."

From Vitebsk we went on to Smolensk. This was a more substantial town; in fact, it had something of that look of a city for which Vitebsk was striving. I remember groups of ocher-colored stucco buildings, horizontal rather than vertical in character. On the afternoon before the concert I took a walk with my accompanist, and he pointed out several items of interest. The city walls, still standing, were now merely decorative whereas they had once been bulwarks of resistance. When we came to one of the principal gates I was amazed to find that it was in ruins! What had been a sturdy barrier now lay open, inviting aggression.

"Why have these gates never been repaired?" I asked. Dulov laughed. "You would have been a great disappointment if you hadn't asked that question," he replied. "Visitors to Smolensk are grouped in two classes: those who do, and those who don't. More than a century ago this town was visited by the Empress Catherine. She was not a Romanov. Her title to sovereignty was shaky. She was an obscure little German princess, married to impotence, who became one of the greatest monarchs of Europe. Her imperial coach, about to enter Smolensk, found the gateway too narrow to admit it. Majesty could not come afoot, Majesty could not be kept waiting. The gateway was forthwith demolished and the coach drove in. The Empress' satisfaction was doubtless expressed in gratifying terms. In any case, the citizens of Smolensk have never replaced the gate."

I thought for a moment. "Catherine," I reflected, "represents to the Russians something of what Elizabeth is to the English?"

"Yes," said Dulov, "the two have certain points in common. But it is easy to exaggerate these. Catherine was an alien, but legitimate. Elizabeth was as English as an oak; but, because of doubt about the validity of her father's second marriage, her claim to royal succession hung by the slenderest of threads. They both had difficult solos to perform on the stage of world affairs. Who could have foreseen the extent of their success, with so many elements in their disfavor? But the parallel ends there. Both physically and mentally the two rulers were direct opposites and in their approach to people they were radically different. It was chance, fortunate for themselves and for their respective countries, that placed their talents in the right place and at the right time."

It is quite true, I thought. Queen Bess would never have demolished a city gate; such an idea would have shocked her sense of economy. She would have dismounted and walked through, confident that the mud would be promptly carpeted by a loyal cloak.

In the morning, Russian towns often look uninhabited. The broad streets and avenues seem to vegetate in silent inactivity. You could almost fancy that you had stumbled on an abandoned exposition site, in tolerable repair as yet, but awaiting demolition.

"Is it," I asked, "a chronic seasonal hibernation, or does Smolensk sometimes awake to activity?"

"On market day," said Dulov, "the streets are crowded, and there is a great deal of life and color. But during the rest of the week it is as you see it now. Most of our provincial towns are not towns at all in the sense that you might expect. They are assemblies of storage houses for agricultural products, distributing plants, and dwelling houses for the farmers. Those who can afford it seek their distractions in Petersburg and Moscow. They have a fling at life and then return to be immured again in monotony. Except for an occasional concert, this routine is rarely varied."

"What a deadly life for those who cannot enliven it with a trip!"

"You are wrong; *they* do not think it deadly. The peasant finds excitement where you or I would be endlessly bored."

"What, then, are his pleasures?"

"According to his lights, he has them in abundance. They are, I must admit, half-way between those of a domesticated animal and those of man as we know him. His enjoyment of food, for one thing; we might well envy such a sharp appetite. The satisfying of it gives him an intense sensation of well-being. He expresses himself, too, in singing and dancing. He gets drunk when he can, which is not often; it is not a vice—it is a necessary exhaust valve. He beats his wife periodically, and enjoys it."

"And the wife?"

"Naturally, I do not pretend that she takes equal pleasure in it; but it is an accepted conjugal custom and its disuse would be resented as a sign of indifference."

"But don't the women complain?"

"Of course they do. It is the chief subject of their conversation and they would not willingly be deprived of it. Furthermore, there are their baths."

"Their baths?" I echoed.

"Oh, yes!" he went on. "I know what you are thinking: How do they manage such affairs in hovels where even the simplest form of hygiene would seem to have no place? But the bath is a weekly ritual, all the same. You know our Russian baths?"

I stared at him in astonishment. Yes, I had even taken one. It seemed to me a very elaborate ordeal—to be parboiled and then beaten with birch branches until you protested against further mortification of the flesh. Surely this was a highly sophisticated taste that must require long initiation. Did the Russian peasant really go through that agony every week?

"It is a fixed habit with them," went on Dulov. "Almost every peasant has a little bath-house. Stones are heated and pails of water thrown over them, producing a blistering hot steam bath. A series of planks mounting gradually over the oven marks the successive degrees of heat to which he subjects his body. Meanwhile, he flagellates himself with birch branches; or perhaps he delegates the beating to his wife—as a compensatory gesture! When he is sufficiently cooked, he goes outside and hurls his naked and reddened body into a snowbank. Then he returns to the inferno and repeats the process several times. It is exhilarating—and grand entertainment. When it is over he is at peace with the world, hungry as a bear, and envying no one. He is not an unhappy animal, when all is said and done!"

In the face of this complacent acceptance of a regime that had come straight from feudal times, I felt suddenly depressed.

"Surely," I remarked, "it cannot last. You do not think it can last?"

"I am," said Dulov, "a revolutionary." He glanced quickly around to reassure himself that the streets were still empty. "All university students remain revolutionaries at heart unless they go into the army, into politics, or into commerce. In that case they become conservatives or reactionaries. We shall have a revolution before long, but it will be the revolt of a minority. The vast majority of our population, the peasants, will neither participate in it nor profit by it. Not for a long time, at least. They will undergo a change of masters, that is all."

"Will it, do you think, follow the pattern of the French Revolution . . . the Terror?"

"It will not only follow it, it will outstrip it in blood and horror. Revolution might have been avoided—that is, the more violent features—if the liberal Alexander II had not been assassinated by an anarchist's bomb."

"In Finland," I remarked, "he is the one Tsar whose name is not anathema."

"Yes," said Dulov, "they even erected a statue to him. He granted practical autonomy to Finland, recognized a self-governing parliament, and opposed conscription. The Finns regarded him as a real liberator. Even today some of them call him 'our Grand Duke.' His death was sad for Finland, but tragic for Russia. The third Alexander tried to carry on some of his father's policies but he, too, was assassinated. Our present Emperor is a kind of Louis Seize—not a vicious man, but the tool of every reactionary force in the country. All the good accomplished by his father and his grandfather has been undone. It can only end badly."

After the concert that evening we went on to Moscow. This is, more than any other place in Europe, the city where East meets West. The Westerner feels that he is definitely in Asia, and I am told that the Easterner, traveling in the opposite direction, feels as if he had reached western Europe. Moscow is not beautiful; it is strident, it is garish, it is blatant. It fails by the standards of any other city; but, after all, why try to appraise it? I was overwhelmed by this jungle of outrageous color, this fairy-tale citadel of cruel chieftains. It left me stupefied, uncritical, entranced.

I paid my first visit to the Kremlin. Its forbidding walls, enclosing an exotic world of architectural color, make you impatient with the incongruously dressed people you see about you. Drab modern clothes are an affront to this medieval splendor. It is a stage setting fit for nothing less than a procession of Mongol warriors headed by Genghis Khan.

In the evening we went to the Moscow Art Theater to see Chekov's *The Three Sisters*. One of the leading roles was played by Chekov's widow. I have never forgotten that performance. Before the curtain went up I thought to myself: "The play is in a language you do not understand. It will be as if you had suddenly gone deaf and were prepared to think beautiful something you could not actually hear." When the curtain went up I forgot all that. It was life itself that we were seeing, shaped by a master cunning in the art of concealing his craftsmanship. Because of the actors' skill we followed the action with what felt like clairvoyant intelligence.

I had a card of introduction from Wolkonsky and we went back and met Stanislavsky after the performance. We expressed our admiration of the company's acting. He agreed with us— it was not in him to assume false modesty.

"There is," he declared, "nothing in the world comparable to it. Unless perhaps—as an individual artist—Eleonora Duse." Then, turning to me, "You have lived in Florence. Do you know Duse?"

I did, I was glad to say.

"Incomparable, supreme! She arrived by the instinct of genius at the same conclusions we have reached as a group. When she comes to Russia to act she is received like a queen. There is never any need to advertise her performance; the news of it travels by mental telepathy, and the theater is sold out long before the tickets are printed."

It was heart-warming to hear this, for to me Duse was a household goddess. I had once had an intimate glimpse of the technical resources at her command. We were seated side by side in the front row of the small theater of Luigi Rasi's famous dramatic school in Florence. Rasi at one time had played leading roles opposite Duse, and she invariably recommended talented students to him for stage training. His graduating class was playing scenes from d'Annunzio's *Gioconda*. More than once, I caught myself watching the play of emotions on the face of the superb actress. She was warmly enthusiastic at the end, and singled out especially the performance of a young woman who stood trembling with excitement at this royal approbation. She praised her voice, her gesture, and her sincerity of emotion. "Too often, however," she declared, "you lose control; you forget what you are doing. You indulge in spontaneous action which looks unnatural. You lack the smoothness of perfect technique. For example, you made an entrance, you rushed across the stage and flung yourself on the couch. How many steps did you take?"

The confused young woman did not know.

"Exactly. You should have known! You should always know. *Ecco!* I will show you."

With that, the great lady rose and made her way to the stage. She dashed from the stage door to the couch with such *élan* that she made the former action look counterfeit.

"Yes," said Duse, "that seemed spontaneous—that looked impetuous. It was neither. It was a completely studied action. I measured the distance with my eye; it is nine of my steps. Furthermore, if you are to fall properly, your last step must be taken by your left foot. Try that out—not once, but hundreds of times, till it comes like second nature. You will not regret it," she ended. "Your talent deserves—no, it demands—this patience."

I wanted to tell this story to Stanislavsky—he would have liked it; but I was too timid, and the story seemed too long.

CHAPTER TWENTY-TWO

I RETURNED to Russia for two subsequent tours, in the seasons 1912-13 and 1913-14. The war clouds were still menacing, but the twentieth century in its early teens was incurably optimistic, obstinately confident of the permanence of peace and progress. The Italo-Turkish war had been fought, and the Balkan wars were in progress; but these seemed remote.

By now André Benoist was playing for me regularly. He had played my accompaniments in the season 1911-12 on my second tour of my own country. His experience had been long and varied. Among the singers he had assisted were Nordica, Schumann-Heink, Tetrazzini, Alda, and Gogorza. In the instrumental field he had played for Jacques Thibaud, Jean Gérardy, Fritz Kreisler, and many others. We became devoted partners in public performance. Absurdly partisan in his outspoken admiration of my playing, he was also quick to criticize and advise when I was not up to standard.

Benoist's first European tour with me was early in 1912. Before going to Russia we visited Scandinavia and Finland, playing numerous concerts in Norway, not only in Christiania (now Oslo) and Bergen, but also in many small towns on the coast and in the interior.

The calendar of traveling comfort was often set back a century. Except for the few railroad lines between main points, which had excellent equipment, we used earlier and more primitive means of transportation: by coastal boat to seaboard towns; by sled over the mountain passes; through fjords and lakes to inland towns. These trips were incredibly beautiful. In the dead of winter, when the sun appears for so short a time, every perception is intensified. The brief day has the terseness of ideal dramatic action. The sun rises, hovers over the irregular skyline, and disappears almost before you have time to say "Now—now!" The black pines are an expression of architecture rather than of Nature. You feel like an intruder. Is this not some forbidden land reserved for a race of Viking giants?

Norway is for me a land of mystery and romance. It seems natural to be silent and reflective there. Its people, you observe, use speech as a necessity, as a commodity, and are sparing of it. They are rarely gay like the Swedes, and never loquacious like the Danes. They would appear taciturn if they were not so amiable. Their gentle courtesy convinces you of their friendliness. They are Scandinavians, and therefore good-looking. They retain the fresh complexion of youth until they are very old.

I remember setting off one morning for Rjukan, an inland town where we were to play that evening. It could be reached only by sled. We left before nine o'clock, when it was still quite dark. Our manager, whose name was Rasmussen, went with us. He was tall, spare, red-haired, and quite un-Norwegian in that he was a great talker; he had, I suspect, Danish ancestry.

"Rjukan," he said, "is one of a series of manufacturing towns you will play in."

"What do they manufacture?" I asked.

"Saltpeter."

Benoist scowled gloomily. He foresaw discomfort. "Where shall we be lodged?" he inquired.

"It is all arranged," Rasmussen reassured him. "You will be quite comfortable. You are to be guests of the Engineers' Club. You will have good beds and good food. Do not be nervous, I beg of you."

But Ben was not sanguine.

"And the sleds, are they quite safe?" He insisted on knowing the worst. "Suppose the horses give out—can go no farther. What do we do? Freeze in this wilderness of snow?"

"No," was the cheerful reply. "You walk."

Ben's gloom deepened. Walking is an activity which he avoids whenever he can; he dislikes it intensely. I tried to change the subject, exclaiming on the scene before us. Ben was aware of it, but he had only one eye for it. The other was still on his creature comforts. "It is," he remarked in a discouraged tone, "all-fired cold." True. Though we were well bundled in furs, the frigid air seemed to penetrate everything. And it contrasted sharply with the moderate temperature of the coastal towns. Rasmussen was quick to explain.

"Most of Norway's coast is bathed by warm currents from the Western Hemisphere. But travel a few miles from the sea and you are in Arctic regions. It would not surprise me to learn that it is forty below zero Fahrenheit."

"That," said Benoist, "is enlightening, but scarcely consoling."

"Have patience," said Rasmussen. "In a few moments we shall stop for cognac and coffee. We are approaching a village."

It was a welcome interlude. We repeated it throughout the day at frequent intervals. My fixed rule of never touching a drop of alcohol on a concert day was modified without misgivings. The liquor provided personal central heating without menacing head or finger control. By the time we reached Rjukan I found that I had consumed six or seven brandies without feeling them in the least.

The Engineers' Club proved to be a long log cabin, low, rambling, and hospitable. It might have been a camp in our own Adirondacks. A group of gigantic men, blue-eyed and with blond beards, stepped straight from a Norse saga to greet us. Some of them spoke English, more spoke German, many spoke not at all. After our welcome there followed the most cordial silence I have ever known. It embarrassed no one.

We were shown to our rooms. They were clean and comfortable. Mine was paneled in cedar wood and smelled delightfully of that healthy perfume. Even Benoist announced himself as reconciled to primitive life.

The concert took place in the Town Hall, a wooden structure with a gabled roof, that might almost have served as a Lutheran place of worship. The hall could not have held more than four hundred. But I wondered where that four hundred were to come from; the entire population hardly seemed so many. However, an audience assembled, and the hall was filled.

"They emerge like moles from beneath the snow," muttered Benoist. "I don't quite believe my eyes. It isn't human, it isn't natural."

When his fingers touched the keys I knew he was secretly as delighted as he ought to be. The concert went well, and the proverbial Norwegian silence was broken by grateful applause.

We returned to the club for a delicious supper provided by the hunters. I cannot remember what the bird is called, but it is midway between a partridge and a quail. The handsome, silent Norsemen became conversational. Their speech was measured, slow in tempo, but without hesitation. They used the odd, yodeling inflection with which Scandinavians speak English. This became more apparent when they were excited or enthusiastic, and it was obvious that music made them both. The concert was discussed in detail. It is odd, I thought, how much at home I feel with these people whose names I scarcely know, and certainly shall not remember.

A friendly bond was established when I mentioned Selma Lagerlöf. In describing my impressions of the day's drive I said that certain of her pages seeemd to spring to life. My bearded hosts stared at me in surprise.

"You have read Lagerlöf?" asked one of them.

In translation, I admitted.

"Are her books much read abroad, in America?"

I said they were.

"And Ibsen, and Björnson?" he went on. "But, of course—how stupid of me! It is so easy to go on, as many of us do, picturing America as a remote settlement. In reality it is you who are the cosmopolitans and we who are insular. Have patience with our surprise."

He did not ask me if I liked Norway. Economy of speech dispensed with the usual conversational padding. I asked him about woman suffrage; a bill to grant this was then pending in the Norwegian Parliament.

"It will pass without a doubt—and this year," he said.

[173]

"Not the first time," I remarked, "that Norway is a pioneer in the world of progress."

He did not deny it. He went on with justifiable pride:

"Illiteracy is practically unknown in our country. And with general education any inequality based on sex is unthinkable."

I asked him about politics, and about their relations with their nearest neighbors.

"They are good," he said. "In spite of some causes for friction, we shall, I think, never quarrel. Our peacetime army is small; you might call it non-existent. It numbers perhaps five thousand men—hardly a police force. If the matter depended on Scandinavia, peace might be said to be permanent."

I could not help reminding him, however, that this pacific land produced materials for war. He frowned; it was not a reflection that gave him pleasure. His troubled blue eyes looked into the distance.

"Yes," he said, "and that is a paradox that puzzles me. I tell myself what I cannot in conscience completely believe: that to make a shell does not necessarily render you responsible for the firing of it, that to fashion, or even to sell, a gun does not make you accountable for the pulling of its trigger. These are some of the half-truths with which we comfort ourselves. They do not satisfy me. And yet, even with an arsenal at hand you do not commit murder if you have peace in your heart."

I went to bed and slept soundly in my sweet-smelling cedar room.

CHAPTER TWENTY-THREE

Y OU reach Bergen by a luxurious train from Christiania. The handsome mahogany sleeping compartments are spacious and well equipped, far better than their counterparts in the rest of Europe. There was little to be seen of the town or its harbor when we arrived, for it was bathed in a heavy fog from the North Sea. When the curtain of mist finally lifted, it revealed a town of homely charm—a town so small that it seemed a kind of suburb of the Bergen I had imagined. But there it was, all there was of it, rising and falling on the gentle promontories that dip down to form the circular harbor. From the windows of the Hotel Norge where we lodged, the dense shipping, too, looked undersized, like so many bantam-weights eager to challenge a heavy-weight sea. The streets were so scrupulously clean that one could, I thought, picnic on their sidewalks without distaste.

Our musical affairs were in the hands of the Misses Rabe, three spinster sisters. They had inherited the musical agency from their father and had been personal friends not only of their own Edvard Grieg and Ole Bull—whose bronze statue dominated the principal square—but also of a long list of international celebrities. They looked alike, dressed alike, talked alike. One almost took them for triplets.

"*Elles sont mal proportionnées pour l'amour,*" commented the irrepressible Benoist, "*mais gentilles quand même.*"

They arrived, breathless and cordial, at the hotel shortly after breakfast. They seemed to belie their nationality, they were so abundantly talkative. Dealing with visiting artists had loosened their tongues. They spoke in gasps, and it appeared impossible for any of the three to complete a sentence she had begun; the thread of the phrase was picked up almost without interruption and resolved by another. They spoke in German. I could not understand half of what they were saying, but it was all very friendly.

It appeared that instead of one orchestral date I was to play three, perhaps four, times in Bergen, at two-day intervals. News of success in Christiania had preceded me; telegrams had been exchanged. Could I please let them have three recital programs? Liberal terms were mentioned. I glanced at Benoist; had I heard right? He confirmed it, not by a nod—that would have been too apparent—but by a slight lowering of his heavy eyelids. I questioned the ladies. After all, they were in business, and I could not see where their profits were to come from. I learned that their commission was three per cent of the net. I protested that the usual agent's fee was ten per cent—none too much for the work they would have to do. I felt like a despoiler of spinsters. My protests, however, were of no avail; the ladies Rabe were adamant.

"Our profit," began one, "has always been three per cent. It has never been raised—"

"Nor lowered," continued another. "If we are content—"

"Why should you," concluded the third, "question it?"

After rehearsal with the orchestra we returned to the hotel. The porter accosted me. There was, he explained, a gentleman waiting to see me. He gave me a card engraved with the impressive name of Ole Bull Grieg. In the public salon a lanky Norwegian rose from his chair to greet me. He was that indefinable type of blond that defies the passing of years. You could not even make a guess at his age. His English was perfect, with a smattering of contemporary slang. He was, he said, editor of the morning paper and had called to interview me. I summoned the waiter and asked him to bring us coffee.

When I expressed my admiration of his command of English he explained that he had made a long stay in the States. He had tried his hand at everything, sometimes with the slimmest of results. When he was down to his last nickel a compatriot had suggested that he apply for a job in a Weber and Fields show. Through a connection in the newspaper world he secured an introduction to Fields, who asked him whether he could sing. He could, after a fashion. Could he dance? He could, against all fashion. Fields put him through his paces. It was not good, said Grieg, but it seemed to pass muster.

"What's your name?" demanded Fields.

"Ole Bull Grieg," came the reply.

Fields contemplated him in scornful unbelief.

"My God," he exclaimed at last, "why don't you call yourself Beethoven?"

"By this time," Grieg laughed, "I, too, was convinced that I was a hoax. I had forgotten that Edvard Grieg was my uncle, that Ole Bull was my godfather. All the same," he added, "I got the job—Heaven knows why—and croaked and hopped my way through an entire season. It fed, housed, and clothed me. And that reminds me—are you not to lunch with the Rabes?"

We were.

"Yes, they told me. I am lunching, too. We will go together."

Benoist looked in vain for a cab and we finally took a trolley up a steep hill to where the sisters lived. The house was one of those weird contraptions built in the eighteen-sixties and -seventies in all lands. We have its counterpart in so-called American Gothic. This house was manifestly Norwegian Gothic of that pseudo period. It made an admirable setting for the spinsters.

When you entered the house you had a momentary feeling of suffocation. Everything was upholstered—even the mantelpieces. An unclothed piece of furniture was apparently not to be tolerated. Every inch of the walls was crowded with badly painted watercolors—the unfortunate fruits of the leisure of one of the sisters. Over the mantel in the sitting-room (how right, I thought, to call it that, there being virtually nowhere to stand) hung a huge portrait of a dour gentleman who might easily have been a founding Mormon. He dominated the congested room and was an effective check on any indecorous mirth or levity. Black-lacquered laurel leaves twisted like a climbing vine over the gold frame, lugubrious evidence of reverence and mourning.

"Our father," chorused the sisters, unnecessarily.

Benoist felt impelled to say something. *"Ein gediegener Mensch,"* he murmured with a sigh.

The ladies were delighted with him. They detected no trace of irony.

We lunched heartily, too heartily. I learned that in Norway meals could be as menacing as in Holland. But lunch, substantial though it was, gave no warning of what might be expected at an evening meal.

On one occasion we dined with Dr. Maartens at five in the afternoon. We sat at table until after ten, during which time repeated courses of soup, fish, and meat were served with relays of wines. "Worse than a Bruckner symphony," murmured Benoist.

Having submitted to one such ordeal I was determined to escape any repetition of it. But it was impossible to avoid such persistent hospitality. When all the plausible excuses had been exhausted and further resistance would have given offense, I decided to play truant after an hour or so of the next dinner. I said nothing to Ben of my dark intentions; it was better, I judged, to play solo.

We arrived for dinner punctually at five. The first courses of soup, fish, and meat I ate with relish. When, however, the second round began, my scheme was put into action. I furtively extracted my scarf pin and pricked my thumb under the table cloth. A few drops of blood on my handkerchief, and I had a well-simulated nose bleed. The entire dinner party was concerned. Benoist was genuinely alarmed; he had never suspected that I was subjct to this affliction. I used what dramatic ability I had and turned, it seems, quite pale. In my eagerness to escape I even persuaded myself that I was feeling ill.

There was a chorus of suggestions. He must lie down. No, that will send blood to the head. An open window—he must have air. A piece of ice at the back of his neck. Alas, there is no ice in the house. Will someone call a doctor? This last suggestion thoroughly alarmed me. No, no, it is nothing! I was overcome with desolation, I protested, that this contretemps should interrupt such princely hospitality. Please let the dinner go on. I would put on my overcoat and sit by the open window a few moments. Would someone kindly call a cab? I would slip quietly out. No, Mr. Benoist must not come with me, I could not bear to spoil his pleasure.

Miraculously, it worked. Even Benoist was unsuspecting. He endured the feast for an additional hour and then departed, anxious and overfed. The third round of dinner was in progress.

When he reached the hotel and observed my complete restoration, the scales dropped from his eyes. His relief gave way to indignation and then to abuse. I finally stopped the torrent of epithets by proposing a movie. To Ben, a movie is as candy is to a child. There are good candies, and better candies—but there are no bad ones.

It is curious that though I played in Christiania oftener than anywhere else in Norway, I recall it less clearly than many other places. In Sweden and Denmark the capital cities dominate the imagination. But in Norway the people and the dramatic countryside come first to mind. In the background you remember Christiania, the capital, as the pale shadow of a city, ashen gray and wrapped in fog. The change of its name to Oslo produced none of the regret you felt in the case of Petersburg. Its absence of definite character would resign you to numerals; it is Norway's number one city without need for further identification.

With Stockholm and Copenhagen, it is quite different. Stockholm has a proud patrician beauty unrivaled in the cities of the North. It is a small city built in the grand manner. Because of the waterways that flow through the city, it is inevitably called The Venice of the North.

The architecture is an importation from the classic French of the eighteenth century. But this northern realm has given it a distinct character of its own. You could no more imagine yourself in a French city than you would look for traces of a Napoleonic general in his descendant now occupying the Swedish throne. The people have an enigmatic aloofness totally unlike the silent but warm friendliness of the Norwegians. Their politeness is unfailing, but it masks an indifference. It is, I thought, about as easy to feel intimate with a Swede as to find homely comfort in a moated castle.

Copenhagen, with a larger population, looks smaller than its neighbor to the north. It is a lively city that invites your affection; it both stimulates and charms. Its narrow, busy streets teem with life and vitality; everyone seems to be in a hurry. The motorcars fly by at a reckless speed; you wonder that there are not more accidents.

If you reduced the Scandinavian countries to the pattern of a symphony, Sweden would be the *Allegro Maestoso;* Norway, the *Adagio Religioso;* and Denmark, the *Scherzo Giocoso.* The Danes are gay and sympathetic. They look English—English who have escaped public-school training. They have few inhibitions and, on first acquaintance, will discuss personal experiences with an unconcern totally incomprehensible to the Britisher.

The architecture, like that of Stockholm, shows French influence; but the pattern of Danish life has altered it to something quite unlike that of its cousin to the north or of its parent to the west. Copenhagen was, in 1913 and 1914, a center of social activity which made Christiania and even Stockholm seem static. Its royal family was allied to practically every reigning house in Europe. On the throne of England sat a half-Dane. A half-Dane was Tsar of Russia. A Dane reigned in Greece.

Maurice Francis Egan, a diplomat of the old school, was United States Minister to Denmark at that time. His keen and sensitive mind had been schooled by Jesuit training, and he could parry embarrassing questions with an adroitness that never seemed to be evasion. A militant Catholic, he was immensely popular in this stronghold of Lutheranism. His militancy was more persuasive than combative. If he had lived in the first half of the sixteenth century he would, you suspected, have followed Erasmus to Basle in self-imposed exile, rather than take arms on behalf of the Papacy.

Of medium height, Dr. Egan's erect carriage made him look tall. His finely chiseled features were set off by a square-cut beard which was a model of manicured perfection, enormously admired; any barber might have coveted it as an advertising display for his window. His well-knit figure defied the advancing years; it was kept in military shape by daily walks. His clothes, square-cut like his beard, were immaculate; he always looked ready to enter the enclosure at Ascot.

Mrs. Egan presented a picture of agreeable concurrence, bustling inactivity, and resigned bewilderment. She navigated her small craft, equipped only for ferry-boat traffic, in the turbulent waters of an international sea. She knew less about more things than a Dickens heroine, and her sympathetic inaccuracies were widely quoted. But she was an admirable hostess and contrived, on meager means, to offer continuous and genuine hospitality. It was said that the Egans had repeatedly been chosen for the more ambitious posts to which his talents were adapted; but they were never tempted to accept.

"Here in Copenhagen," he said to me, "my own tiny income plus the ministerial salary of $8000 allows us the pleasant exhilaration of a tobaggan coast down a not too abrupt mountain slope. We have the zest of danger without the risk. In London, Paris, or even Rome, the salary would be doubled, but the anxieties would be multiplied a hundredfold. It just couldn't be done."

Friends had provided me with an introduction to the Egans, and on my arrival in Copenhagen, I left cards at the Legation. My call was returned within two hours. We were lodged at the Hôtel d'Angleterre, which faced the principal square. Our wants were efficiently attended to by a manservant of superior talents who was floor waiter, valet, index of information, and arbiter of manners. He appeared at the door breathlessly to announce the American Minister.

"He must not be kept waiting," he insisted, disregarding the fact that I was in a bathrobe. I pleaded for five minutes' grace in order to dress properly. They were reluctantly allowed me while he stood by the door to make sure I did not abuse his indulgence. He was plainly relieved when I completed the task with one minute to spare. He eyed me appraisingly, hastened to the chest of drawers for a clothes brush to give me a final polish, adjusted my hastily knotted tie, and led the way down to the large palm court where our Plenipotentiary was sitting.

"I have ordered tea," whispered this amazing Admirable Crichton. Then, straightening his shoulders and projecting his voice as though he were a court seneschal, he announced:

"Mr. Spalding, your Excellency."

Egan rose and greeted me. Some people have the art of communicating a quiet warmth and cordiality without suggesting premature intimacy. Egan had this to a remarkable degree.

"Tea—what a genial idea!" he exclaimed, as it arrived with surprising despatch.

I told him about the floor waiter's solicitude on my behalf. Egan laughed.

"I might have guessed as much. Morissen is a character here—far more important really than the hotel manager. When in doubt consult him about everything. You will not go wrong. He is, I am glad to say, a good friend of mine."

Egan was anxious to know my plans. How long was I staying? How many concerts, and when? Whom did I know in Copenhagen? The vacuum was, it appeared, to be speedily filled by new acquaintances.

After tea, Egan proposed a walk. His daily quota, imposed rain or shine, was incomplete. He consulted his watch.

"We have time," he said, "for a nice walk along the waterways. It is about two miles. You are kind to keep me company. Often I must trudge it alone. My wife says that in order to insure companionship I resort to bribery."

"Bribery?" I echoed.

"Yes. It's quite true. Do you like Danish oysters?"

I had never tasted them.

"Something is in store for you. A mile or so along the waterfront there is a place famous for them. Will you accept my bribe?"

We walked along at the leisurely gait that suited him. At a street corner he paused to chat with an old woman selling flowers, and for a silver coin received a sweet-smelling bunch of the first spring violets. This was evidently a daily affair to which the flower-vendor attached great importance. Her eyes had brightened at our approach, and she raised her apron to execute the semblance of a curtsey. Egan's Danish was limited, and as leisurely as his gait. In drawing-rooms he restricted himself to English and to his excellent French and German. But he used his modest Danish vocabulary in his daily conversations with this old woman. She looked at him with adoring eyes as he assured her that Mrs. Egan enjoyed her violets, keeping them always in a small vase by her bedside. Would there be some fresh ones tomorrow or the day after? Good, she must reserve a bunch for him. He would surely come by for them.

We went on. I had now met two of Egan's devoted friends in Copenhagen: Morissen and the old flower-seller.

CHAPTER TWENTY-FOUR

TWO days later I was to meet more of Dr. Egan's friends, under different circumstances. Dinner at the Legation was followed by an evening reception. The dining-room was strained to its utmost to seat some twenty-odd guests. The domestic personnel was, I suspected, hard pressed to cope with such an invasion, their sparse numbers having perhaps been temporarily augmented from the outside. But there was no lack of good food and wine served quickly and efficiently under the quiet direction of our hostess. This she managed with the most disarming ease, never letting it disturb the steady flow of her conversation.

"How does she manage it?" I asked the wife of one of the secretaries who was crowded next to me at the dinner table.

"Mrs. Egan," she replied, "is blessed as are few other women. She completely lacks self-consciousness. It is her greatest charm. She has read a great deal and remembers more than she has read. In assimilating historical facts, her enchanting imagination alters both time and place. Her reactions to a question are seldom relevant, but always entertaining. She was born to be a diplomat's wife. See, now, how interested the old Comte de Beaucaire is."

So he was. With a glass poised in his hand he sat in rapt attention while Mrs. Egan's animated talk went ceaselessly on. The French Minister, dean of the diplomatic circle, was obviously engrossed. My neighbor went on:

"He may have asked her some question about Wilson's Mexican policy. Or perhaps a more innocuous one—how the opera season at the Metropolitan was going. Do you think that he will be in the least disappointed that her reply has nothing to do with Wilson, or Huerta, or Carranza—that she will not mention Caruso's splendid voice or the magic of Toscanini at the Opera? Why lose time on such matters? Quite probably she is telling him of a wintry evening in the Berkshire Hills when the Stockbridge Indians, avid for scalps, besieged her grandfather's house; how they were stood off hour after hour by a small group of men and women armed with flintlock muskets; and how rescue came at the last moment with the arrival of the militiamen."

"Did it really happen?" I asked.

"I don't know. Does that matter? She may have read it all in Fenimore Cooper, or somewhere else, but it is quite real to her. Moreover, her way of telling of it has a fairy-tale quality. See how pleased M. de Beaucaire looks—he seems ten years younger! It is a dream of his youth come true: America is not, after all, the sophisticated, industrialized land that everyone has been telling him about; it is the land of backwoodsmen, of Indians, of adventure. Do you wonder at his gratitude?"

I turned to my neighbor on the left. The lady, advanced rather than aged in years, presented an astonishing appearance. Her coiffure looked more like heavy passementerie than human hair. It must have taken her maid countless hours to get so unreal and startling an effect. I found myself staring, quite forgetful of manners.

"No, I assure you that it is *not* a wig," said a rich contralto voice, plainly American. "Everyone thinks it is. But do not feel embarrassed. I should have been disappointed if you hadn't noticed it." Her dark eyes flashed. They were large and deepset and still held the sparkle of youth.

I was abashed despite her reassuring cordiality.

"You are the young violinist. Do you play as well as they say? I hope so, for we have had altogether too many mediocre samples, extolled to the skies—a lot of pretentious publicity with but little to justify it."

I sought in vain for a proper answer, gave it up, and remained silent.

[185]

"Of course," she went on, "you are hardly the one to give an affidavit of your own powers. Your playing must do that. We are all coming. Play well. Do not disappoint an old woman. I am, you know, an American, and I was once something of a musician myself."

Who *was* this woman? I recalled, among the many introductions in the salon a long, hyphenated, Danish-sounding name, and now, under cover of the conversation, I glanced at her place card: Mme. de Hegermann-Lindencrone. A bell rang in my memory. Could this be the celebrated Mrs. Charles Moulton of Second Empire days in Paris, whose salon had been such a famous music center, whose rich voice—admirably trained but exercised only as an amateur—was said to rival the best professional voices of the period? Gradually it was coming back to me. She had grown up in Boston and Cambridge, had married Charles Moulton of our diplomatic staff in Paris, and had early become a distinguished diplomatic figure. After Mr. Moulton's death she had married the Danish Minister to the United States, Hegermann-Lindencrone, and with him had lived in many European capitals. Even now, her book *In the Courts of Memory* was being sold and read widely. I spoke now of this book. Had I read it, she asked. I had, of course; everyone had.

"It never occurred to me," she said, "that those random reminiscences would find so large a public. Today, it all seems very far away, very unreal."

Did she regret the passing of that time, I asked.

"No!" said the old lady, decidedly. "The essence of my life has been change. I am not afraid of change. Today and tomorrow have always been more important to me than yesterday. And if I remember yesterday with pleasure, it is only because of its contribution to today and tomorrow."

I glanced at her quickly. Manifestly, her spirit was youthful and unfaltering. I recalled one of the pleasant anecdotes in her book. Someone in her salon spoke of the advanced years of Auber who was then eighty years old. He was there, and overheard it. He protested that he was not eighty—he was merely four-times-twenty.

"A trick of words," said Mme. de H.-L., when I mentioned

this; "but how comforting, how rejuvenating! I do not take quack medicines, but I am a firm believer in the power of suggestion.

"You are new to Copenhagen," she went on. "You have met a number of people tonight and can remember scarcely a single name. Why should you? Your memory is trained for crotchets and quavers. Do not crowd it with useless things. But, for this evening's convenience, I will catalogue some of the guests. First and foremost, the French Minister and his wife, the Comte and Comtesse de Beaucaire. I see by your expression that you already know. . . ."

The Comtesse, I presumed, was the highly enameled bisque figure who sat at Mr. Egan's right.

"Yes," said my entertaining informer. "Isn't she wonderful? No one ever sees her in the daytime. She is fit only for candle-light. Even electricity profanes the secrets of her cosmetic mausoleum. For evening entertainments she consents to exhume herself."

"She must," I hazarded, "be years younger than her husband."

Mme. de H.-L. looked at me witheringly.

"Where is your eyesight, young man?" she demanded. "The smooth glaze you see at a distance masks as many wrinkles as I have. Oh, she is decorative, I will admit. That dazzling expanse of white bosom is pushed up by the corset-maker's art. The choker of black velvet and diamonds supports a sagging throat. She is never without it, and it serves as a reminder that she may pivot her vacant head just so far to the right or left. You are fortunate to have me and not her as a dinner partner."

I knew it; she knew it; there was no need to agree. On the other side of Mr. Egan sat a woman, no longer young, but still lovely. She was restful to look at after the unreality of the French Minister's wife.

"My daughter," said Mme. de H.-L. "She is the Countess Raben. Her husband is that distinguished-looking man sitting to the left of Mrs. Egan. His family dates back to Viking days. Isn't she beautiful? Do not say 'No' or I shall be disappointed in your taste."

Quite sincerely I reassured her.

"They have three children, all grown. That is one of the daughters sitting over there," pointing to an attractive girl diagonally opposite from us. "One son, whose name is Siegfried. He's a nice boy, though hardly a Wagnerian hero. It is fortunate that they have American blood. You cannot expect such healthy growth in the arid desert of aristocracy."

Clearly the old lady, for all her international experience, was still a Yankee at heart.

"Next to my granddaughter sits Haakon Schmedes. His brother, Eric, was a well-known opera singer. Used to sing Wagnerian roles at the Metropolitan. I never liked his voice—or rather, I never liked the way he used it. The voice itself is a good natural instrument, but he uses the traditional Teutonic method of forcing the tone up through the vocal cords so that it comes out as a muffled explosion. Tone should float. No one knows that better than a violinist."

There was no argument.

"Yes, I was a singer—a good singer. Why should I be ashamed to say it?"

I saw no reason.

"Haakon is also a musician of sorts. He was a gifted—even, at one time, an accomplished—violinist; he studied with Ysaÿe. He made several débuts—each fell just short of real success. His talent is not quite great enough to take him to the peak of Parnassus. It always seems such a tiny stretch, that last lap; such a temptation to pause, rest, review, and rejoice in the ascent already made. And it is just this pause that must not be made. Once the drive toward the top is relaxed, it is rarely regained. You may be tired, you may be breathless; but you must forget fatigue and push on, with a kind of insane will to win. . . ."

She was looking sideways at me as she spoke. This was, I felt convinced, meant for me rather than for Schmedes. True to herself, the old lady was more interested in today and tomorrow than in yesterday.

"Then, too," she went on, "Haakon has been cursed with too easy a life. Good family, modest but comfortable means. He has, also, a gift for marrying. He has had two wives already, both of them nice women who adored him. He will marry again and again. His type always does."

"Is he, then, a widower?" I asked.

"His second wife is still living, but not for long."

"She is ill?"

"Not ill, just sliding down the slope of wasting vitality. There are many women like that—willing victims of men like Haakon Schmedes. They are drawn to his vigor like moths to a flame. He should," she said reflectively, "have been a Mormon. It would have been better for him, and healthier for his wives. After dinner you must talk to him. You will enjoy it; he is genial and will welcome conversation with a musician. He pretends to be satisfied with his *dolce far niente* life, but you will detect a nostalgia whenever the subject of music comes up."

It was quite true. When I joined him, Schmedes wanted to talk of nothing but music. We had friends in common—Ysaÿe, the Thibauds. He had spent a short time in the States; had even, for a time, played in the Boston Symphony Orchestra under Gericke.

"I see," he said, "that you are playing some unaccompanied Reger. Unless you play it better, far better than I have yet heard it played, I shall plan to arrive after that number."

I stoutly defended Reger.

"Well," he conceded, "I do not suppose you would play it unless you liked it. But his self-imposed neoclassicism wearies me. It smells of the midnight oil. Do you know Reger personally?"

I did. Two years before, he had been in the front row at my recital in Leipzig and had led the applause like a Yale cheerleader.

"Oh, yes, he rather rules the roost in Leipzig, and it was shrewd of you to play his music there. But here in Copenhagen . . ."

I assured him that the sonata did not take longer than twelve or thirteen minutes.

"Of boredom?" he retorted with an upward inflection. "I can perhaps resign myself to that. The interest of listening to a new fiddler will help. You knew that I played? Yes, I can see that you did. That irrepressible old lady, Mme. de H.-L., has probably told you more than all there is to tell about me. Hasn't she?"

I was grateful for an interruption in our conversation. We were joined by a tall, good-looking young man who was talking in Danish with Schmedes. Then, in excellent English, he asked me about the latest American slang terms. I told him all I knew. The young man looked disappointed. He was already acquainted with those, and knew others that were new to me.

"What about the latest Broadway tunes?" and he hummed one that I recognized as the current hit called *Snooky-Ookums*.

I rose to the occasion lamely but bravely with other recent popular favorites that occurred to me.

Would I perhaps play some at my forthcoming concert? It sounded like a joke, and I replied that my banjo technique was suffering from disuse and I would therefore confine myself to simpler efforts.

"Highness," remonstrated Schmedes, with a shade of mockery in his voice, "Mr. Spalding's concert will, I fear, be an immense disappointment to you. His instrument, his program, his playing, will all sound quite European to you. At best, if you come late, you can hope for some Viennese waltzes by Kreisler as encores."

Highness' interest in me abated considerably. After a few polite remarks he moved off to another group. "Who is he?" I asked Schmedes.

"Oh, didn't you know? But, of course, how could you? That is Prince Aage, the King's nephew: playboy of the Eastern World. You mustn't feel in the least embarrassed that you didn't address him as Highness; he thoroughly enjoyed his temporary incognito. And, of course, he was pulling your leg part of the time. Toward the end of the conversation I slipped in the title for your benefit. You will, of course, be properly introduced to him by Egan later on. It would not have been my place to do so."

The formal introduction did, in fact, take place a few minutes later. The stiff figure standing at attention was quite unlike the carefree young man whose earlier greeting had been as casual as that of a club member just off the golf course. It was, I thought, a more than doubtful advantage to have been born in a royal bed.

Each successive concert was receiving increased public favor; and I played a good many private engagements in addition. Fees were modest by American or Russian standards, but they paid our expenses and showed a comfortable profit.

The music-publishing house of Hansen very flatteringly requested some recent pieces of mine which I had played with success both publicly and privately. Benoist suggested that I let him handle the business transaction.

"What business transaction?" I asked, surprised. "They will offer the usual ten per cent, I suppose. Do you expect to do better?"

Ben cocked his head to one side.

"The pieces are not usual," he said speculatively. "Your success here is not usual. It is not usual for a publisher to do the approaching. Why be satisfied with the usual percentage? You have an excellent business head for everything but your own affairs. Let me have a try at this."

Not too hopeful, I let myself be persuaded. I was due for lunch with the Rabens. When I returned in the afternoon I found Ben taking his ease in the largest armchair, lazily indulging in the luxury of an opulent Havana cigar.

"Have one," he offered, impudently.

"Where . . ." I began.

"Yes," he interrupted, "I've been wasting your money prodigiously, *mais c'est pour une bonne cause.* I ought by rights to charge you a thundering good commission. But I am modest, unassuming; in short, I have all the virtues. Only you are blind to them. You begrudge me a good smoke. There is, obviously, no gratitude in you."

"They took the pieces?" I asked.

But Ben was not to be cheated out of his drama. He savored each delay, as obstinate as Dame Nurse with the impatient Juliet.

"Light up your cigar," he suggested. "It is a long story. It is more than a story—it is a ritual."

I resigned myself; after all, the cigar *was* good.

"I arrived at Hansen's about twelve-thirty. I had telephoned and they were all there waiting for me—the Hansen brothers, and Jespersen, the female fortress shrouded in black who presides over the accounts. We met in the upstairs salon. Coffee was served. I drank altogether too many cups. It is not good for my liver."

"You had the manuscripts with you?" I put in.

"But, no! It would have been premature; this was a social call, an opening of pour-parlers. You must not hurry these things. Remember, I was born in Paris, and here in Copenhagen it isn't only the architecture that shows a Gallic influence. We talked about you, your playing, your music, your personality. It was all very tiresome, but the coffee helped. I explained that you were greatly touched by their wish to publish your pieces, that nothing would please you more. Perhaps it could be arranged. In the meantime you had certain commitments at home, and also in Russia, where you are shortly due."

"Commitments?" I echoed in bewilderment. "What commitments?"

"Hush," said Ben. "Don't spoil my story with silly trivialities. Present or future, your wide public is awaiting you. If I anticipate the date somewhat it is because I am a prophet rather than a reporter. When, after the fourth cup of coffee, we adjourned for lunch, they were half persuaded—so was I, for that matter—that the time is *now*. . . . So, as I said, we paused for lunch."

"You came back to the Angleterre?" I asked.

"On the contrary, I lunched with them. And a very good lunch it was, too."

"Still talking about the contract?"

"Decidedly not. No business at the midday meal! I told them anecdotes of Nordica, Tetrazzini, Kreisler, Schumann-Heink. I was very entertaining."

"Seasoning it all, I suppose, with some of your shopworn and unmentionable stories—"

"My stories," said Ben, looking hurt, "were all new to them. They were enchanted. It would be interesting to speculate on how substantially those stories contributed— But I must not get ahead of myself. After lunch we separated for a brief interval.

I returned to the hotel for the precious manuscripts. Suddenly I realized that something was lacking. There would be more coffee, of course. Cigars would be a nice touch. I stopped at that excellent importer's on the Leif Eriksen's Gade. Many's the time I have looked longingly at the Larranagas in the window."

"To the tune of twenty-five kroners or more a box," I remarked ruefully.

"I never knew you," said Ben, "to be so stinkingly stingy before. You will regret it. I bought a box—with *your* money. Let that sink in! I stuffed my pockets with eight or ten of these tokens of peace and goodwill. The remainder of the box was sent here by the shop. See, it is there on the mantelpiece. Then I went back to Hansen's to wind up the campaign."

"And the conclusion?" I asked.

"The conclusion," said Benoist, "was not a coda, but a recapitulation à la Bruckner—endless repeats of theme, sub-theme, more developments, more and more coffee, skirmishes, alarums, retreats, recoveries. They offered the usual ten per cent."

I suspected a trap, and waited quietly for him to continue.

"Gently," said Ben, "I explained to them that such a proposition could not be even considered. I made as if to go. It was all part of the game. They countered with a request for your terms."

"And what are my terms?" I asked, genuinely interested.

"Your terms? You have no terms. An artist does not think of such matters; he is too absorbed in his art. I made that clear to them. I offered them cigars. The precious aroma mellowed the atmosphere. What then, they asked, was my suggestion? I murmured that the initiative must come from them, in the form of an offer, if they were really interested. An offer commensurate with your talent and success. A substantial advance royalty on sales, a good publicity campaign; in short, an offer that I could without embarrassment transmit to you."

"But my pieces may not sell," I protested.

"Perhaps not," said Ben blandly. "Such matters are not your concern. The fact is that Hansen apparently thinks they will. In any case, here is the contract. And here," he ended triumphantly, "is your advance royalty."

He threw a handful of hundred-kroner bills onto the table. "Count them! There are eight hundred kroners there—more than you make on a successful concert. Now begrudge me those cigars!"

That night we celebrated with champagne and ended the evening with a visit to the local circus. Our indispensable Morissen had told us of a clown there who was making a worldwide reputation with his original stunts. We were not disappointed. This man raised buffoonery to an art that was creative, spontaneous, and irresistible. His name was Grock.

CHAPTER TWENTY-FIVE

A DAY or two later we left for Finland and Russia. We traveled via Stockholm, then by night boat to Abo (now Turku). Until late spring these small boats have to plow their way through fields of almost solid ice. We looked at the minute cabins, the narrow bunks.

"Do they expect us to sleep in these?" asked Ben. This was his first trip across the Baltic.

I offered the doubtful consolation that, with the noise and jarring from continuous ice-breaking, we could not in any case expect to sleep very well. However, the dinner was excellent. But, since it consisted chiefly of smoked fish, we ordered some bottled water. The only kind to be had was called Salus, and it fully justified its name, being so saline as to act as an astringent on our already parched throats.

"I feel just the way a herring tastes," muttered Ben.

We went outside. It was clear, and there was a moon. A few clouds floated across the blue-black velvet of the sky. The ice and snow through which we laboriously traveled was a luminous white. The sound of shattering ice punctuated the Northern silence. It was eerily beautiful. Occasionally an unusually large cube of ice was catapulted into the air, flashed like a mammoth diamond in the moonlight, and crashed to fiery splinters. It was a setting for a Hans Andersen fairy tale.

We arrived at Abo early in the morning, and a short train ride took us to Helsingfors. Here we had a warm welcome from the Fazers, from Kajanus, and from Jussi Snellman, the actor. Sibelius I did not see on this trip; the composing fever was on him, and no one knocked on his door at such times.

Ben liked Helsingfors; he liked the Finns. I should have disowned him if he hadn't, for I felt a proprietary pride in their qualities. Could they possibly be the same on this trip? The recollection of your delight in these people always seems to have been a pale understatement when you rediscover them. The struggle for material necessities liberates rather than fetters their minds. They think with an individual freedom, with an originality that drives home to you a lesson of spiritual values.

Even Benoist seemed to become less conscious of his creature comforts or the lack of them. He accepted the bowl and pitcher instead of running water, the remoteness of the bathroom facilities, and the necessity of using his legs as the main form of transportation. This unusual mildness of spirit did not, however, prevent him from voicing his disgust with a language that consisted of nothing but vowels, or his annoyance at finding a "drugstore" that was merely an apothecary's, barren of all those delights which enterprising American merchants were beginning to add. He sought distraction in the local newspapers. Those in Finnish he could not make head or tail of. The ones printed in Swedish, however, he scanned page by page, seeking in vain for announcements of our forthcoming concerts.

"Not one word," he protested to me. "A swell kind of house you can expect tomorrow night!"

Then I looked—it was quite true. Something must be wrong. Calling Fazer's office on the phone, I was told that he was on his way over to see me. Indignant, I prepared a self-righteous dissertation on the plight of artists whose interests were jeopardized by a careless management. When Fazer arrived I sailed into him. His round face grew rounder; his eyes widened. He opened his mouth several times to speak, only to give it up as a bad job.

"Oh," I went on, "I know what you will say tomorrow night when empty benches yawn at us: that someone has had a wedding, or a funeral, or a reception. But in the meantime there is no publicity. No publicity today—the eve of the concert. What have you to say to that?" I paused, breathless.

"But, Mr. Spalding," said Fazer, wildly, "I have been trying to tell you: your house is sold out. It was sold out several days ago, after the first announcements. There was no need to spend more money. You are well remembered here."

I was completely flattened out. I dared not look at Benoist, who was secretly convulsed. When I had recovered my wits and my manners I ordered some coffee. It was gratefully accepted. Fazer showed no resentment. He explained that when you have the complete answer to an accusation you rather enjoy it. "Sometimes," he added, "the answer is not so satisfactory. Then is the time to be irritated."

We talked about the concerts. After my recital there was an orchestral engagement, then two provincial towns to visit.

"Then another recital, after which you depart for Petersburg. But, after your concerts there, will you return for two more recitals in Helsingfors? The demand is strong; I can, if you like, spend more money on preliminary announcements. . . ."

CHAPTER TWENTY-SIX

TRAVELING to St. Petersburg we went from the frugal freshness of Scandinavia and Finland to the pungent aroma of an oriental bazaar. The contrast was as startling as ever. At the border my passport was scrutinized with what seemed to me more than the usual care, and my baggage was inspected item by item. A large, wicked-looking Finnish knife I had in the top of my suitcase was an immediate object of suspicion. Though a sinister tool, I had come by it innocently enough. It had been given to me by an admirer as a souvenir. But it seemed cause enough for further questioning, and I was led into another room. Busy hands passed over me in search of concealed weapons. I was somewhat relieved to find that they were not going to make me strip. Recently Casals had had to undergo that ordeal. There were more questions which I answered as best I could, first in French, then in halting German.

The tension relaxed little by little, and at last I was allowed to go, although they kept the knife. I would not, I decided, accept another such present unless I were traveling west, not east. The train, fortunately, had waited. It is amazing, I thought, how much you can be upset by a trifling event; I was ready to consign Russia, concerts, all my plans, to the devil in a blind, unreasoning white rage. And you feel so helpless. My anger, however, soon passed, and I was delighted to find the Hôtel de l'Europe unchanged. We ordered a regal breakfast as compensation, not forgetting to order glasses instead of pots of coffee.

The pageantry of Petersburg again unfolded itself. The old

friends were there to greet me, and I found some new ones. Leopold Auer, the violinistic autocrat of all the Russias, was an unexpected ally. He proved to be kindness itself, coming to all my concerts and bringing with him many of his pupils. Had I been one of his students he could not have shown more interest or enthusiasm.

We had dinner at his home with Mengelberg and Glazunov. At the head of the table sat Mme. Wanda Stein, who later became the second Mrs. Auer. She was tall, blonde, high-cheek-boned, with a sort of equine good looks. She was an excellent pianist and often played joint recitals with the aging master.

Mengelberg was making a brief visit as guest conductor. At one of his concerts Auer played the Beethoven concerto. Despite waning technical powers, it was a remarkable performance. Great purity of style and breadth of conception governed his phrasing, and in the lyrical passages his innate sense of poetry was deeply moving. More than once his left hand faltered over the elaborate and difficult cadenzas—his own; but it scarcely mattered. The result as a whole was richly rewarding. He was given a merited ovation and, in response to repeated demands for more, played the *Romance in F* by Beethoven with seraphic simplicity.

At the opera Chaliapin still reigned supreme. His unequaled portrayal of Boris dwarfed everybody else's, and his voice was still at its unapproachable best, an instrument of infinite color, power, and variety. Even rarer than the voice was his use of it. With his sense of space-phrasing, compelling and right, his free rhythmic impulse, Chaliapin always dominated the stage from his entrance to his exit. He contrived to make everyone else look only half alive.

One evening he played Ivan the Terrible in the seldom-given opera *The Maid of Pskov* by Rimsky-Korsakov, and it was unforgettable. I recall Ivan's first entrance. The decrepit old Tsar, a skeleton of fragile bones, sat limply on a magnificent white horse that stamped its way to the edge of the stage "so proudly as if he disdained the ground." The contrast between horse and rider could not have been sharper. The feeble figure sat astride an animal of splendid vigor; the reins hung loosely from tired

[199]

hands; the head was toppled forward; the sparse strands of white beard spread like thin trickles of water over the barbaric costume. On the stage and in the orchestra pit there had been a steady diminuendo both in sound and in action. The chorus, representing the waiting multitude, stood hushed and still; the orchestra muted its tones to a murmur.

The audience waited, alert and quiet. Three centuries dropped away, and we had become part of the scene. The suspense was oppressive. An almost imperceptible movement rippled through the figure on the horse. With a superhuman effort his body slowly straightened. Inch by inch the slack of the reins was taken up. The shoulders squared themselves. Only the head remained bent—the last part of this sagging body to draw into place. Eventually, with majestic deliberation, it lifted. The eyelids opened wide; and the personification of power and ruthless evil looked straight at his people, both on the stage and in the audience.

Over an orchestration still low and indefinite, Ivan began to speak in measured recitative. The tones, at first hushed and hollow, slowly acquired depth and quality. The return of vitality and eloquence from the dim past was made convincing and compelling. It was one of those portraits that hang in the gallery of my memory untarnished by the passing of time.

There were many other memorable spectacles that season. One was a ballet performance held at the Marinsky Theater during the celebration of three hundred years of Romanov rule. A galaxy of stars performed at this gala event. Nijinsky and Karsavina danced with a company of colleagues scarcely less famous. The music of the ballet—*Don Quixote*—was not distinguished, but the dancing was superb. And the thronged theater was almost as colorful as the stage. The Court was there in all its splendor. Tatar chieftains wore fantastic and barbaric costumes topped by headdresses of peacock feathers and jewels. The women were all beautiful; I looked in vain for a plain one. Every treasure chest from the Caspian to the White Sea had been rifled to deck them out.

By great good luck—I suspect through Wolkonsky's influence

—we had been given a box from which to witness this kaleido-scopic pageant; tickets were not available at any price. Indeed, the twilight celebration of the Romanovs in January 1914 held no hint of impending disaster. There was actually less talk of war than there had been in 1910. The last ominous incident, the appearance of the German ship *Panther* at Agadir, now nearly three years old, had subsided, and the international sea was as serene as any inland lake. Disturbances in the Baltic were regarded as schoolboy problems. Like the "growing pains" of adolescence, they seemed unlikely to disturb the balanced judgment of adult nations.

The management of my Russian concerts was in the hands of Charles Koehler, whose association with the Diedrichs' impor-tant agency gave him influence. I had met him on my previous visit to Russia, and his energy and integrity gave me far greater confidence than Magnus' shrewd but questionable behavior. It was a wise change; for Magnus had recently damaged his repu-tation by a series of unwise ventures and had, temporarily at least, disappeared from the musical scene. Koehler managed my affairs excellently. Better and better engagements were procured. I played at the Alexander Siloti concerts with gratifying suc-cess; and Russia was beginning to be an audience eager for re-peated visits.

One evening at the Diedrichs' I met a new star in the field of conductors, Serge Koussevitzky. Still a young man, he was abandoning his spectacular career as the wizard of the bull fiddle to assume generalship of an orchestra, his marriage having made this financially possible; he could take the short cut to popular acclaim. He formed an orchestra and, ignoring the ex-pense, trained it at innumerable rehearsals. Consequently he achieved a polished perfection that few European orchestras could rival. His concerts in Moscow and Petersburg were practi-cally sold out by subscription, though even at that the deficit must have been considerable at the end of each year.

About once every two years Koussevitzky and his orchestra made the long trip down the thousands of miles of the Volga, giving concerts every night or so on the west bank; on the return trip they played in the towns on the east bank. It was suggested that I go with them as soloist on the spring trip of 1914. The offer tempted me; I was anything but unwilling to put off my return to Occidental Europe. But I had fixed engagements there, and my New England conscience held* me to my obligations, marshaling a series of virtuous arguments against my great desire to accept this exotic adventure. Virtue won—and I have never ceased to regret it, for the trip that I told myself I was merely postponing disappeared in the blackout of war and revolution.

One day Auer asked me to come to a class lesson. He had several extremely gifted students; one, in particular, he was anxious to have me hear. I remembered that some weeks earlier Kreisler had been full of praise for a small boy he had heard there. Was it the same one, I wondered?

When we arrived at the Conservatory the following afternoon, Ben and I were shown into the large, low-ceilinged classroom. Small chairs flanked the walls. The grand piano stood like an ebony island in the center of the room. The students, instruments in hand, silently waited for a summons to play. Some were accompanied by parents who masked, as best they could, any suggestion of jealous rivalry. On my arrival they all rose and stood until Auer's welcome ended and we were shown to our chairs.

A small boy stood up to play. He had only recently graduated to a full-sized violin, and it made him look even smaller than he was. One of Fra Angelico's seraphs seemed to have stepped from his background of goldleaf, disguised himself in modern dress, and exchanged a trumpet for a fiddle. He played the Ernst concerto. It is not one of my favorites; its unsubstantial themes might have had a naïve charm if treated simply, but faithful to the tradition of the day they were a continuous scenic railway of coasting thirds and ascending octaves, the work being designed to amaze rather than to please. Needless to say, its technical difficulties tax the most seasoned veteran. What a cruel test, I thought, for a child!

But I quickly found that there was no need for apprehension. The first flourish of fingered octaves was attacked with a kind of nonchalant aplomb; the tone was firm, flowing, and edge-less, the intonation of fleckless purity. A kind of inner grace made itself felt in the shaping of the phrase. I completely forgot the tawdriness of the piece in the elegance and distinction of its delivery. I had never heard such perfect technique from a child.

Jascha, they called him—Jascha Heifetz.

While the boy was playing, Auer strode nervously about the room, glancing at me now and then to appraise my reactions. His dark, restless eyes danced with delight as the wonder boy threaded his effortless way through the tortuous technical prob-lems. He expected nothing less than paralyzed astonishment from me—nor was he disappointed. He would turn away with a helpless shrug of the shoulders, as if to say: "Was there ever anything like it?". Other talented students performed later, but they were eclipsed by this miniature wizard in his early teens.

In those days, public favor in Russia made itself felt in more ways than one. In addition to fees substantially higher than were paid in the rest of Europe, the visiting artist often received un-expected anonymous gifts. A handsomely bound edition of a work I had recently performed would be left at the hotel with the inscription: "From a group of music-lovers." Once I found a violin bearing the Jacob Stainer label—an instrument that I myself had already admired in an auction salesroom. I had put in a modest bid for it, but it had been knocked down at a higher price. The purchaser, whose anonymity was jealously preserved, sent it to me with a card on which were written two bars of a Bach concerto and the date of my performance of that work. The violin, though it proved not to be an authentic Stainer, was an excellent old copy of the German master's craft.

Sometimes the booty bestowed by the generous Russian public disregarded the fact that I was traveling a great deal. On the eve of my departure for Western Europe a large wooden case was delivered. An unsigned note explained that the writers had observed my enjoyment of a smoked fish called *sig,* or *sigui,* ob-tainable only in Russia, and they were wishing me bon voyage with one of these fish as a gastronomic souvenir. It proved to be an embarrassing traveling companion. At frontier after frontier,

I had to explain its presence to incredulous customs officials. This is what would happen:

"Have you something to declare?"

"Only personal effects." Then, remembering, "Oh, yes—I have a fish."

"A fish? What kind of fish? Where is it?"

I pointed to the huge box. The officials, sometimes curious, sometimes suspicious, went into a perplexed huddle. How much did it weigh? What was its value? Was it for sale or for personal consumption? Only to the last question could I return a satisfactory answer. Time after time I fully expected the white elephant to be confiscated; presently I found myself hoping that it would be! But the fish and I were invariably allowed to proceed after I had paid a small duty. Sometimes, irked by a problem to which there seemed no ready answer, the officials passed it with the label *In transito*.

After some weeks of travel I brought it home to Florence. Though my mother was not easily persuaded that it was edible, her adventurous spirit triumphed over her housewifely misgivings; she was enchanted by the manner in which it had been given to me and by its eventful Odyssey. She therefore planned a large dinner with the *sig* as pièce de résistance. She consulted with Angelo, the cook. He appraised it clinically; he approved. The fish was served, admired, and consumed to its last fragment.

CHAPTER TWENTY-SEVEN

THE spring season of 1914 was drawing to a close. I had played some fifty or sixty engagements throughout Europe and a series of recitals in Egypt. I had signed a contract for a South American tour in the summer of 1915. The subsequent winter seasons were to be alternately allocated to concerts in my own country and in Europe.

Peace appeared to be a permanent fixture. No storm clouds hung on the horizon. I remember walking home along the banks of the Arno one evening when a brilliant sunset turned to pink the low Renaissance buildings. It was June twenty-eighth. At the newspaper kiosks small groups of people were assembling, and I noticed some excitement. An Austrian Archduke and his morganatic wife had been murdered in a town called Sarajevo in the Balkans. There was obvious anxiety until it was learned that the outrage had been committed by a Serb. *Misericordia!* One had feared it was an Italian—Franz Ferdinand was unpopular in Italy—and if so, there might be international complications. But a Serb—that was different.

At my home, the affair was discussed with academic interest only. It seemed a curious paradox that the heir to the Austrian Empire should meet violent death at the hands of a Slav. Had his policy not been proclaimed as Pan-Slavic? It looked like one of those silly crimes that make no sense. My father had a keen, clear-cut way of discussing the news that was always interesting though not always prophetically accurate. Austria would, he believed, demand and receive summary satisfaction from the troublesome Serbs. There would be a speedy trial and conviction of the assassin, a searching investigation of subversive agitation, and guarantees of good behavior in the future. This highly normal view was shared by practically everyone I saw during the next few days. In the meantime, we were busy packing for our yearly migration to the States. We sailed from Cherbourg about the middle of July on the North German Lloyd liner the *Crown Princess Cecilie,* still serenely unaware of the smoldering volcano that was soon to erupt so violently.

The summer season in Europe looked even more brilliant than usual. The French President departed on a friendly visit to the Tsar. King George's gray topper and Queen Mary's unique turbans made their annual appearances at Ascot and Wimbledon. The Kaiser was having one of his spasms of uncontrollable irritation, but these were by now so familiar that they were no longer feared. The present one seemed warranted, indeed: the All-Highest would naturally react violently against this lèse-majesté, this outrage on the Divinity of kings.

Aboard ship the affair was not much discussed. Among the passengers—largely American—there was more talk of the Mexican problem, of Wilson's policy of "Watchful Waiting." Only at the Captain's table did one feel any tension. Captain Pollack made fewer appearances at table than usual. The weather was fine, and there was no fog; but when he did join us he seemed preoccupied. This was recalled later rather than observed at the time. No one dreamed of what, indeed, must have been true, that he had sealed orders, as well as oral instructions, probably, in connection with the sinister emergency.

When we arrived in New York we learned of the ominous ultimatum from Austria to Serbia—which at that time everybody still called Servia. It was so sweeping in its demands as to be unacceptable by any sovereign state. But even this threat to peace seemed local. Serbia, acceding to the insistent urgings of England, France, and even Russia, agreed to comply with practically every demand in the ultimatum. Apparently this was not enough, however. Austria, backed up by Germany, was determined on a punitive and annihilating war against her small and troublesome neighbor. The assassination of a prince could be expiated only by the wholesale murder of millions

Overnight there was a sudden revulsion of feeling. Sympathy for Austria disappeared. She was no longer an injured nation. At the bidding of Wilhelmstrasse she was prepared to rend the tenuous fabric of peace so patiently woven over many decades. War was declared on Serbia, and the Austrian invasion began. Even then—in the very last days of July 1914—there was still hope that the affair could be localized. All eyes were focused on Berlin. Would Germany exert her influence toward a pacific solution, reinforcing the efforts of Grey and the British Foreign Office? There were pious protestations that she would—provided Austria were given a completely free hand. Germany, it appeared, had always been eager for peace—on her own terms. From the middle of the nineteenth century her policy had followed this pattern, and for more than fifty years its success had satisfied the German people.

The difficulty was Russia. Russia, it seemed, was not going to be docile; she was not going to repeat her submission of 1908; and Russia mobilized. At once, on August first, Germany declared war on Russia, and at the same time sent an ultimatum to France demanding—as guarantee of her neutrality—the delivery to Germany of such frontier fortresses as Verdun, Toul, and Epinal. France refused, and adhered to her alliance with Russia; whereupon Germany declared war on France, and started the invasion of Belgium.

For the main attack was not to be made on France directly. A quicker road to Paris lay through a neutral country of whose inviolability Prussia had been one of the guarantors in 1830. But that guarantee of Belgium's neutrality, said Chancellor Bethmann-Hollweg, was only a scrap of paper. It was a scrap of paper, however, that had real significance across the Channel. Great Britain, therefore, in turn delivered an ultimatum to Germany, and by midnight of August fourth was at war with her.

Public opinion in America was stunned. The vast majority in our country aligned itself immediately with the Allies. There were, however, important minorities—German-American groups, a great many Jews, some Irish, and some Scandinavians—who hoped for a German victory. President Wilson's proclamation enjoining strict neutrality "in thought as well as in deed" went unheeded; certainly we were not neutral in thought, at least.

August and early September rolled up for the apparently invincible German armies a succession of victories which we followed in the papers with bated breath. The inexorable march on Paris continued. The small British Expeditionary Force—the "contemptibles," to quote the eloquent Kaiser—were having difficulties in Flanders; the retreating French armies were facing defeat and annihilation; only a miracle could avert it.

The miracle occurred. A stand was made at the River Marne, and the overextended right wing of the German army met unexpected resistance. For the next four years this spirit was to stand as a symbol of faith and courage.

Two years and a half went by; the sanguinary war continued. The deadlock on the Western Front looked as though it might last till doomsday. The submarine was becoming an increasing menace to both belligerent and neutral shipping. When the *Lusitania* was sunk, American lives were lost, and endless diplomatic notes were exchanged. The 1916 elections came around and Woodrow Wilson was returned to the Presidency by a narrow margin on the doubtful slogan that "He kept us out of war."

A revolution took place in Russia. The Imperial Government was overthrown and a new government was set up under Alexander Kerensky. It looked for a while as if the democratic front were purging itself of doubtful and reactionary partners.

Early in 1917 Germany violated her pledge to restrict submarine warfare in accordance with the international code, and embarked on an all-out program of "Sink on sight." Under Wilson's leadership this was denounced as an act of piracy. The famous Zimmermann note to Mexico came to light. In seven-league boots we were striding toward war. And within a few weeks after the inauguration of a President elected on a peace slogan, the United States went to war.

Meantime, I had been playing almost continuously throughout the States. For three successive seasons I had given an average of sixty or seventy concerts each year. In spite of very active competition from distinguished colleagues who flocked to the one

remaining market for music, I enjoyed an increasing and gratifying share of public favor.

Best of all, I got to know my own country as I had not known
it before. West of the Mississippi Valley the vast prairie land
stretches like an arid sea to the horizon. The occasional towns
seem to be intruders on forbidden territory. The scorched, bare
plains present a striking contrast to the congested industrial East
and to the prodigal fertility of the great valley between. They
make you feel solitary and insignificant. Only animals, and perhaps Indians, can really feel at home on these plains. There is
drama in the way Nature has planned in placing this unpromising approach to the unbelievable architecture of the Rockies
and to the Eden that lies beyond.

It was an experience I shall never forget, my first acquaintance
with this mighty land, and it came at a crucial moment, when
the troubled times demanded answers to many questions within
oneself. My answers were given by the land itself, not by the
people who dwelt there. They were, for the most part, indifferent
to the issues of the war. I was impatient with their comfortable
assumption that our unprecedented economic power carried with
it no obligation or responsibility beyond enjoyment. Liberty, I
thought, can never be preserved by mere walls of defense or by
insular retreat. It remains a heritage only to those who are willing to rededicate themselves continually to its renewal; and this
renewal entails risk.

Too often I was no match for a skillful debater who could
make the entire struggle appear to be one of power politics, with
little to choose between one side and the other. In detail there
was much to support this argument; and its obvious conclusion
was that neither our interests nor our ethics were involved in
the outcome of the war. But even while smarting with defeat
I knew that these details were of only minor importance. The
main point stood like a fixed star: Is Force, or Reason, to prevail as the ultimate weapon in adjusting differences between
men? Can Force, even when victorious, bring more than a temporary advantage, dependent on the steady accretion of more
and more force? Can the exchange of ideas gain by the support
of physical power? These were, I felt, the questions to which we

[209]

must seek the answer. To remain indifferent to them was a childish renunciation of our maturity.

Germany had chosen Force, and the Allies must meet it with Force; but always their intention was to return to Reason as the ultimate. That selfish interests were in action, as well as high resolve, was of little importance. The main question was clearly defined.

I was in Salt Lake City early in April 1917, when Wilson delivered to the Congress his momentous message announcing our entrance into the struggle. The news came to me as a profound relief. It was as if we had awakened from a long and troubled sleep. At once I felt more alive and at the same time anxious to participate. The months passed with feverish quickness as the remainder of the season's concerts were played. I made frequent trips to Washington. The confusion was bewildering; I trekked from one office to another, confident that the next visit would solve my problems.

Would I enroll in the Red Cross? Would I volunteer in the Y.M.C.A.? Would I join the entertainers' organization?

It was explained to me over and over again that if I did any of these I should be exempt from military service. I disavowed any intention of trying to escape the draft; indeed, active service was my object. I was answered with raised eyebrows. What? With your hands? And I heard overmuch about the need to safeguard such specialized talent.

In the strictly military offices I found more direct and sympathetic reactions. For immediate service? What could I do? Languages? Yes, French, Italian, some German. Good. Military training? None. Law? None.

Presently I was taking examinations at Governors Island and elsewhere. Action in the matter seemed imminent. I was to get a commission in the near future, probably as a liaison officer. Meantime I registered at Red Bank, New Jersey, for the draft, hoping that the commission would come through first. Toward the end of August I received a long telegram signed by the Adjutant General. I was directed to go to a recruiting office in Newark, there to be enlisted in the service for immediate duty overseas. This action would relieve me from the draft, pursuant to this or that mysterious article, and this or that omnipotent authority. I complied immediately. The physical examination proved me hale and hearty; it was but one of many that I underwent that summer. Apparently even a fiddler could be a sound specimen.

The recruiting officer had likewise heard from the Adjutant General. He did not impart any details of the message, but merely ordered me to report at once to a camp at Mineola on Long Island. I was now a soldier, not supposed to ask questions.

With great satisfaction I traveled from Newark to Mineola at Uncle Sam's expense. A strange, new life was about to begin. At Mineola I was ushered into a small shed, a temporary office for the Signal Corps, of which the Air Service was at that time a branch.

Seated at the desk was a small man with graying hair who spoke with a southern accent. His name was Captain Swann and it was no surprise to learn that he came from Tyler, Texas. He received me kindly. Before him stood an obvious greenhorn, still in civilian clothes and totally inexperienced in the ways of the Army.

We were, he explained, due to sail overseas at any moment. Was my home near by? Near enough for me to take advantage of eighteen hours' leave? Good! He wrote me out a pass, and told me to return not later than noon of the following day.

I wasted no time getting home for those last precious hours. It was not easy to announce the day's events to my father and mother. My mother especially was unable to face its suddenness with the stoicism she tried to assume; she kept biting her lip in a vain attempt to prevent tears. My father, with the nervousness of an adolescent, made futile jokes to conceal his own emotion. And I was ashamed that I was unable to show the tenderness I felt.

Jacques and Marguerite Thibaud stopped by for a moment. They had been our neighbors all summer, they and the Pierre Monteux. Jacques hugged me, Gallic fashion, and advised me to practice shooting with my feet, *"pour épargner les mains."* Marguerite, or "Didi" as we called her, looking and speaking like a reduced version of Sarah Bernhardt, said little; she kept exchanging surreptitious glances with my mother as though they shared some secret. Both women maintained a hostile silence before the inept jokes we males indulged in.

Jacques and I had been quite inseparable during that 1917 summer. We played tennis, golf, and a great deal of music together. He exemplified the adventurous spirit of Gascony; the sun-shot warmth of southern France illuminated his smile. He could tell a tale with enthralling zest. The same grace and charm that individualized his violin playing was evident in everything else he undertook. He was irresistible to women, young and old —and was as proud of this power as he was modest about his musical genius. He cannot have been unaware of the spell which his inimitable playing could evoke; only a fool or an insensitive man could fail to know it, and Thibaud was neither. His wife adored him. She accepted his frequent infidelities as the price of his companionship.

Jacques asked me if I meant to take a fiddle with me. I thought doubtfully of the restrictions of a soldier's kit, but— remembering Captain Swann's good-natured face—said I would try to manage it. I had a modern instrument that could take quite a bit of punishment. My mother's face brightened considerably. Both Thibauds felt this modulation to a major key and proceeded to develop the theme. Didi, when she became animated, had a curious trick of manipulating her head; she could make it recede into her shoulders, or emerge, as though she had a vertical lifting and lowering device. Turtles can do it, but it doesn't seem quite human.

The Thibauds remained longer than they had expected to. It was a Samaritan act. There are moments when personal relationships are subject to an extraordinary strain. The closer the bond and the deeper the feeling, the more absolute is the chasm between human beings—a kind of No Man's Land where every familiar object is lost in a heavy fog. The part of you that yesterday was so much part of them is suddenly no longer there; in its place is a stranger, speaking another language.

Jacques and Didi had appreciated the situation and remained to resolve our dissonances. The modulation came almost imperceptibly; little by little my mother's gloom lifted. She remembered that Jacques had risked his life for his country. She remembered her own passionate partisanship for the cause of the Allies. Suddenly she was herself again, cheerfully proposing sandwiches and beer. We were all hungry; dinner, several hours before, had been left almost untouched. It was late when we went to bed.

Our good-bys the next morning were brief and stoical. I took the early train to New York and thence to Mineola to report on time.

At headquarters I found myself in the presence of two other officers besides the friendly Captain Swann. A tall, eager-looking blond was senior in rank. He was, I learned, the commanding officer of a detachment of some hundred and fifty cadets destined for flying training abroad. His name was Leslie MacDill, and he looked absurdly young to be a major; but there was the note of authority in his voice as he snapped questions at me. Name; civilian occupation; military training; languages. My reply to the last brought a gleam of satisfaction to his eyes.

"What languages do you speak?"

"French, Italian, some German, sir."

"Do you speak them well?"

"Yes, sir; that is, French and Italian. German less well."

He turned abruptly to the third officer. "Examine Private Spalding," he ordered briefly, "and report to me."

I saluted stiffly and followed my examiner to an adjacent room. It was empty but for a table and two chairs. The officer was short, stockily built, dark complexioned. His regular features had been minted, I suspected, in a Latin country. His movements were quick and nervous but well co-ordinated. He took a chair at the table and motioned me to the other one.

"At ease," he said. His high-pitched, rather metallic voice sounded slightly out of key with his decisive personality.

Terse questions followed—in French, in Italian, in German. I answered satisfactorily and with ease. The lieutenant's frown relaxed.

"No overstatement as to your abilities in that line," he commented. "How does it happen that you are not a commissioned officer?"

I described my efforts of the summer, told how the results of my examinations had apparently vanished into thin air, or into the archives of the War Department. His small, restless hands contracted as if to clutch some unseen object.

"Don't I know!" The heavy eyebrows met again in a frown. "Well, you're a soldier now. I've heard you play, and I know what a good fiddler you are. Will you be as good a soldier?" He looked at me quizzically.

I looked back at him for a moment. "Yes, sir," I said.

Once more the frown relaxed. "I believe you!" His voice borrowed for the moment a deeper, more personal note. A hand shot out to shake mine.

"You'll have your commission, some time, some way," he said. "Meanwhile, things may be strange, difficult, but you'll get on all right. You've had no training whatsoever—know nothing of military regulations?"

I had, I replied, gone through quite a number of preparatory books on the subject. He waved his hands at this, as if to imply that it was inconsequential.

"Better to be alert and unprepared, than prepared and dumb. But," he allowed me, "you are not dumb."

He went on to explain some immediate plans.

"We are not to sail tonight then?" I asked, surprised.

We might, we might; but probably not for several days. I must get some injections at once; inoculations, vaccination, antityphoid serum; a pity that they must all be taken in one day, but the pressure of time left no alternative. Too bad, also, that my status as soldier meant steerage on the steamer and not the first-class privileges enjoyed by the flying cadets.

"You will not fly?" It was more of a statement than a question. I signified my eagerness to do so.

"How old are you?"

"Twenty-nine," I told him.

"Hm. There is an emphasis on youth for flying. I agree with that emphasis, and—and why jeopardize talent if you don't have to? Don't look discouraged. You'll risk your hide plenty before you're through!"

He called in one of the cadet pilots who was acting as sergeant for the detachment—Elliot Springs, he called him. The new recruit was consigned to his care.

The temporary sergeant was, I could see at once, a rare lad. Sturdily built, with a shock of unruly blonde hair, keen eyes, and an infectious smile, he was totally unlike the dour drill-master I had been taught to expect. The only quality that suggested the senior non-commissioned grade was a hoarseness in his voice which he must have cultivated in order to bark his orders in the approved manner.

I tried to copy his smartly executed salute as we left the office. Springs asked me where I had been to ground school. It was humiliating to explain that he had mistaken my status, that I was not even a cadet, merely an auxiliary soldier. This painful revelation did not seem to damage me irretrievably.

"You were a long time with the Congressman," he remarked cheerfully.

"Congressman? What Congressman?"

"Didn't you know? Our outfit has a Congressman—the little lieutenant is Representative from a New York district. He is fiery, aggressive, and an able fighter. Perhaps the House is too small an arena for him, and he is trying the European theater. His name is LaGuardia—Fiorello H. LaGuardia."

Springs spoke with a pronounced southern drawl, and I had to ask him to repeat and spell the name; I had never heard it before.

Springs showed me over the barracks, introduced me to group after group of cadets, and piloted me through the ordeal of serum injections—which proved extremely unpleasant. The last shot in the arm gave me a dizzy spell; I lost consciousness and would have fallen if Springs hadn't been there. He caught me and laid me out on a cot. I was grateful, when I came to, that he hadn't laughed. Perhaps I was not the first greenhorn he had had in tow. He was, I decided, an excellent sergeant.

We spent the next few days awaiting embarkation, in exasperating inactivity. My arm troubled me considerably; it was alarmingly swollen and I felt feverish most of the time. We were given frequent short leaves to New York. My reiterated good-bys to my family lost their sting. It was as though I had already departed; these subsequent meetings, though cherished, were, in effect, cinema reproductions of the first farewell.

I wrote to Mary Pyle asking if she would see me. Our paths had not often crossed in the last few years. Five years before, I had asked her to marry me. But, with my career not yet firmly established either artistically or financially, this would have meant an engagement of indefinite length, which would have been unfair to her and therefore distressing to me. Time, distance, and separation found me unchanged. But to Mary it might perhaps have meant the end of our relationship. The way to find out was to write.

Incredibly, she had not married during the interim. Incredibly, too, I got a prompt answer to my note. We met in New York one afternoon for a brief hour. I spoke again. She didn't say "Yes," but she didn't say "No." It was agreed that we would exchange letters. How much more than I had a right to hope for!

Two days later we sailed.

CHAPTER TWENTY-EIGHT

Our ship was the Cunard
liner *Carmania.* Strict secrecy governed all the details of our departure. Until we were all but out of sight of land I saw nothing
of the boat except the steerage quarters in the hold where the
enlisted men were bunked. Quarters were cramped, but not too
bad. Four of us were together in a cube-shaped cell where full-
length occupancy of your bunk was the only comfortable position. I was fortunate in my companions. They were, like myself,
auxiliary soldiers assigned to the flying detachment. In view of
the limited amount of fresh air, I observed with relief the personal cleanliness of my immediate neighbors. Because it was not
scrupulously shared by the bulk of the military personnel
crowded into every nook and cranny of these nether regions, by
mutual consent we kept our cabin door shut as much as possible. When the stench of unwashed bodies rose, mingled with
the smell of stale fish, you found yourself limiting your breathing to a minimum.

The big fellow in the bunk opposite yawned, grimaced, then
grinned. "They might have issued us some gas masks," he remarked. There was a chorus of agreement. A bit of humor
made you forget the lack of oxygen.

"I never thought," I said slowly, "that the time would come
when my only conscious organ would be my nose."

"Yes," said the big fellow; "it makes you forget stomach, sight,
touch, sex—"

This last proposition had immediate consequences. The other
two woke up to claim that, for them at least, the reproductive

instinct would be proof against even the present circumstances.

The big man's name was Kingsley Moses. He exchanged amused glances with me while we listened to the untiring recitation of experiences proving inexhaustible manhood. It could not be called rewarding, but it passed the time.

Moses was not, on first glance, prepossessing. His heavy, dark beard only partially concealed a disfiguring birthmark which spread like a blot of red ink over one side of his face. But it was curious how quickly you forgot that and remembered his quiet manner and keen, intelligent eyes. I liked him; and I think he took to me.

Finally the long wait came to an end, and we were allowed on deck. The last vestiges of land showed low on the horizon. Invigorating sea air filled our eager lungs. The enlisted men were, at first, restricted to those portions of the lower decks which had been the steerage class. They were close quarters for the hundreds of soldiers of the Ninth Infantry; and a more liberal area was soon allocated to them. Only the upper promenade deck was reserved for the exclusive use of the officers, cadet-pilots, Red Cross nurses, and the few civilian passengers.

The fresh salt air immediately produced an insistent appetite. The trumpet call to evening mess was a welcome sound, even though it meant braving the unpleasant odors below. But this situation, too, had changed for the better. A few hours of ventilation had disposed of the worst pungencies, and only a faint reminder of stale fish still persisted.

The food was abominable: ill-cooked, uninviting, inexcusably bad in quality. The Cunard Line must have made a substantial profit on the passage money paid by Uncle Sam for each of his soldiers; certainly it was enough to have insured good food. But we were hungry, and therefore the food was devoured in spite of our distaste.

It was no better next morning: tasteless coffee that might have been the German Ersatz brand, accompanied by hunks of fish in pans of cloudy water tinged pink with blood. This was, for the most part, refused with ribald resentment. The Ninth Infantry had a vocabulary.

Captain Swann made his rounds below that morning. He

asked me how I was getting on. Fine, I said, although I was really hungry. Whether he had heard rumors about the food I don't know; he didn't say. But surreptitiously he slipped me an orange as he assured me that he had my fiddle safe in his cabin. He proceeded on his way leaving me enchanted with the army.

The urge for food teaches you to be resourceful. At the midday meal I forced myself to eat enough to dull my hunger. Afterwards I found myself in a corridor leading toward the second-cabin pantries. Was I or was I not out of bounds? I didn't quite know. The original boundaries had been enlarged and relaxed. I followed my nose, which had detected the inviting smell of food. An undersized kitchen boy stood in a pantry doorway—the wiry, terrier type of underprivileged Briton. Clad in his undershirt, he looked as though he had just been drenched with sweat and grease. As he saw me approach his first impulse to warn me back to my quarters gave way to an expression of unbelieving recognition. An avalanche of misplaced *h*'s followed:

"Swelp me hif hit hain't Mr. Spalding! You are Mr. Spalding, sir, hain't you?"

What luck, I thought. Perhaps he has heard me play. Surprisingly enough, he had. Perhaps I could turn his recognition to good use. No harm in trying. It was not easy to convince the boy—Dick, his name was—that my private's uniform was not a masquerade, that I was not an officer. In good time I broached the important subject of food. Dick was sympathetic; he was generous. I had gained a firm and valuable ally. Dick led me into the pantry and provided sumptuous fare: a plate piled with cuttings from the joint, gravy, and potatoes. Profound gratitude established a bond between us. From then on we were not only friends but accomplices. And my fodder problems were solved. Dick tipped me off on how to work it. I was never to come at mealtime, but at off hours. My dinner table was the pantry sink. In front of the sink hung a tarpaulin apron. Dick stood guard at the door. With the approach of danger in the form of the Officer of the Day, Dick's low whistle warned me to dive under the sink where I was concealed by the tarpaulin curtain. Inspection over, another whistle announced "all clear" and the banquet was resumed.

[219]

It worked miraculously for a time. But I had hungry comrades and I could not for long keep this precious source of supply to myself. I shared my secret with Moses, with others. Dick's capacity as a provider was stretched to extraordinary lengths in response to his increasing clientele. They were, alas, not all so discreet as I had been in observing Dick's warning to come only at certain hours. One day the whole bunch was caught redhanded by the Officer of the Day. There were no dire punishments, but our clandestine café went out of business.

Years afterward, when I was playing a series of radio dates, I recalled this story in answer to persistent requests for human-interest material. The sponsor's press agent was enchanted with it; he broadcast an invitation to Dick to dine with me in return for his generosity. Dick, it turned out, had multiplied himself: he was living in practically every state of the Union; and all these Richards had convincing reasons for preferring the equivalent of the dinner and transportation in the form of cold cash. In every case, investigation proved the candidate spurious.

After two days we put in at Halifax and sailed again in a few hours—one of many ships in an immense convoy that was taking arms and men overseas. After seven days below decks my status was suddenly altered. I have always suspected that the chief influence in this change was the fiery little Congressman—now Captain LaGuardia, his promotion to the rank of company commander having come just before our departure.

He told the commanding officer on the ship, the Colonel of the Ninth Infantry, that my services were required to pound the rudiments of Italian into the cadet-students. They were, he said, headed for flying training at Italian camps where the pilot instructors would speak only Italian. No time must be lost in giving them an elementary knowledge of the language. The Colonel agreed, but was profoundly shaken when he heard that the teacher-to-be was a private—Buck Private Spalding, who would have to be raised to cadet status in order to have access to books, as well as elbow space for correcting lessons. Everything in the Colonel revolted at this threat to a rigid caste system. West Point steeled itself to firm refusal. But LaGuardia's

Congressional technique throve on opposition; he reminded the Colonel that my status as a private was due to an oversight of the War Office where, in fact, my commission was probably hidden in some forgotten cubbyhole, and that public interest transcended technicalities. In short, he appealed to the commanding officer's broad judgment. West Point tradition faltered under this barrage of political persuasion, hesitated, gave way. The lowly private was ordered to sit among the mighty, and couldn't quite believe it.

I found myself quartered with three cadets. The first-class stateroom seemed to me sumptuously spacious. I was made to feel in no sense an intruder as, duffel-bag in hand, I stood hesitating for a moment on the threshold. I was greeted as though a lost fraternity brother had just been found. One of the three, a quiet lad by the name of Adams, told me of his love of music. He was shy about it. We were friends at once. Another offered me his typed book of ground-work studies. Would I like it? I was grateful for this assumption that I would eventually fly. The fourth—whose name was, I think, Halleck—invited me to make a fourth in their conversation. The subject was an ambitious one: fear and death. I was a bit bewildered, but at the same time touched, at this admission to immediate intimacy. I looked from one earnest young face to another. Each with a kind of mature and considered honesty confessed the occasional presence of fear. It was, I reflected, a high testimony to their courage.

"Only a fool is completely unconscious of fear," rationalized Halleck. "Don't you think so, Spalding?" he asked, inviting my participation.

I agreed that complete disregard or complete unawareness of danger probably denoted insensitivity.

"What we were talking about," explained Halleck, "is not exactly that. Take, for example, a man who nine times out of ten faces danger unafraid. The tenth time he is seized with unreasoning panic, and his courage fails. Is he a coward?"

"Not necessarily," I replied. "But he cannot escape the responsibility for the consequences of his act."

Adams was still shy, but he found a voice to express his belief in the goodness of God as his contribution to the discussion.

"If you really believe in God," he said, "the presence or awareness of fear is reduced to a shadow."

With that he brought out a small Bible and read a Psalm. We were, all four of us, strangely moved. It is not only my quarters, I thought, that have been improved. I got out the volume of the *Dialogues* of Socrates that was in my duffel-bag, and read aloud some of the *Apologia*. It followed appropriately.

Dinner in the main saloon—ambrosial!—was followed by a game of bridge in the lounge. When it was discovered that I played a tolerable game of bridge, my social status was firmly established.

The days went rapidly by. I conducted the Italian classes and studied the vocabulary of technical aeronautic terms, with which I was totally unfamiliar. I also plodded through the volume of ground studies, learning some things that proved extremely valuable to me later when I was given permission to take flying training. I practiced the Morse code every day and became quite proficient at it.

We rounded the north of Ireland and landed at Liverpool after a fourteen-day trip. The presence of submarines in the Irish Sea caused a certain amount of excitement. It was almost disappointing that no dramatic incident occurred; under cover of fog we slipped uneventfully into port.

At the dock we received a complete change of orders. The student-pilots were not, after all, to go to Italy, but were assigned to Oxford for training. Major MacDill, Captain LaGuardia, and the few enlisted men were ordered to Paris. We caught a train immediately for Southampton. From there, after a two-day wait, we crossed the Channel to Le Havre in an ancient craft of doubtful seaworthiness. In its long-departed prime it had been a cattle-ship answering to the name of *Courtfield*. Now in its decrepitude it spent its last energies in ferrying men and material to and from the Continent. It took its time; the narrow span ordinarily negotiated in three or four hours required a full night and a day.

My job as language instructor had vanished with our cadets and taken my temporary privileges with it. Relegated to the crowded hold, I enlarged my acquaintanceship with a new set of odors. Curiously enough, I found this stench less objectionable; it had a healthy sting; it was endurable.

There was an issue of bully beef in tins, and some hardtack. Something of a novice in the opening of cans, I watched how others did it. Crowded with us was a large detachment of Australian troops on their way to rejoin their regiments. They were a magnificent-looking set of men. It was as if all the animal energy of the world had been poured into their veins. They had an aggressive and lusty good humor. One of them, seeing my predicament with the tin, offered to show me how it should be opened.

"Here, see?" he said. Pulling out a bowie knife, he sliced the can open with a circular sweep. The weather-beaten hand tore off the lid with economy of time and gesture. Paying little attention to the rather ugly cut in his hand left by the jagged edge of the can, he wiped the blood off on his breeches and handed me the open can. I thanked him and diffidently explained that I had been a musician in private life and was therefore unconsciously careful of my hands.

The huge Anzac stared at me for a moment; then, with a huge guffaw: "Sweetheart!" he roared. "How was I to know?" And he gave me a resounding slap on the back to show there was no hard feeling.

As night fell, the boat, shrouded in darkness, continued on its snail-like way. The Channel was choppy, but not unduly rough. The hours hung heavy. You were not allowed to smoke in the hold or on deck. Even the tiny glow of a cigarette was dangerous in these submarine-infested waters.

The relative comfort of the officers' quarters did not exclude boredom. Someone (was it LaGuardia?) remembered the presence of a fiddler aboard. Could he be summoned to entertain them? I didn't wait for a second invitation. Grateful for the warmth and light in the cabin, I was quite ready to play as long as they would listen. My fingers felt as if they were made of butter, but never mind! I plunged into the longest pieces I could

[223]

think of—sonatas, concertos, even the Bach *Chaconne*. I was regaled with sandwiches, beer, and a precious smoke: a princely fee.

The entertainment over, a return to my quarters below decks was in order. I determined, however, to play truant; armed with a greatcoat and a blanket, I stole up on deck. The night was so dark that you had to feel your way about. A muffled tread here, a muttered comment there, punctuated the silence.

The *Courtfield* had a ventilating system of rather original design. Funnels slightly elevated from the deck looked like truncated metal caricatures of bergère seats, and into one of these I wedged myself. It was not too comfortable, but the air was delicious. I promptly fell asleep. I woke up an hour or so later, stiff and acutely conscious of my jack-knife position. I crawled from my lair and stretched full-length under the blanket. This invited discovery, but my aching and rebellious bones demanded it. Anyway, perhaps my luck would hold. Some of the blackness seemed to have lifted—or was it only that my eyes were getting used to it? Suddenly a figure loomed up, and a voice spoke. By it I identified one of the young subalterns. There was no reprimand in his voice; to my astonishment, he was making a request.

"Do you mind if I join you under that blanket? You look so damned comfortable!"

"I'm afraid I'll have to explain, sir," I said. "I'm not an officer but a soldier. In fact, I am probably out of bounds. But," I added, "if you're not afraid of contamination . . ." I rolled back a corner of the blanket.

Lieutenancy was shaken; lieutenancy hesitated. But temptation won.

"I'll risk it," he muttered and slipped under the inviting cover.

With the approach of dawn, prudence woke us both and I made my way back to the hold unperceived.

Two decades later I was playing a concert in Colorado Springs. Summoned to the telephone, I was told that the Commandant of an adjacent army post, Major Saulnier, wished to speak to me.

"Major Saulnier?" The name was unfamiliar.

"I felt I must telephone you, Mr. Spalding," said a cultivated voice. "I am going to ask you to turn the calendar back twenty years. Do you remember a certain Channel crossing at the beginning of October 1917?"

I did. Who could forget it?

"What do you recall of it?"

I recalled it all, step by step.

"I was that young officer," laughed Saulnier; "and on the strength of our having slept together you will perhaps forgive this intrusion!"

Paris, in October 1917, wore its three years of war with unconcern. Except for the frequency of uniforms it would have been difficult to believe that trench warfare was going on not many miles away. True, civilian clothing was predominantly black; but to anyone who knew peacetime France this did not necessarily mean mourning, for French women wear black a great deal of the time.

France was in the grip of an invader. But, in the midst of her suffering, Paris was conscious that she was, for the moment at least, the center of the Allied world. Her brilliant lighting was somewhat dimmed at night, but there was nothing approaching a modern blackout. In fact, the element of danger added zest to the night. Every restaurant, every theater, every movie, was crowded. The length of days might be shortened, but the sense of life was heightened.

So far as the war went, there was no hint of the coming reversals of early 1918. In October 1917, Russia, under Kerensky, still held a long line. Italy had not yet suffered the Caporetto defeat. Nivelle's ill-fated offensive was on the eve of its optimistic launching. And the Yanks were coming. Were not some of them already at hand?

LaGuardia left after a day or two for Italy. He was to command one of the camps near Foggia where American pilots were being trained. Major MacDill, who remained in Paris, told me to report for assignment to duty at the Air Service headquarters at 45 avenue Montaigne. This immense building was honeycombed with offices. I cooled my heels in first one and

[225]

then another before I got any attention. At length I found my-self facing authority in the person of Captain Carroll, who was adjutant to Colonel R. C. Bolling. I felt like a stray mongrel in a pedigreed kennel. How soon was I to be kicked out?

The door opened. It was the chief of Air Service, Colonel Bolling. His eyes traveled past me. A faint look of recognition . . . then doubt . . . then recognition again.

"What is your name?"

I saluted and told him.

"I thought I was not mistaken. What are you doing in a private's uniform?"

"Is it a mistake, sir," I asked, "to be one of two million Americans?"

The Colonel apparently liked this, for the shadow of a smile appeared in his eyes.

"Come inside for a moment," he ordered. "I want to talk to you."

Inside, he invited me to be seated. Omnipotence offered me a cigarette; had often heard me play.

"You would not, I assume," he said dryly, "object to becoming an officer?"

I told him about my several attempts in that direction.

"Well, that's settled then," said the Colonel. "My cabled request will be put through to Washington today. As a rule there is very little delay. It has, of course, to go through Chaumont— through the Commander-in-Chief's office. In the meantime, report to Lieutenant Colonel Milling's office; he will assign you to temporary duty until your commission arrives. By the way, how did you happen to come to this office?"

I explained that it was by accident, that I was in the wrong place.

"Don't regret it," rejoined the Colonel. "You'll get on in the army if you contrive to make the correct mistakes. I'm glad to have seen you. Good day."

A few months later he was killed in a car that came under direct enemy fire at the front, and I learned of his untimely death with a sense of deep personal loss.

While waiting for my commission I worked in the personnel

department at 45 avenue Montaigne. It was largely routine and did not present any problems. But routine of itself was alien to the life I had lived until then, and I was impatient with this comfortable immunity. The comparative remoteness from danger eventually made me restless.

"You are here, ready to go anywhere," I told myself, "ready to do the thing that will be of the most use. Who are you to decide, anyway?" But this sensible rationalization was no help at all. Even the commission, when it came, hardly seemed mine; I had done nothing to deserve it.

My violin lay untouched for many weeks. In the evening I had neither the heart nor the energy to tune up its relaxed strings and urge my still more relaxed fingers to recapture their agility. But the consolation of music had not departed altogether. I found great pleasure in the mental photographs that memory could evoke of score after score; in the silence of my room I could thus recall performances I cherished. At first somewhat elusive, this trick of memory became increasingly absorbing and even exciting. The printed pages of the scores grew clearer and clearer. I found it second nature to translate some of this experience into a kind of abstract practicing of my own. The violin lay untouched in its case, but some of my best work was done in those hours.

In the meantime, I had my first plane flight. I occasionally met a young chap called Leslie around the Air Service building. Canadian by birth he had been a distinguished flyer in the R.A.F. He was assigned to instruct American pilots at the air field outside Paris. One afternoon he invited me to go up with him. I was eager to accept and, my work completed, permission was easy to obtain. Leslie was small, dark, shy as an adolescent, nervous as a hare.

"Have you ever been up?" he asked. He was astonished when I shook my head.

"And you want to be a flyer?" he continued. "Sometimes a first flight cures that wish."

On the flying field the two-seater Spad looked terribly small. Was that contraption, hardly more than a kite, capable of winging its way—winging *our* way—into the sky? I felt very clumsy getting into the fuselage.

"Just like me," I thought, "to stumble at such a moment. Leslie will suspect that it is nervousness—which perhaps it is!"

Before I could reflect, the engine was roaring and we were off. Breathless, I awaited an ascent that seemed dangerously postponed. We were headed straight for a line of trees; it looked as if we should inevitably collide with them. The noise from the motor was deafening. Suddenly I felt, not that we were ascending, but that the earth was dropping away. The tops of those menacing trees were cleared. The angle of the climb became more abrupt. We were apparently aiming for dizzy heights. A fleecy cloud was our objective. We approached it, pierced it, came out on the other side. Miraculous! Leslie looked back and yelled something I couldn't hear. I managed a nod and a wave of the hand in reply.

Reassured, he proceeded to initiate me in the mysteries of air acrobatics. Nose dives, side-slips, and tailspins followed each other in rapid succession. My emotions were undergoing such violent shifts and shocks that they felt like a pack of cards being shuffled.

When we glided to earth again I expected to feel dizzy. I wasn't dizzy, but my breath came with some difficulty. It was about ten feet in front of me—hard to overtake.

"Were you scared?" asked Leslie.

My voice, when it came, sounded somewhat displaced. I decided to be honest and admit fear coupled with excitement.

"That's all right then," said Leslie. "Chaps who say they're not afraid are generally lying by the clock. There's enough blood left in your cheeks—you'll enjoy your dinner tonight. And maybe you will be a flyer."

CHAPTER TWENTY-NINE

THE facile optimism of the early autumn faded with the approach of winter. The fall of Kerensky's government and the rise of the Bolshevist dictatorship threatened the defection of an important ally. And the Italian disaster at Caporetto came as another stunning blow.

An old family friend, the Countess de Saint-Maurice, called me excitedly on the phone one morning. She had just heard the news of Caporetto from a government official; it was not yet shouted on the streets nor displayed at newspaper kiosks. Grace de Saint-Maurice was a vivid personality whose career had been more colorful and crowded than a patchwork quilt, Trained as a newspaper woman, she still had a peculiar talent for scenting an item of dramatic news as if by instinct. And it never lost in the telling.

"Albert," she said, "the Italian Army is in complete rout. I have it from an unimpeachable source. No, I can't tell you—at least, not over the phone. But the situation is desperate. The Germans and Austrians are pouring in. There is nothing to stop them. Venice is already lost. By tomorrow they will be in Milan and headed south. I'm thinking of your father's lovely home in Florence. Before it's looted I might be able to save some things— perhaps a picture or two, a tapestry. If I can get a plane—and I think I can—shall I fly down before it is too late?"

Her kind generosity touched me, though I knew that Grace was secretly enjoying the prospect of adventure.

"No," I said slowly, "don't do that. If the disaster is as complete as all that, there is nothing, or very little, that you could do. You'd only get into trouble." And I expressed my gratitude for her offer.

It is difficult to deflect newspaperdom once it is set to go, and Grace was disappointed; but she reluctantly agreed not to start until she had seen me. When we met that evening the news had been confirmed, though not quite as in the advance rumor. The break-through and encirclement had been considerable, and many prisoners had been taken. But the Austrians were not yet in Venice, nor were they pushing on toward Milan. British and French divisions were being hurried to bolster a re-formed line which it was hoped would hold.

Grace was wearing a smart dress and looking her best. I proposed some good food, and we went to Voisin's—a sober landmark that looked reassuringly permanent. The same two black-clad women presided at the desk, monotonously checking gastronomic entries into ledgers. The dark woodwork and somber upholstery were part of the tradition of an eating-place that had no patience with supplementary distractions. It would have seemed sacrilegious, an intolerable affront to the maître d'hôtel, to open our conversation before giving our order. Since Grace was enough of a conformist to recognize this, we ate our petite marmite in ritualistic silence. Then, refreshed and relaxed, we faced each other. I compared my few items of news with hers. She nodded impatiently.

"I have been," she said, "all this afternoon at the War Office."

"With Clemenceau?" I teased her. It did not take. No—it was not Clemenceau, but it was someone very close to him. The situation was graver than anyone realized. Nivelle's failure, the deplorable losses in the autumn offensive, the complete loss of Russia as an ally—all these were beginning to look as if a separate peace might be made. Now this Italian rout opened up a new front—a fresh liability to the Allies. The endless wait for the Americans—would they never come in numbers sufficient to turn the tide? Above all, the war weariness of the British and the French was perhaps the most serious element of all. The outlook seemed gloomy indeed.

"Is there not," I asked, "a war weariness on the other side? In Germany?"

"Oh, the Boches." She shrugged her shoulders, waved a nervous hand. "They are not human beings, they are machines. They do not think; their individuality has been carefully stamped out. Furthermore, although the same energy may be expended on an offensive as on a defensive action, the former produces less fatigue—incalculably less. G., of the War Office, has just said all this to me in so many words. And he is right."

I decided to try other tactics. Abandoning my incurable optimism for the moment, I switched to dark forebodings. What was, then, the prospect? Did she think we would have some sort of arranged peace? A stalemate? With a free hand in Russia, perhaps Germany would agree to a return to an approximate status quo in Western Europe. . . . This worked beautifully. Grace straightened her shoulders, and her fine eyes flashed.

"What?" she cried, looking at me incredulously. "Never, never did I expect to hear you, you of all people, suggest such a thing. The result of a peace like that would be no peace at all. It would be a nightmare!"

"But if there is no alternative?" I went on, though by now it was hardly necessary.

Grace, chameleon-like, fired at me a barrage of convincing reasons for being sure of the ultimate victory of the Allies. And our evening closed on this bright note.

Early in 1918 I was transferred to Italy. On one of his brief trips to Paris LaGuardia had asked me if I would like to be assigned to his command. I would, indeed. The request was thereupon made, and granted. With my new chief I traveled south to the east coast of Italy where, at the flying field of Foggia, I took up my duties as adjutant.

I was hoping that at last I might be trained as a flyer. But La-Guardia was adamant, implementing his refusal with excellent reasons, such as my usefulness in other lines, and my mature years. (I was in my late twenties.)

"In short," he would conclude, "I didn't ask you to come south for that purpose. I wanted a good adjutant—not a mediocre pilot!" But this was said with so quizzical a look that I have always suspected that his real preoccupation was with a fiddler's fingers, which must be kept safe against the return of peace.

It was a new and vital experience to work under LaGuardia. I learned to have a deep admiration for this unpredictable man. A dynamo of energy, he appeared to be immune to fatigue. Apart from his military duties, the retention of his seat in Congress meant a constant flow of correspondence on political matters at home.

LaGuardia's memory was prodigious and irritatingly accurate, and he expected the same faculty in his subordinates—or from this subordinate, at least. When, with methodical zeal, I wrote down a number of instructions, he looked at me with scorn.

"What are you doing that for?" he snapped.

"To insure against oversight, sir."

"Use your memory. Fix what I say in your mind. You won't forget. Or, if you do, you'll get hell, and you won't do it again. Anyway, what use is that bit of paper to you? If you're pinning your faith to that, you'll probably lose it, and then where will you be? Use your memory—that's what it's meant for."

He was right, of course. I disciplined my memory as best I could, and soon got so that I did not often forget. When I did, the expected explosion was tempered with mildness. LaGuardia's natural impatience was checked by his recognition of my obvious, though unexpressed, chagrin. I never once tried to alibi myself on these occasions, for with him that would have been fatal. It was incredible that he should like me, but he did. We lived together almost like brothers.

When he was made representative in Italy of the joint Army and Navy Aircraft Board he kept me with him as his assistant. Italian factories were producing planes for the American armed forces, the agreement to do so being contingent on our supplying the necessary raw materials, chiefly copper, steel, and ashwood for propellers. A steady stream of these raw materials was already flowing in convoys across the Atlantic, but they were allocated to British and French factories; and meanwhile the Ansaldo works in Genoa, the Fiat, the Isotta Fraschini, and the

Caproni—all in Northern Italy—were waiting in vain for their share.

But LaGuardia does not accept—or even recognize—an impasse; the very word challenges his ingenuity. One evening, after work, he unburdened his mind.

"This delay," he declared, "is impossible. But there must be a solution for it. What do you think of this?" And he outlined his plan of action.

"There is," he said, "an abundance of copper, steel, and ash lying close at hand—a good deal closer than the U. S. A."

I thought quickly. In Spain, he meant?

"Yes, in Spain. There it lies, unused, 'frozen.' Spain is probably more afraid of Germany's displeasure than she is of our pressure, so she has put an embargo on her exports. Still—still, there are ways. There must be ways."

Half suspecting what was to come, I held my breath.

"Smuggling is an ancient art," LaGuardia went on. "It has been practiced before, it will be practiced again. It is what I am suggesting to the Chief of the Air Service, General Foulois. Here, draft this wire. I can see by your expression, Al,"—he is perhaps the one person who has ever called me Al—"that you are all for it."

The wire was sent. Apparently the idea caught fire, for we were both ordered immediately to Paris for consultation, and LaGuardia's plan was approved at once. General Foulois and his assistant, Colonel Dunwoody, expressed immediate enthusiasm. LaGuardia and I were authorized to proceed to Spain, in civilian clothing, armed with letters of credit, to get what we could from that forbidden source of supply. It was explained to us, however, that final authorization had to come from the Commander-in-Chief himself—from General Pershing. General Foulois lacked the power to sanction this special mission, but the request would be put through to Chaumont at once, and there was no doubt that it would be granted. There might be some delay—perhaps ten days—but the orders would certainly come. LaGuardia said nothing, but I could see that he was far from happy.

Once outside the office, my instructions came in quick staccato. I was to attend to the details of our immediate departure for Barcelona, to get civilian clothes and reservations on tomorrow night's sleeper.

"Tomorrow night?" I paused, bewildered. "But—"

"But what?"

"Our orders," I protested. "You heard just now that it will be a week, perhaps two, before they come. We should never get over the border without them. We couldn't even get our transportation countersigned by the Provost Marshal without them."

"We leave tomorrow night," insisted LaGuardia. "Tickets, clothes, orders—those are your affair. I didn't specify what kind of orders. You have an imagination—use it! Any kind of orders that will do the trick. They'll be O.K. by me. I shan't ask any questions; nor do I expect any questions from you. I'm off to the Embassy for our passports, and to General Dawes' office for the letter of credit."

I knew, of course, what he wanted. I was to fake some kind of bogus orders that would slip us past the eagle eye of the military police, through the cordon of French vigilance. They would have to be good, I thought. Well, there is nothing like trying.

Colonel Dunwoody's desk was a repository for any number of official seals. If my role as forger was to be successful, I had to get at those locked drawers. I decided that my only hope lay in Doris, his confidential secretary. She was a young woman, half French, half English, sensitive, intelligent, and keen as a razor blade. It seemed unfair that she should also be so attractive. After the war she became Mrs. Halsey Dunwoody.

Choosing a time when I knew the Colonel was absent from his office, I sought Doris' sympathies and co-operation. I was not, I believed, risking military secrets, for, as the Colonel's confidential secretary, she knew at least the outlines of the venture. But she was not easily won over. Her interest was aroused, but she hesitated at being an accomplice to this enormity. I protested that she must, in effect, know nothing of it.

I seated myself at her typewriter and spent some little time composing a document that would carry conviction. The real orders, from General Headquarters at Chaumont, would have the ring of supreme command—of General Pershing himself—and would be signed by James W. McAndrew, Chief of Staff.

My masterpiece, when it emerged in printed characters, read smoothly and boldly that Captain F. H. LaGuardia and 1st Lt. Albert Spalding should proceed to Cerbère, France, and thence to Spain—"to such points in Spain as may be necessary, to carry out the instructions of the Commander-in-Chief." I enlarged upon why this travel was necessary to the service. To sanction it all, Lt. Colonel Dunwoody's name was invoked. The Colonel was a rare and admirable combination of West Point technique and intuitive imagination. He had been a good friend to this expedition from the start, but in case we came to sudden grief he could have no choice but to disavow our flagrant anticipation of orders. I decided that, face to face with the military police, only an impressive manner on my part was going to carry the thing off!

"Now then," I said to Doris, "all I ask is that you leave the Colonel's desk unlocked. There are some interesting sights on the street. Just keep looking out of the window for the next five minutes. If this plan goes sour and I get into trouble, you'll know nothing about it. Now be a sport."

Would she do it? The spirit of adventure prevailed and without a word she consented. Over the face of the doubtful document I plastered seal after seal. In the top left-hand corner I marked the paper "Secret" in red ink; this word was sometimes an effective talisman. The five minutes up, Doris turned. She was an admirable actress. Without a word but in excellent pantomime, she registered dismay at her oversight in leaving a desk drawer unlocked, and hastened to mend the error. A half-smile flickered at the corner of her mouth in answer to my "So long, and thanks." This was, I knew, a completely forgotten incident.

First lap. So far, so good.

Next I went to the Belle Jardinière, where I bought two civilian suits, cheap, serviceable, nondescript. I had to guess at LaGuardia's measurements, but I was sure he would be unconscious of anything short of the most outrageous misfit. As a matter of fact, his uniform always looked as if it had been made for someone else.

[235]

The next job, perhaps the most ticklish one, was to get my document countersigned by the Military Police. The men who make up this redoubtable force are a fearsome lot; I suspect them of living exclusively on cactus plants, for everything within and without is thorned and bristly.

I was careful, before going to the head office in the rue Ste. Anne, to change to civilian clothes. This would make the whole affair more mysterious, and might stem the flood of embarrassing questions. Civilian clothes felt odd after so many months in uniform. From the looking-glass a stranger looked back at me. The coat sleeves were somewhat too short, the trouser legs somewhat too long. I wore a broad-brimmed sombrero hat. Was it only a guilty conscience, or was I facing an escaped prisoner?

At the rue St. Anne a typical M.P. Sergeant glared at me across a desk. "Who are you?" he growled in a regular M.P. voice imported directly from the Zoo.

I told him.

"What the hell are you doing in that outfit?"

I decided that a little show of authority was called for. "Sergeant," I snapped, "lower your voice. Look over this paper. You can read?"

He paused for a moment. His eye caught the red-inked word "Secret." He glanced hurriedly over the paper, a little shaken, but far from convinced. (Why on earth should I begin to sweat so? The day was not warm.)

"But who are you?" he repeated.

"I've already told you, Sergeant." I pointed at my name in the orders. Then, as he still hesitated, I risked even bolder tactics. "If you want further confirmation you may, of course, ring up Air Service headquarters. Ask for General Foulois." (Was I managing to get a conspicuous irony into my voice?) "If that does not satisfy you, perhaps you would like to call up Chaumont and talk to General Pershing himself. Do it if you want to—but, seeing the nature of this document, I do not envy you the experience! But go ahead and try. . . ."

The Sergeant looked me over. It was an ordeal. My knees felt weak; would they hold, I wondered. Would he call my bluff and telephone? At last he grunted. The day was won. The precious counterfeit was signed and stamped, though the Sergeant's eyes had not lost their habitual look of suspicion. I had to walk slowly out of the office; but once on the street I ran like a hare for three blocks.

The railroad reservations and the French countersignatures were child's play after this. My chores were done hours in advance of our departure. LaGuardia, too, had been busy; by now he had our passports, as well as two letters of credit munitioning Captain LaGuardia and Lieutenant Spalding to the extent of five million dollars.

Once on the train, the chief relaxed. The secret of his galvanic energy is that it can be shut off at will. He rests as intensely as he works. These periods of relaxation would come as suddenly as the return to activity. They were usually heralded by a joke, sometimes completely irrelevant. LaGuardia loved to laugh, and his laugh was infectious and hilarious.

I knew that, for the moment at least, all thought of our trip was to be put aside. LaGuardia talked about home, about the girl to whom, once the war was over, he was to be married. He showed me her photograph; she was frail and delicate-looking, as fair as an Illyrian spring. You could not imagine two greater opposites, I thought, contemplating the volcano of vitality at my side. It was plain that he was ardently and romantically in love with this gentle and lovely girl. Confidence invited confidence, so I told him about Mary, and it made home seem very near.

CHAPTER THIRTY

Barcelona was blindingly bright in the May sunlight, appearing blithely unconscious of the war. It was strange to arrive at a station not under strict military control, where a passport examination was a minor formality. But there was also an uncertainty, the insecurity you feel at the first absence of some familiar restraint.

We were immediately reminded that Spain was a happy hunting ground for German propagandists. Even before our luggage was assembled, a bystander offered us some postcards. Sales resistance did not deter him; he insisted on pressing them on us as gifts. They were attractive photographs of some of the great Goya canvases in the Prado.

"The Spaniards are generous in their welcome," I remarked to LaGuardia as we went on toward our hotel.

Then we examined the cards more closely, and both the nationality and the disinterestedness of the donor vanished. The hand-out was patently propaganda. The Goyas reproduced on the cards were his dramatically brutal pictures of Napoleon's troops shooting down Spanish civilians. There was no date; even the name of the artist was omitted. The only text was the caption reading *French Atrocities in Spain*.

"Blatant, but clever," said LaGuardia.

"But is it so clever?" I protested. "Who will be taken in by this?"

"More than you think," said LaGuardia. "That is the way the Germans work. They don't care about the few who will recognize Goya's hand, who will realize that this took place a hundred years ago, during the Peninsular campaign. The Germans are aiming at the mass of people whom they can influence by a dramatic picture—a single phrase. And there are many such. Yes, these are effective." Then he turned to a new subject.

"This looks like a city of violent contrasts," he said. It was true. The glaring Mediterranean sun threw everything into blacks and whites; atmospheric grays were conspicuously absent. And the contrast was just as sharp in the activity around us. The people either hurried through the streets or relaxed into an almost lifeless repose. The ornate churches, proclaiming the splendors of life eternal, seemed indifferent to present-day misery. The profuse array of spring flowers in the street stalls mocked the pallor of the vendors' hungry faces. This city was, indeed, a cavalcade of contrasts.

Breakfast over, I looked expectantly to my chief for orders.

"Orders? There are none. For the moment, at least, we are tourists, and tourists who must watch their steps or they'll stub a toe. Today there is a bullfight. Have you ever seen one?"

I hadn't, and doubted if I should like it.

"Neither, perhaps, shall I," said the Captain. "Nevertheless, we'll go. It's one of the sights. No doubt we shall be watched, and not by friendly eyes, either. This trip is a mission, but it's also an adventure. You ought to be pleased"—this somewhat quizzically. "There is an element of risk."

It was, I admitted, not unlike a Phillips Oppenheim tale.

"Yes," said LaGuardia; "he would have all the materials for a thriller here. Only with this difference: in fiction the hero's mistakes can be repaired by a benevolent and omnipotent author. You and I have got to see to it that no mistakes are made. Above all, don't talk to anyone; commit nothing to writing; don't even write home."

Were there to be no further orders? There were. I was to make a thorough examination of newspaper files for the past two years and to list the merchant shipping lost by Spain and the respective losses of each large shipping company. I could see what the chief was after—he wanted to find a pro-Ally steamship company. The result was illuminating: one company, the Taja Line, had lost more than all the others put together.

"We shall call on Mr. Taja tomorrow," announced LaGuardia; "and go to a bullfight this afternoon."

The savage pageantry of a bullfight appeals to primitive emotions. It unmasks another self to you, disclosing an inner world of disturbing violence. There is a stately formalism about the spectacle that is engrossing. The scorching sun beats down on the arena of yellow sand. The amphitheater holds a dense and colorful throng of people. You think, The last act of *Carmen* is about to be enacted here and at once. That hungry, desperate-looking man at the corner might easily be Don José, and in the initial procession there were an army of Escamillos. The procession is ritualistic, almost ecclesiastical; if we turned the calendar back three centuries we might be on the point of witnessing an auto-da-fé. The heat is intense, almost intolerable.

With the entrance of the bull the crowd's excitement takes on an ominous, smoldering quality. The silence is punctuated by muffled and guttural mutterings, low and threatening. The bull, dazzled by the sudden sunlight, bewildered by the size of the arena after his recent confinement, and sensing the presence of enmity, stands irresolute, idly pawing the sand. Slowly he advances to the center of the ring. Here he is taunted with capes of flaming color. Rage mounts within him; in blind fury he charges. The sharp horns, seeking a victim, find only empty air. His dexterous tormentors, graceful and sinewy as dancers, are safely away. But death is avoided by a slender margin. This ballet, tempting fate, builds up the tower of anger like an emblem of phallic power. Instinctively the bull knows he is there to kill or be killed.

The second stage of the sanguinary ballet is the introduction of the banderilleros. These dancing harlequins—treading, it would seem, on air—advance and retreat with incredible swiftness. In each hand they carry the pointed arrows, the banderillas, which at the moment of greatest peril they dart into the neck of the tormented animal. It is like a sleight-of-hand trick—over before you realize it.

I glanced at LaGuardia. Though he disliked the performance, he was as absorbed in it as I was.

Next came the picadors. The melancholy horses, unhappy descendants of the raw-boned Rosinante, stood trembling like victims in a torture chamber. Their riders made not the slightest move to avoid the charge of the maddened bull; they were intent on prodding him with their long, sharpened poles or *pics*. The bull, finding at last some living substance to attack, stabbed his horns deep into the pitiful animals. The disemboweling operation was ghastly; I closed my eyes till it was over. The dead horses were hastily removed from the arena. A mingled smell of sand and blood rose sickeningly on the hot air.

Again the weakened bull was receiving the painful attention of the banderilleros. This time the irritating darts carried a small explosive charge which detonated in his flesh. How much further could the imagination go in devising exquisite torment?

The last moment of the drama approached. The chief matador stood erect and confident in the center of the ring. Sword in hand, draped by a scarlet cloth, he looked vulnerable, incapable of self-protection. Again and again he provoked a rhinoceros-like charge from the menacing beast. Again and again he evaded what seemed like certain death by a slight movement of his body. It was pure economy of action. Each episode had an increased element of impudent daring, and each was greeted by a mounting roar from the excited crowd. I found my admiration compelled by this display of skill and bravery. The final thrust of the sword was, apparently, executed in the classic and approved style demanded by critics of the arena. I was not a discriminating judge of these niceties, but the uncontrolled ovation from the thousands of *afficionados* testified to its virtuosity.

The program called for the killing of six bulls. After this first emotional ordeal, how could I sit through five more? I looked at LaGuardia. He, I could see, shared my inclination to get out at once; but a slight shake of his head reminded me that we were the guests of an Italian agent, who, like his other guests—all Spaniards—was an ardent fan of the bullring. They would regard our desire to escape as a breach of good manners. So we sat on to the bitter end; both, however, managing to shut our eyes each time to the unbearable and debasing episode of the horses.

[241]

Back at the hotel, as if by mutual consent, not a word was spoken about the afternoon's experience, and neither of us had much appetite for dinner.

The next morning we called on Señor Taja. He was the squat, round-headed type of Iberian, slow in gesture and mild in speech. His gentle, tolerant eyes were capable, however, of expressing implacable resentment on occasion. He was, I discovered, an intimate friend of Pablo Casals, who told me some years later that Taja had served as model for Blasco Ibañez's novel *Mare Nostrum*—for its hero Ulysses, in fact. Like Ulysses, he had lost his only son, victim of a German submarine's torpedo. His hatred of the Hun was an unquenchable flame. LaGuardia's uncanny instinct had led us to the man who could help us most in this mission. Taja was to prove not merely an agent, but an ally and an accomplice. Quietly he listened, approved, and advised. He outlined whom we were to see, whom to avoid, whom to trust, whom to suspect. In an incredibly short time he had planned a program that seemed to leave little or nothing to chance. We followed his advice to the letter.

The next few days passed quickly in the methodical activity outlined by Taja. Metallurgical factories were visited, agents for ashwood called on, quantities and prices settled. Taja himself undertook the ticklish business of port clearance or evasion.

We had decided that it was prudent not to see Taja oftener than we had to, for already we were being followed and spied on. More than once our hotel rooms had been visited during our absence, and there was evidence that alien hands had searched our personal effects for documents that were not there.

Once, through an Italian purchasing agent, we met a so-called Mexican who was bent on interesting us in a new type of air locomotion. The new invention, he explained, could ascend and descend vertically like an elevator, with no need for take-off space; he called it a helicopter. He was plausible—too plausible. LaGuardia had misgivings about this eager promoter, but he listened attentively to the detailed description of the new invention; it had promising features to recommend it. Little by little the Mexican brought up comparative estimates of well-known motors and planes, mentioning quantity outputs and other more or less confidential details, in a tentative fashion that was not exactly questioning but that certainly invited indiscreet answers. The corners of LaGuardia's eyes stiffened slightly; he was alert and on guard. Not so the Italian agent, who—completely taken in—was all ready to correct the errors in the stranger's statements. But just as he started, the chief created a diversion. He was sitting with his chair tilted back, and suddenly he seemed about to topple over. In a successful effort to regain his equilibrium, his legs shot out, he balanced precariously for a moment, and then his left foot stamped down on the Italian's instep. The Latin winced, but graciously accepted LaGuardia's profuse apologies. He looked a trifle bewildered when the Captain reminded him of our pressing engagement elsewhere, and was about to protest. But LaGuardia's voice occasionally has a metallic ring to it that unmistakably demands obedience. We therefore said hasty good-bys to the promoter, whose face wore a mystified look as he, too, took his departure.

The Italian was equally mystified. LaGuardia lost no time in enlightening him; repeating his apologies, he said, "That fellow is a German spy, sure as you're a foot high!" Though the Italian was incredulous, LaGuardia had succeeded in sowing doubt, and it was not long before our naïve companion seemed persuaded that a bruised instep was a small price to pay for being rescued from an enormous indiscretion.

That same Mexican, together with his Teutonic wife, was arrested some months later in France, charged with espionage. They escaped the death sentence only because their conviction came at the time of the Armistice, when the extreme penalty was not enforced.

"Albert," snapped LaGuardia, when we were alone, "the more I see of the Allies, the less I think of the Germans." The Germans, he explained, had bungled chance after chance offered them by our stupidities. The thoroughness of their planning was offset by a total absence of imagination; real initiative was lacking. The Allies would pull through, in spite of their blunders.

A few evenings later we sat outside a café whose tables, continental fashion, overflowed to the sidewalk. As we idly sipped our drinks, any casual observer would have thought us innocent enough. At nearby tables, however, sat more interested watchers. We knew that each day of the ten we spent in Barcelona was bringing us under increasing surveillance. Tonight there was, we sensed, a whole posse at our heels. This was all right. From now on, our activities were to be entirely innocent. We were no longer acting as agents; our mission was smoothly under way. And it was all to the good if we now received the attention that might otherwise be focused on those raw materials which were, perhaps at that very moment, on their way toward Taja's ships in the harbor. About a million and a half dollars' worth eventually reached an Italian port safely.

The next evening we took the night sleeper to Madrid—still shadowed. The adjoining compartment was occupied by a man and a woman who probably spent as sleepless a night as we did. More than once the door to the lavatory between the two compartments was stealthily tried; but it had been securely bolted on our side. Several times, too, the corridor door was unlocked and partly opened, which could have been only with the connivance—the bribing, perhaps—of the wagon-lit's guard. An instantaneous "Who's there?" brought a muttered apology, and then privacy again.

We reported to the Embassy in Madrid, where the entire story of our mission was committed to writing and dispatched in the Embassy pouch to Paris. Meantime, we received from the hands of the Military Attaché, Major Lang, our legitimate orders, which had been forwarded from General Pershing's office to the Embassy. Our activities had now been rescued from bastardy: they were properly sanctioned at last.

Outside the Embassy door I was accosted by a large Negro.

"Gawd bless ma soul, if you ain't Mistah Spaldin'. You *is* Albu't Spaldin', isn't you?"

Puzzled, I admitted my identity.

"An' I is Jack Johnson. Jack Johnson—*you* know! I was champeen once!" I stared at him. What was he doing in Spain? Then I remembered. Of course: white wife—Mann Act—deportation. What could I do for him? Plenty, it seemed. Johnson was anxious to get into the U. S. Army. He was in trouble with the

[244]

law, but that didn't affect his patriotism. He looked as if he meant what he said.

I told the Captain about Johnson, and he was at once interested. How much better to place him in a Negro regiment and let him re-earn his citizenship than to leave him knocking about neutral countries! He promised to do what he could about it, although he confessed that he was afraid the Mrs. Grundys who would decide the matter might see it in a different light. Unfortunately, officialdom ran true to its narrowest, most bigoted form: Johnson's plea for service was denied.

We spent two days in Madrid, and paid a memorable visit to the Prado to see those strange, elongated transfigurations by El Greco which make other masterpieces look anemic in their more conventional realism. Then the two smugglers left Spain for Paris, whence, after an oral report to the Avenue Montaigne, we returned at once to Rome. The change from civilian clothes back to uniforms made our fortnight in Spain seem as remote as a vivid but evanescent dream.

CHAPTER THIRTY-ONE

IN Rome one Sunday after-
noon LaGuardia and I attended a performance at the Augusteo
of Perosi's fine oratorio, *The Resurrection of Christ.* The orchestra was ably led by Molinari and the baritone role of the Christus
was sung by the veteran Battistini, then a sexagenarian, and, I
think, the greatest vocalist I have ever heard. The passing years
had brought no impairment to the effortless production of golden
sound, which poured itself forth with astonishing opulence. He
phrased like an instrumentalist; breathing became an expressive
punctuation rather than a physical necessity; and he had a sustained legato that was unbearably beautiful.

LaGuardia was as spellbound as I was. "You don't have to be
a trained musician," he said, "to recognize art at that level."

He was curious to know more about Perosi, that obscure Catholic priest whose works are so rarely played or sung. This strange
talent, I explained, had puzzled many people. There were all
sorts of contradictory rumors about him. At present, it was said,
he was in disfavor because of certain heresies; had he not refused to officiate at Mass because he no longer believed in tran-
substantiation? He was rumored to be under observation because
of an unsettled brain. One hobby in which he had made himself
quite a virtuoso, and in which he took an inordinate pride, was
his ability to memorize railway time-tables. He had learned every
train schedule throughout the length of the Italian peninsula, so
that he could tell you precisely where any given train was at
any given moment. You had to hear him do it to believe it—
and, even then, you didn't quite believe it.

"Well," sighed LaGuardia, "it certainly is astonishing, but I think it's still more important that he should write music, and that Battistini should sing it!"

That evening we took a train for Padua just behind the Italian front, and at the station the following morning were met by young Colonna, whose father, Prince Colonna, was Mayor of Rome. We were, he informed us, to have dinner that evening with the King. A car would call for us at seven and bring us to the villa where the King had his headquarters.

During the day we witnessed some experiments with parachutes at the flying field. These were the early days of the use of parachutes, and you wondered if there were suicidal tendencies in the volunteers for this dangerous sport.

Midday mess we shared at G.H.Q. with General Diaz and members of his staff, including Badoglio. Diaz was a forceful man who inspired great confidence. He had had the unenviable job of reorganizing the remnants of a badly beaten army and of convincing the world that the men who had fled at Caporetto would stand firm at the Piave. Italy had suffered not only the humiliation of defeat, but also the contempt of her neighbor and ally, France. The help of the British and French troops which had been rushed to stem the advance of the Austro-German armies was acknowledged and appreciated; but it was clear that the advance could not have been checked by two or three divisions alone. The Italian army had not been so bankrupt as Gallic gibes implied—gibes that created a resentment which was to grow until it influenced Italy's policy for years. But hardly a trace of this appeared at the time. For the moment, the young stepsister of the Entente swallowed her pride. In the spring of 1918 the war had still to be won, and there was little hope of an early victory.

Diaz calmly discussed the recent situation on the French front where the German break-through had so nearly crumpled Franco-British resistance. Defensive action had its limitations. To the threat of an overwhelming offensive there had been propounded a new answer—not mere resistance, but a counter-offensive. Its author, one of the junior French generals, was given supreme command of the Allied Forces; his name was Foch. Diaz expressed satisfaction at this selection.

"The defeat at Caporetto," said Diaz, "was not due to any lack of valor in the Italian soldier. It was those in authority over him who were responsible. The army's personnel department thrust into division after division thousands of men hastily mobilized from factories and fields, inadequately trained and badly equipped—and just hoped for the best.

"It is folly to hope for the best," he went on, "when your actions lead directly to the worst. What had we done? We had taken sorely needed technical workers from our factories to furnish our front with cannon-fodder. It is the system, or rather the lack of system, that failed."

LaGuardia asked him if he thought there would be a general attack in the near future. "I do," said the General, quietly adding, "We are prepared for it."

Back at the hotel we surveyed our somewhat shabby uniforms; they hardly looked presentable enough for a royal dinner, so we begged help from the black-eyed chambermaid. She took a needle and thread to our frayed collars, and went over us vigorously with a clothes brush. We added a pair of immaculate white stocks preserved for important occasions. We could do no more. Our cameriera-valet was indefatigable on behalf of the two Americanos who were to receive so signal an honor; Italians, high and low, adored their King. But she didn't realize that she was being addressed when LaGuardia called her *Signora*. She moved to one side to make way for the unseen "lady" who must be there. When it dawned on her that the title was hers she gazed at the Captain with rapturous adoration. Fiorello, utterly unconscious of this, went on snapping out his staccato instructions. In anyone else his tone would have sounded cross; to the beaming peasant girl his voice was silver-toned. *"Che brava persona, l'Onorevole,"* she murmured to me.

Punctually at seven Colonna arrived in a sumptuous limousine to escort us some thirty kilometers to the royal headquarters. The King was staying in one of those enchanting villas to which the Venetian merchants retire from time to time to remind themselves that the world contains green fields. The rooms were commodious, but not large. We assembled in a living-room that opened onto a flagged terrace. The evening was mild and through the open windows one could hear the distant rumble of field artillery.

In addition to LaGuardia and myself, there was the King's personal retinue (of whom the least rated a Brigadier's commission) and several guests from the General Staff. Altogether, we were fourteen or sixteen. There was a certain amount of protocol, and etiquette followed court procedure even here at the front. The master of ceremonies was a corpulent general of remote gravity, apparently a contemporary of the present ruler's father, Humbert. His general appearance, the cut of his hair, the shape of his mustache, were patterned after the royal model of two decades ago. Everything about him bristled; his mustachios and even his eyebrows stuck out like a porcupine's quills, and he wore a perpetual frown.

"You will sit at the right of His Majesty," he warned LaGuardia, and waited for that awesome intelligence to sink in before turning to me. "And you," he added no less impressively, "will be seated at His Majesty's left."

Following my chief's example, I bowed as low as I could. We went on waiting for the Presence, the silence punctuated only by an occasional voice. What is it, I wondered, that gives the zero-hour complexion to such moments? Why should the arrival of Royalty be so funereal? Were we, after all, at a wake? Suddenly the double doors leading from the hall were thrown open and a voice announced:

"*Sua Maesta, il Re!*"

Victor Emmanuel came in, walking with short nervous steps, and wearing the gray-green uniform of a Lieutenant General—a modest rank for a king, I thought. The presentations were quickly and simply made. I observed that LaGuardia, who even then spread horizontally rather than vertically, towered above the King, who must have been less than five feet tall. It was a rare experience, and I wondered if it gave LaGuardia secret satisfaction.

The King greeted us both in English which he spoke fluently. Shortly afterwards, when he learned that I, as well as LaGuardia, spoke Italian, we reverted to that language. His manner was informal and direct. He was, you felt, as impatient with the elaborate court etiquette as General Mustachios was delighted with it.

Dinner was announced and we filed into the dining-room. The King's place was not at the head of the long table but at the middle of one side. As had been announced, LaGuardia and I sat on each side of Majesty; but I found my appetite for the excellent dinner quite unimpaired by the proximity.

The King eagerly discussed the current situation. He spoke with penetrating observation, and one saw that it was not mere flattery that called him an able strategist. He inquired into LaGuardia's estimate of industrial production in northern Italy. Efforts had been made to redouble production in the Fiat factories in Turin, the Ansaldo works at Genoa, and those of Caproni and Isotta Fraschini in Milan. Was the Captain satisfied with the progress being made?

LaGuardia gave an encouraging rejoinder; progress had indeed been made. "But, Majesty," he went on, "may I permit myself the liberty of certain less cheerful observations? They have to do with co-ordination—the co-ordination of the total war effort. We have just recently visited Genoa. I saw with satisfaction the excellent showing of the Ansaldo works—Pio Perrone is an able industrialist." The King nodded his head in assent. "Under his management those factories are turning out planes, guns, trucks, and mobile units. There is real accomplishment. But those results, good as they are, could be bettered. And it doesn't depend on Perrone—"

"On whom, then?" interrupted the King.

"Majesty, I will tell you. The capacity of the Ansaldo works is almost double its present output. The machinery is there; the manpower is there. And there, too," said Fiorello, slightly raising his voice, "at the docks of that same city, lie tons of precious raw materials. They remain at the docks indefinitely. Idle dock hands by the hundred lounge around in the sunlight, but it is a *dolce far niente* that can spell death and defeat at the front."

The King was silent for a moment. "Why do you say this to me?" he asked, at length.

[250]

"When once I have a chance," said LaGuardia, "to speak to the fountain head of the government . . ."

Victor Emmanuel interrupted him: "The Head of the Government? What a mistake you are making! Speak to the Foreign Minister, speak to Nitti. I am only the King."

The King was engagingly simple when he talked of his family. He never used their titles; not once did he say "the Queen" or "the Prince of Piedmont" or "the Princesses." Always it was "my wife," "my son," or "my little girls." Referring to the somewhat unusual names of these last—Yolanda and Mafalda—he said:

"Both my wife and I liked these names; but, as you know," he explained, "a Catholic child must be christened with a name from the Saints' Calendar. Had there ever been a Saint Yolanda, a Saint Mafalda? We doubted it. Fortunately, however, careful search proved that there had been."

He gave a great deal of attention to his son's education. The Prince was to be simply and austerely brought up, disciplined and inured to hardship; a future king must not be pampered.

"I cannot conceive," said he with conviction, "asking from any man in the army a sacrifice that I would not be willing to demand of my son."

At this moment a telegram, evidently an urgent one, was brought in. Eyebrows looked his disapproval of this interruption, but said nothing. The King tore it open and gave an exclamation of satisfaction.

"Mata Hari has just been shot at Vincennes!" he announced.

I felt it almost treasonable that I could not share the general satisfaction, and I secretly court-martialed myself. A dangerous enemy spy had been disposed of—but she was also a beautiful woman. . . .

Succulent pastries were served with the coffee. It was strange to have sweets for dessert; they were rare in a country in which sugar was now an all but unknown commodity. I eyed them with pleasure when they came round a second time—with so much pleasure, indeed, that I failed to notice that after the King's refusal of a second helping the platter went round the table untouched until it reached me. My sweet tooth, and my failure to observe this procedure, betrayed me into a situation of unparalleled gaucherie: I took a second helping! Opposite me, Eyebrows seemed on the verge of apoplexy; his color deepened dangerously; his hirsute appendages bristled, and he glared at me and my offending plate. I realized that something was wrong, but for a few embarrassed moments was at a total loss for an understanding. His outraged glance, however, soon enlightened me. Well, I thought ruefully, it's just too bad! What shall I do? I can't eat it; I can't stow it away in my pocket. Perhaps, if Eyebrows would look away for a moment, I might dispose of it under the table; though that, even if successful, would hardly be anything to write home about.

Meantime the King, still talking to LaGuardia, had somehow become aware of my distressing situation. Looking at my plate, he said, "You took a second pastry. How right you were! They *are* good. I think I will join you and have another one myself."

I have seldom felt such gratitude. The situation was saved; even Eyebrows seemed to relax, though he still managed to convey an extraordinary amount of disapproval.

Presently LaGuardia was extolling my merits as a musician. The King responded politely and amiably, but I knew he had no interest in my vocation. For the head of the House of Savoy was notoriously tone-deaf; in fact, musical sounds were acutely painful to him. It was no secret that he preferred an hour in a dentist's chair to an evening at the Opera.

The King's good-night was the signal for our departure. The same lordly limousine took us back to the hotel.

"An essentially good man, the King," said LaGuardia.

LaGuardia was very much in demand as a public speaker. His fluent Italian had none of the oily redundancy of the current Italian style of oratory. It was terse, direct—even astringent. He had, moreover, a gift for holding and moving his audience. It was a voice from the New World, heartening, invigorating, spontaneous. The crowds stamped and roared their approval of this fiery little man.

It was fortunate for us that we had such a speaker in Italy.

[252]

Our industrious Bureau of Information was not always prudent in its selection of the men it shipped overseas, presumably to inform the war-weary Europeans of the transoceanic reinforcements that were to turn the tide in such short order. One wondered why such representatives were sent; but they came in great numbers.

One in particular I remember with rueful amusement. He was expansively built and wore an outsize sombrero. His clothes fell loosely away from the slopes that bulged from shoulder to stomach, and from stomach to knee, in shapeless confusion. He represented the Order of the Moose. (Was it by a typographical error only that the Italian papers printed this "the Order of the Mouse"?) Because he was an American, he was graciously received, and the Italians never failed to give him the title of "Honorable." They thought he must be at least a Member of Congress. When he made no disclaimer, I saw signs of mounting irritation in my chief. One morning LaGuardia greeted him with: "Good morning, Congressman. Just what district do you represent?"

The "Honorable" was not a bit embarrassed. He explained his status in the noble Order of the Moose; to him, the correction raised rather than lowered his prestige. In gratitude for his secret amusement LaGuardia forgot his annoyance—it would have taken a better man to deserve his anger!

The "Honorable" made a speech a few days later at a mass meeting in the Colosseum. The immense amphitheater was crowded, and many dignitaries were present. In the speakers' rostrum, where LaGuardia and I sat, I noticed our own Ambassador, Thomas Nelson Page, whose admiration of Woodrow Wilson was almost an obsession; Marconi, looking less like an Italian Senator than an English intellectual; and many others.

Page read his dignified speech with more modesty than carrying power, but it had the virtue of brevity. Italian orators rolled their r's over the glorious past of Rome and the brilliant future of Wilsonian democracy. A place of honor had been reserved for the Order of the Moose. He was ready for it, unafraid, unabashed.

"Friends, Romans, brothers," he bellowed, "I bring you the greetings of all America." He spoke slowly and, the word Amer-

[253]

ica being one intelligible to the multitude, they drowned his voice in a chorus of bravos. After this auspicious beginning the Moose warmed to his task.

America, he informed us, had never lost a war. America, he said, loved peace; but when she fought a war—and she had fought five of them to date—she always won. After this comforting assurance he proceeded more specifically to console Italy. America, he said, knew of Italy's plight—knew that Italy was down and out. Well, he went on, Cuba had been down and out, too—and now look at Cuba! Italy (being just like Cuba, of course) might hope for a similar recovery.

I could see a grim smile on Marconi's rather tight lips. LaGuardia gave a muted groan; this was almost too true to form to be amusing. The Moose went blithely on. He pictured himself as a combination of Mark Antony, Theodore Roosevelt, and Buffalo Bill. All his life had been but a preparation for this moment—and how sweet it was! The few people present who understood English were appalled, but the others cheered the Moose to the echo.

Occasionally LaGuardia, when he was unable to keep a speaking engagement, would call on me to be his deputy. He was deaf to my protests of inexperience.

"Nonsense!" he would say. "You know Italian. You are used to stage appearances. You are not inarticulate—write your own speech. Hang it on a handle which you feel deeply about and, above all, keep it simple." It was not a bad formula.

My first important appearance took place in Orvieto, that miraculous hill city dominated by its dreamlike cathedral. On the trade route from the Orient, the sober Romanesque churches are decked out with colors straight from the treasure chest of India. They are singularly unchurchly; they are even heretical. What a trial they must have been to the true Inquisitor!

The meeting at which I was to speak was held in the Communal Theater one Sunday afternoon. There were other speakers, the event signalized being the naming of a street for President Wilson. Ambassador and Mrs. Page had come up from

Rome. He seemed quite nervous when he learned that I was to replace LaGuardia.

"You will read your speech, of course," he said.

No, I had memorized it and would talk from notes. Seeing his concern, I assured him that I would *not* liken Italy to Cuba. He apparently relished the allusion, but I do not think he drew a quiet breath until the afternoon came to an end. Surprisingly enough, the speech was successful. From the first phrase I felt the warm current of sympathy that sometimes flows out to you from a responsive concert audience, inevitably spurring you to do better than you know how.

CHAPTER THIRTY-TWO

WHEN LaGuardia was transferred to the Italian Front to command a squadron of American pilots, his post as representative of the Army and Navy Aircraft Board was filled by Major Robert Glendenning. He was an older man, a banker from Philadelphia, with a pre-war knowledge of aeronautics that made him an excellent candidate for the post. He was less intransigent than Fiorello had been about my desire to take flying training, and was willing to endorse my application provided it did not interfere with my work as his assistant. The solution appeared to be that I should train as an observer, not as a pilot. There was an excellent school for observers at the flying field of Cento Celle just outside Rome. In due time the necessary authorization was received and I embarked on a new phase of life.

The hours were long, for I had to do double duty. I reported at six in the morning for flight training, instruction in wireless telegraphy, aerial photography, navigation, bombing, and machine-gunning—first against fixed, and later against moving, targets. All these numerous techniques were necessary, for in the Caproni bombers to which I was eventually to be assigned the observer, not the pilot, was in command of the plane.

I had to be back again at the office by ten or eleven in the morning to deal with the endless chores piled up there. I have forgotten the many titles that accrued like barnacles to my job. I was made Judge Advocate and on occasion had to conduct courts-martial. This meant additional hours of reading military law, of which I was completely ignorant. I went back to the camp in the late afternoon for a few hours more of training. And at night I was never troubled by insomnia. From Fiorello came a letter affectionately and passionately profane about what he termed my insanity—a characteristic document.

The autumn brought a sudden close to the desperate four-year struggle. It was over as abruptly as it had begun. A delirium seemed to possess the world. It was too feverishly excited to feel any real happiness or to welcome the responsibility that went with peace.

My flying training had been completed too late for me to be assigned to combat duty before November 11. I felt no regret at packing away, untried, this newly acquired skill. The next few months were busy ones. Tying up the loose ends of unfinished business was followed by demobilization and a return to civilian life.

In the meantime, Wilson made his historic visit to Europe. His coming to Rome was heralded as if the whole country were Seventh Day Adventists awaiting the arrival of the Prince of Peace. Unfortunately, his Fourteen Points were stretched and contracted to form arguments in favor of every clashing set of selfish interests and every expansionist dream. The frantic adoration of the Apostle of Democracy had no sound foundations, crumbling away at the first indication that Wilson was stubbornly opposed to the Italian thesis that the Adriatic should be a Latin lake. Overnight, the posters that had endowed him with angel's wings were now redrawn with scales on those wings to indicate his Mephistophelian treachery. This violent shift from love to hatred was very disturbing. Was the War to End War to be followed by a Peace that was to end peace?

Toward the middle of February 1919 I was demobilized at the camp of St. Aignan. Civilian clothing felt very strange after a year and a half in uniform. I accepted a series of concerts in Italy, beginning with an appearance in Rome at the Augusteo with Molinari conducting.

Meantime, I had received from America a flattering contract from the Wolfsohn Musical Bureau, headed by Pop Adams. My last two seasons in the States had been successfully managed by George E. Brown, to whom I was warmly attached. I wired back an acceptance of the Wolfsohn proposal, contingent on their including Brown in their managerial personnel. Pop Adams, it seems, growled that he had bargained for an artist, not a clan—but in the end he agreed; and George Brown has been a faithful member of that organization ever since.

During my soldiering, André Benoist had played accompaniments for two years with Jascha Heifetz, whose brilliant success not even a world at war could dim. He would, he wrote me, return to our musical partnership the following season.

I went back to the concert stage with a certain amount of misgiving. Although I had never been entirely separated from my instrument, it was only rarely that I had had time to play. There were stiff hinges to oil, and a rigorous spring cleaning to undergo, before a semblance of concert pitch could be recovered. However, the leisurely days seemed to hold limitless practice time, and mechanical facility returned much more quickly than I had expected.

Toward public appearance I had a curiously detached sensation—a total absence of the stage fright that used to exact its paralyzing tax. I wondered whether my long absence from the stage had brought immunity from its attendant fears. Apparently it had. Excitement returned, but it was a stimulus, not a deterrent. I found myself stepping onto the stage of the Augusteo with the same confidence I might have felt if I had left it successfully only the night before.

I played a series of twenty concerts in Italy that spring. Home in June—and happiness! Mary Pyle and I were married on July 19, 1919. It was a quiet wedding in the little white church at Ridgefield, Connecticut. Mary was as opposed as I to making this intimate event a public spectacle, so only our families and a very few friends were at the church. Music by Jacques Thibaud, with André Benoist at the organ, was a delightful wedding present.

We spent our honeymoon in a white frame cottage in the village of Mendon, Vermont—the epitome of shabby comfort. We were taken care of by a general house servant, Mary Flynn, as

Irish as the shamrock. Once or twice a week we would drive the four miles to Rutland for provisions. There were long practice hours in the morning, picnic teas in the afternoon. A nearby lake, the town reservoir, was a favorite spot. We could canoe to a miniature island in the center and, while Mary boiled the water for tea, I would disturb the peace by stripping for an icy plunge. Evenings we spent reading aloud to each other. These outwardly uneventful days may not sound exciting, but they are an excellent recipe for contentment.

The summer ended all too soon, and we began an arduous season for which the Italian concerts the previous spring had been only a curtain-raiser. It surprised me again to see our immense and ever-growing auditoriums, although previous experience ought to have accustomed me to them. They were, I reflected, altogether too large for the intimate type of recital dear to the hearts of Europeans. Subjective playing had to be modified in favor of broader, more objective brush strokes. I remember my dismay at the vastness of the Denver auditorium. I had played there before, but part of the hall had then been partitioned off so that it held a mere four thousand. The enterprising Oberfelder—"Obie" to his friends—had by now so enlarged his subscription list that the whole theater was to be used.

"But," I protested, "I'll have to change my program, especially the opening numbers. I have some quiet old Italian pieces—a modest sonata by Porpora, for instance. They will never be heard."

Oberfelder agreed, and we substituted the Mendelssohn concerto. Its brilliancy should carry if anything could.

In the opening phrases I found myself coolly appraising the sound of the familiar E minor phrase as "up it wings the spiral stair." At such detached moments you often do your best, your freest playing. But I had not reckoned with the perverse tricks that memory can play on you with even the most familiar musical material. There are three kinds of memory: the almost photographic memory of the printed page; the ear memory, or association of shifting intervals and harmonies; and the very compelling muscular memory—compelling, but hardly dependable. These three reinforce each other unconsciously; it is sometimes very hard to tell where one leaves off and another takes over. In those rare instances when all three play truant, you are left defenseless—it is like a sudden blind spot. Such a blind spot assailed me on that first page of the Mendelssohn concerto. I found myself helplessly going round and round in a circle. Benoist tried to hammer out some key notes that would extricate me, but to no avail. I circled—was it six, was it eight, times? I could not seem to resolve out of the eternal E minor. I was on the point of stopping to apologize and start over again when— *click*—out of the blue a G sharp appeared! The temporary resolution to A minor had come in at the door, and from there we sailed on serenely. Excitement of this kind sometimes adds a zest, a gusto, to the rest of the concert, and this one ended on quite a triumphant note. We were due to catch a midnight train. "But do," I said to Benoist, "arrange with the news-stand at the hotel to send tomorrow's papers on to us in Chicago. I am curious to hear how accurately my blind spot is recorded."

A few days later the papers reached us—a whole sheaf of them. The reviews were long; they were as flattering as obituary notices. Never, it seemed, had I been in better form; but—"but what had happened to Mr. Benoist in the first movement of the Mendelssohn concerto?"

Ben said nothing; he merely looked at me with Asiatic inscrutability. He expected, and obtained, the propitiation of an excellent cigar. Later that evening we met Jacques Thibaud and Harold Bauer in the lobby of the Congress Hotel, a familiar rendezvous. The story of the Mendelssohn was too good to keep —it was told at once. Jacques whooped with delight and insisted on hearing it in detail several times. It was followed by similar anecdotes from first one, then another. Charlie Hart, Jacques' accompanist, exchanged commiserating glances with Ben. Theirs to do and die, theirs not to question why, when others blundered.

The imp of suggestion added an ironic sequel to this tale. My orchestral dates kept me in Chicago for several days. Thibaud had a recital in a nearby town. We met again on his return. He put on a fiery show of Gascon indignation.

"What species of malicious animal are you?" he demanded. "Knowing full well—as you did—that my program last night included the Mendelssohn concerto, you deliberately fabricated a story, loaded with every kind of contagion, knowing full well—as you did—that I would forget—as I did—in the self-same place! No, comrade, it was *not* the act of a brother!"

Charlie Hart had something to say about it, too. There was, after all, he confided to Benoist, some justice left in the world. Only a few nights previously he had been subjected to a kind of Chinese torture such as only the irrepressible Jacques could have thought up. The first page of the Beethoven sonata which they were to play had been doctored and distorted by the alteration of accidentals, sharps being substituted for flats and vice-versa. The score was a pernicious cryptogram. After the first shock, Hart had broken out in a cold sweat. To avoid complete disaster he took a chance on his memory and shut his eyes during the playing of the first page. Surely the torture was not to be prolonged throughout the entire piece? When he heard the page being turned he opened his eyes to find an enormous "Bravo" scrawled in Jacques' boldest manner at the top of page two. "So," added Hart, "I thoroughly relished the merry-go-round last night in Mendelssohn!"

At this moment we were joined by Pablo Casals, who was to play a recital the next day, Sunday, in Chicago. We had planned to attend it. No string player ever denies himself this privilege unless conspired against by the tyranny of time-tables. "It is music itself that speaks," said Thibaud, referring to Casals, a few moments before he joined us.

What was it, I wondered, that was so compelling in the presence of this unobtrusive little man? He stole quietly into the room. Unimpressive physically, he gave you a sense of power and authority almost as if by inversion—the sensation you sometimes have in a museum when, as you face walls crowded with brilliant canvases, a single picture (it may actually be the lowest in key) suddenly claims all your attention. The claim grows in strength, in intensity, and you feel yourself drawn more and more to it.

The great Spanish musician's conversation was as profoundly simple as his cello-playing. I don't remember exactly how the subject of personality came up, but "Personality," observed

Casals, "is a much-abused term. I constantly dread its misuse."
Then he told the following story.

"Some years ago a young student came to study with me.
Ysaÿe had praised his gifts, though he warned me of the trouble
I should have in trying to bring some order out of uncontrolled
chaos. The young man played for me. He had some good qualities, clouded by ungoverned and distorting impulses. He had
unbounded self-confidence—not a bad trait, though in his case
a little premature. He said to me: 'Master, I have come to learn
the secret of some of your tricks!' Tricks, I thought ironically.
However, I concealed my amused irritation and nodded gravely.
I would try to teach him my tricks, such as they were.

"We set to work—from the ground up. The lad, as I have said,
had talent. He had application. In a short time he had made
great progress—without, however, any sense of where he was
going. Each problem solved was to him a necromancer's trick
rather than a foundation stone on which to build a true edi-
fice. When I would show him how, by the elimination or sub-
stitution of a needless or unidiomatic shift of position, a phrase
could be restored to its natural modesty, he would pause and
give me a sly wink as if to say, 'So that is the way it's done!'
This, of course, dismayed me. However, as I said, I was not dis-
satisfied with his general progress, and when the occasion arose
for him to make a public appearance I gave my consent willingly.
He was, I thought, quite equipped to play the concerto requested.

"I attended the concert with no misgivings. It was imprudent
of me. Rarely have I passed so uncomfortable a half-hour. Such,
I reflected bitterly, are the results of my teaching. What kind of
teacher are you after all, I asked myself. The boy played with
all his old, arrogant self-confidence. Rhythm, discretion, control
were thrown to the winds, and what came forth was an impudent array of vulgarity. Not one cheap effect did he miss. It was
a caricature of the music—and worse than a caricature!"

"And what did you say to him?" asked Thibaud.

Casals took a reflective puff from his inevitable pipe. "I did
not trust myself to go behind stage that night," he said. "I decided to have my say the following day in my studio."

"And then?" I asked.

"And then . . ." Indignation still spoke in a measured fashion, the ironic voice scarcely raised from an inexorable monotone. Casals, it seems, had asked patiently what had happened to provoke such disorder. He was willing, almost anxious, to hear and accept the excuse of extreme nervousness. But no—that was not the reason, it appeared.

"Master," the young scoundrel had said, "this was my first chance at a public appearance. I realized that I must forget for the moment everything you had taught me. Otherwise people would think that here was another Casals playing. I must let my own personality speak!"

At this Pablo Casals could contain himself no longer. "Get out of here," he had roared at the astonished boy, "and never let me see your face again. 'Personality'—*I* have not taught you anything of *my* personality. Nor could I. It would be easier to graft my finger tips onto yours—manifestly an impossibility. What I *have* tried to teach you, imbecile that you are, is a true, simple, and reverent regard for music. But you have not the character to see it. The shabby costume you falsely call 'personality' will neither cover nor disguise the vacuum that lies beneath."

It was not difficult, one thought, to understand Casals' subsequent distaste for the term.

When he learned that we were staying over for his concert the next day, Casals was as naïvely pleased as a child. With such colleagues at hand, he said, the vacant spaces would pass unnoticed.

"Vacant spaces?" we protested. "But that is impossible!"

The suggestion was, we felt sure, a libel on Chicago; but Casals was not sanguine. For a favorite tenor was singing at the Auditorium, and what could a cello—a mere cello—offer against such competition? He was right, and we were wrong. The theater was not large, but even so it held plenty of empty seats. The small band of musicians huddled in secret conclave.

"It's sacrilegious," said Thibaud, "for us to be here on invitation! Let's go out to the box office and pay for our seats."

The figure behind the grille had almost to be shaken from his somnolence before the truth penetrated. "Mr. Casals wouldn't like it," he said hesitantly.

"He is not to know anything about it," we insisted. "Nor is anybody else. It is a matter of conscience. Let it go at that."

We returned to our seats to enjoy the performance. We were in this man's debt for many unforgettable experiences; could it be that memory had magnified them, had created an ideal that a fresh experience could not equal? With the first commanding phrases of a Handel sonata, however, we knew that memory had played us no tricks. This, then, was Casals. As he played, a kind of renascent beauty flooded the dingy, all but empty theater. It was achieved by an extraordinary absence of display, a baffling simplicity to be appreciated only by those who think and feel deeply. His pulsating rhythm is a miracle in itself. It has none of the mechanical beat of the metronome; it has the elasticity of nature, and its inevitability. And Casals' technique—rarely spoken of because how he says a thing is so easily forgotten in the significance of what he has to say. All the facilities of a craft developed over a thousand years seem to have been brought to a point of effortless ease.

"It is abominable of him to disguise difficulty with such unconcern," whispered Thibaud. After the Handel sonata, he played a Boccherini concerto. The solo phrase in the slow movement opens with a long note played in half voice, but with incredible and increasing intensity. As the bow, drawn slowly from hilt to tip, nears its end, there occurs a little passage, a turn, articulated almost in the spoken manner. With a hardly perceptible movement of the wrist, Casals played this turn in the same bow stroke, as a kind of parenthetical addition. Here again was the picture—low in key, and compelling in power.

Following Boccherini came one of the Bach suites for the unaccompanied cello. In these the art of Casals ascends to perhaps its greatest heights. He speaks with the voice of a prophet imparting some of the wonders and mysteries of an unreachable universe. The present-day level of solo cello-playing owes its eminence to this master's influence; the great virtuosos of today are the first to admit this truth. We were few in number who heard him that Sunday afternoon, but we cheered so lustily that he forgot we were not a multitude and continued with piece after piece long past the set program.

[264]

There were trains to be made. Thibaud and Casals were headed east, Ben and I toward California. But Casals knew from the expressions on our faces, from the clasp of our hands, and from what we were too moved to say, that he had played one of his greatest concerts that day. It was an imperishable memory.

CHAPTER THIRTY-THREE

ON the train going West I was practicing, as was often my habit, in my compartment. With the doors shut, and the neutralizing noise of revolving wheels, this had never before annoyed my fellow passengers. However, we live and learn. My compartment was in the observation car. Benoist had gone in search of a periodical, or perhaps in search of chance companionship. I am, he tells me, an unsociable person to practice while traveling—and Ben is gregarious by nature. Nor was he disappointed on this occasion. In the next chair, idly turning the leaves of a magazine, sat a pretty young girl. Ben, who has an eye for comeliness, observed that something seemed to irritate her. Could it be the sounds from our compartment down the corridor? Ben was loth to believe it, but the evidence was becoming unmistakable. As the frowns on young-and-pretty deepened to distress, he decided to learn the worst.

"You do not like music?" he began pleasantly.

"Music!" the girl snorted. "You call *that* music?"

"It sounds rather good to me."

"There is nothing so painful," was the severe reply, "as inferior violin-playing to ears accustomed to the best. The very reason this disturbs me is because I *am* a music-lover."

"Do you go often to concerts?" Ben asked.

"Indeed I do." Pointing to advertisements in the Los Angeles paper on the table, she continued: "If you really want to hear what the violin can sound like, I advise you to attend *this* concert."

[266]

Benoist's eyes followed her finger. It pointed to the announcement of my concert the following night.

"Did you enlighten her?" I asked him when, a few minutes later, he interrupted me to share this tidbit. Ben looked at me with scorn. "And lose a customer? What do you take me for?"

The long stretch of land that slopes down from the Sierras to the largest of oceans never fails to fulfill its fabulous promise. After the endless reaches of prairie, and the arid and forbidding mountains, Nature was reckless with her incredible opulence. Even in the train, that first shaft of brilliant sunlight has a new quality, tempered from its desert harshness by a fresh, green world. You savor it for an exquisite moment, remembering that presently you will be invited to admire it too often. Californians wear their climate ostentatiously.

I have often wondered what would happen to Californians if their visitors stayed at home. Or whether, indeed, they have any real occupations? They all seem to have limitless time at their disposal to devote to the newcomer. I would try always, I thought, always to be a newcomer! It would be all but impossible to maintain the unabated enthusiasm without which any resident is considered disloyal.

Los Angeles always astonishes me. It continues to grow without developing. Some of the buildings are very fine. Others are in the feverish process of building. But you rarely have the feeling that they belong, that they are anything but transient. San Francisco is quite different—but one must not mention San Francisco in southern California. It is less sacrilegious to speak of New York and the East.

But why do we spend so much time and energy in poking fun at California? Having once seen it, we long always to return to it; but with human perversity we hunt and cherish what flaws we can to humanize its excess of magnificence. It is perhaps impatience with the utter inadequacy of the spoken word to describe the silent majesty of Creation, which

> "With Nature's calm content, with tacit huge delight,
> Does welcome what it wrought for through the past."

Let only one voice, I thought, be spokesman for this land. And let that voice be Walt Whitman's.

For the musician at least, Los Angeles in 1919-20 held a new interest, a new excitement. A major symphony orchestra had emerged, owing to the princely generosity of one of our musical Maecenases—William Andrews Clark, Jr. He had two hobbies: the collecting of rare books, and the creating of a symphonic orchestra that was to rival any in the land. To lead this new and beautiful instrument he had engaged his old friend Walter Rothwell. Rothwell was a distinguished musician. He had had his schooling under Gustav Mahler, whom he idolized—as do all Mahlerites. His knowledge of orchestration was profound. I had had the advantage of supplementing my earlier studies by a long course in orchestration under his guidance, and he was an excellent drill-master. Added to this, he had fastidious taste and excellent judgment. Practically overnight he had produced an orchestra with a tonal beauty that would have done credit to any city. This is the test of the true conductor.

"Public appraisal of a conductor," Ossip Gabrilowitsch once said to me, "is seldom trustworthy. And the present custom of more and more guest conductors, and fewer and fewer permanent ones, is only adding to its untrustworthiness. People start from a false premise. They assume that they can judge a new leader much in the same way that they would a soloist. But it isn't so. With a soloist, you often know, with the first phrase, whether a singer, a violinist, or a pianist knows or doesn't know his job. Of course, even here, the decision is sometimes relative; it takes repeated hearings to get the full bearing of the artist. But with the first impact you can generally form an opinion. But it's quite different with a conductor. He does not do the playing. Others do it—under his guidance, his planning. He is like the general of an army. You do not judge a general by a skirmish; sometimes not even by a battle. It is the result of a campaign that counts. The public forgets this."

"And the critics, too," I ventured.

"The critics! They are the worst of all; in fact, it is they who are largely responsible for the premature judgments that in some cases have given mediocrity a long lease, and kicked excellence out of doors in others."

How entirely like Ossip, I thought, this straightforward, yet highly original diagnosis! This gentlest of gentlemen, and most poetic of pianists, had a trenchant way of expressing himself.

We dined often with Clark and the Rothwells in the old-fashioned, rambling house that sheltered his literary treasures. We gaped wide-eyed at the array of first editions, manuscripts, and priceless incunabula which patient and persistent collecting—plus unlimited means—had assembled here. This impressive collection, for the pleasure of a single individual, made you wonder at a system that could permit it. It would have been almost intolerable, were the collection not (you remembered) destined to return eventually to the general public. All the same, it was a privilege and a joy to handle these books. And Clark's unassuming pleasure in them was disarming.

We were on the threshold of that decade of reactionary political philosophy and popular thought. The phrase "Return to Normalcy" had not yet been coined, but the desire it embodied was already alive and growing. This was, after all, to be the best of all possible worlds if we could forget the responsibility and refuse the leadership which the war had thrust upon us. Surrounded by protecting oceans, we could and would withdraw from international entanglements and problems. With the senility of second childhood we believed that an Arcady of milk and honey was once more at hand if only we could maintain the resolve to be "too proud to think"!

CHAPTER THIRTY-FOUR

IN the spring of 1920, the New York Symphony Orchestra, led by Walter Damrosch, made a tour of Western Europe. Damrosch was no longer young, but you had long known that he would never be old. Our friendship and artistic collaboration, begun twelve years before, had sealed and soldered itself with the passing of each year. It was my privilege to accompany the orchestra on this tour as one of the two soloists. The other was John Powell, the composer-pianist, as Virginian as tobacco and so utterly and endearingly Jeffersonian that I marveled that he had not chosen the fiddle and bow rather than the keyboard. He was to play his own *Negro Rhapsody,* which had already earned him golden opinions. But he was as distrait as the artist is popularly thought to be, and we often wondered whether he would turn up at the appointed time.

The orchestra itself was composed of virtuosos; many of the men in the string section, I reflected, could and should take over my role. Prominent in the wood-wind section was the familiar black beard of Georges Barrère, whose wit and Gallic philosophy went hand in hand with a transcendent art. Hearing him, you did not necessarily have to be a pagan to believe in Orpheus.

The concerts were a succession of gala events. The tour began with three concerts held at the Paris Opéra. To welcome this new visitor, the famous auditorium seemed to drop, in a moment, more than half a century—to forget the Third Republic, to forget the nightmare of the recent struggle. Its burnished gold

[270]

shone again, reflecting the pomp and circumstance of the last Napoleonic Empire.

Paris is often called an unmusical city. Paradoxically, however, it boasts many symphony orchestras—one, I should think, for every arrondissement. They all starve, perhaps not to death, but at least to emaciation. They seldom if ever rehearse, and if by chance they do, the rehearsals are attended by substitutes. But the individual French musician is admirably trained and a marvelous sight reader; in consequence, admirable results are sometimes obtained with these guerrilla, catch-as-catch-can tactics. Too often, however, the valiant individual efforts of the underpaid, under-rehearsed musicians produce a performance that is as hard on music as it is on the listener. The advent of a well-disciplined American band must have been something of a revelation.

We attended a reception given by Widor at the Institut de France in honor of Camille Saint-Saëns, who was then eighty-six. The gathering included practically every familiar face from that famous gallery of French intelligentsia, the Academy. They were as bearded as ever; in France the male still avoided the razor as though it were an emblem of effeminacy. Their wives, too, were like a race apart. Their bodies seemed to be confined in upholstered armor. Obviously, the shifting modes of the Rue de la Paix had little influence on them. "They have all of them," Mary whispered to me, "stepped straight from the pages of a Balzac novel. Certainly nothing more recent!"

In spite of the fact that the wardrobes of these ladies flatly ignored a changing world, the wearers retained a style and an elegance of their own. Their finery became them, and they knew it; wore it with quiet confidence and pride. It was a tacit rebuke to 1920. Mary, looking her best—which is very good indeed—in a new Callot gown, seemed like a misplaced piece of modernism in their midst.

Glancing around the spacious rooms, I saw a few consoling figures linking us to the present day. Margaret Damrosch and three of the four daughters—Polly, Gretchen, and Anita—were at hand; like Mary, they were imprudently dressed in the clothes of today. I found them comforting and delightful to look at.

Polly's wide-set eyes and generous smile went straight to every heart; the passing of years, happy or tragic, would neither change nor diminish that smile. Gretchen—or Gay, as we called her—who was on the trip as a prelude to her honeymoon with Tom Finletter, was already formulating those endless and intriguing questions with which she was forever to flatter and trouble her contemporaries. Gay has always contrived to make you feel more intelligent and alive than you really are—though you know that she knows that you know it is not so. Anita, tall for her sixteen years, was trying very hard to look ten years older and almost getting away with it. It was somehow reassuring to look around and find, in this world of yesterday, the bright promise of today and tomorrow.

The phalanx of French femininity dominating that scene closed its ranks as far as the amenities would permit. The women must have regarded these strange encroachments on their sacred precincts with the distrust peculiar to their caste. However much they might differ in age, in feature, in general set up, they were uncompromisingly alike in type and manner; not four thousand years of Chinese art has produced a more unyielding convention. One guessed the reason why France, in some ways the most civilized of all countries, would be one of the last to give the vote to women. The women themselves would not want it. Why seek an outward symbol of emancipation and forgo the silent dominance so indisputably theirs? A survey of this assemblage, representing perhaps the greatest amount of power to be found in any one place, left you in no doubt where lay the driving, sustaining, and curbing forces behind that power.

Meantime, Saint-Saëns was being fêted and cheered by his colleagues. His ready wit, his whistling lisp, were as evident as ever. And his fingers were ready, too, to defy the years with their nimbleness. With the gusto of a youth he played the piano part of his septet with the famous trumpet part—bidding you at once never to be frightened of growing old. The septet is not a great piece; it will hardly go on being heard frequently in our concert halls. But on this occasion, at least, it went with a fine

[272]

swagger, and I shall never forget the audience alive with concentration.

Our tour took us to Bordeaux, to Marseille, to Monte Carlo. In the famous gaming center the outrageous flamboyance of the buildings is somehow less offensive than you expect it to be. And the theater in the Casino is reassuringly true to type. Prudently they kept it small—a miniature opera house. Spectacles, concerts, even ballets were but incidental interludes in the real business of this playground of the Mediterranean world. But for this occasion its modest capacity was strained far beyond its limits. I played two pieces at this concert: the Bach E major Concerto and the *Poème* by Chausson.

Joining our party for a cup of tea after the performance was a man of imposing presence. I wondered why his face was so familiar. He addressed me as though we had already met, and to my delight, solfèged with incredible facility some of the intricate figures from the Bach concerto. Why should I, I asked myself, be so pleased by this man's enthusiasm? And who *was* he? I was soon to learn. He and Damrosch picked up the threads of a time-honored friendship and recalled anecdote after anecdote. I knew then that sitting with us at tea was Tristan—Faust —Lohengrin—in person. I had never had the privilege of hearing this, one of the world's greatest dramatic tenors, who in certain roles had set a standard never since quite reached. It was Jean De Reszke.

Our luggage packed and dispatched, Mary and I took a brief stroll on the waterfront. Approaching us was another figure of operatic fame. Even at a distance the familiar swinging stride proclaimed Mary Garden. Her companion was an Englishman, neither young nor old, neither artist, industrialist, nor diplomat, but from that incognito world of elegant indolence that flourishes so abundantly on the Mediterranean coast. Plainly, the rhythm of her walk taxed his energy. They, too, had been at the concert, and were enthusiastic about the Bach and the Chausson. Not that this was important in itself; but delivered as it was in Mary Garden's inimitable French with that rich sauce of Scots burr, it took on distinction. This mode of speech she deliberately clung to; it had become a valuable trade-mark. Doubt-

less it sprang from the same impulse that later prompted Leopold Stokowski to cultivate a strong Polish accent in place of
his previous Oxford English. My wife so enjoyed meeting
Mélisande and Louise—on top of the thrill of having met Tristan and Lohengrin—and voiced her enthusiasm so well, that
the conversation threatened to prolong itself beyond train time.
We barely made the station platform as the train pulled in.

Over the border, at Ventimiglia, scenery, architecture, and type
of people change at once. The scene sobers; the architecture
loses its theatricality and becomes a part of nature again; the
people are better-looking. Mary and Gay Damrosch made a
game of picking out the handsome old peasant women whose
finely chiseled features set them apart as a type. But also, on
crossing the border, our hitherto easy trip became suddenly more
difficult. Trains no longer even pretended to run on schedule,
and the dining-car, which in France had been conveniently at
hand, vanished.

We arrived in Genoa late, many hours late, but with optimistic visions of bath and food and rest when the hotel should
be reached. Room and bath were available, but the inner man
was to be denied, for a general strike was in progress in the
North of Italy. Not a restaurant open, not a scrap of food in
the hotel. A few maids (were they strike-breakers?) scurried
through the corridors doing their bewildered best for the tired
and exasperated travelers. But their best could not supply a
crust of bread. Mary was all in, and took to her bed at once.
With me, hunger triumphed over fatigue, and I went below
to see what could be done.

In earnest consultation with the hotel manager was Walter
Damrosch, whose resourcefulness and diplomacy were being
exerted to the utmost after first meeting a stone wall of denial.
The Italians are a kindly and co-operative race, especially when
their hearts and their imaginations are tapped. Walter had, it
was evident, been patiently and persistently softening the hotel
manager's heart.

Finally the manager whispered that if we were to take the
first turning on the left, then the third on the right, and go
straight on to the fifth narrow street again on the right, we

should come to a house with green shutters—tightly closed, of course. Making sure that we were quite alone on the street, we were to knock a certain signal—was it the SOS of the Morse code?—on the second shutter. Perhaps it would open. Perhaps we would be vouchsafed some food. The Latin sense of drama was active, and we were loaded with dire warnings of the dangers involved in this adventure; there was an opera-bouffe touch in the affair. So we promised to be duly careful—we were certainly too hungry to feel frightened. Out we streamed, a whole band of us, looking somewhat like an untrained chorus in the first act of Seville's *Barber* about to intone *"piano, pianissimo."* The streets were dark and deserted. No traffic was circulating— not a taxi, not a trolley. Private cars were safely shut in their respective garages. Chalked on walls in bold scrawls were "Viva Lenin!" and "Evviva Communismo!" We found no police on the streets. Was the dark shadow of revolution at hand?

Eventually we reached the designated house. No one was around, not even a stray cat. Somewhat nervously we knocked. Nothing happened. We knocked again. After what seemed like an interminable wait, we heard the shutters being unbarred. From a peep-hole a scared eye appraised us, detected no ruffianism in our appearance. Hurrah—we were to be admitted! Once inside, our eagerness permitted no pause to discuss a choice of food. We set to, gratefully and voraciously, on the delicious cold ham and coarse bread that was set before us.

I was able to smuggle back to Mary a paper bag containing a leg of cold chicken and some bread. Sitting bolt upright in bed, wide-eyed with hunger, she greeted my treasures with unfastidious rapture. Yesterday's menu at Monte Carlo paled in comparison with this homely satisfaction.

When we awoke the following morning Genoa seemed to have recovered somewhat from her paralysis. There was traffic in the streets. I rang the bell for the waiter, and was astonished when he materialized and, in some confusion, took our order for coffee. Apparently the fever of the General Strike had abated. Today at least, there would be no revolution.

The concert took place at the opera house that night before a packed house. And our train left for Rome the following day without too much delay. Rome showed few signs of the strike. Less industrial than the three northern cities of Turin, Milan, and Genoa, it smiled its hospitality in a truly festal manner. The plaudits at the Augusteo were, as usual, directly descended from the excitement of an arena rather than a sober concert hall. A bit exaggerated, but heart-warming just the same.

At the Grand Hotel where we lodged we found the Robert Underwood Johnsons, the President having recently appointed Mr. Johnson to replace Thomas Nelson Page as Ambassador. It was not an easy role to fill. It would have taken an astute interpreter, indeed, to explain to the Italian people why Wilson's obstinate idealism was to make itself felt at the exclusive expense of Italy's "justified" aspirations. It was significant, too, that the Embassy in Rome during the Wilson administration was given as a reward for literary distinction rather than for party prominence. And the literary dynasty was continued when the Republicans were returned to power, for the next plenipotentiary was likewise a writer—Richard Washburn Child.

The Johnsons must have welcomed the orchestra as an interlude in the endless and perhaps painful discussions with the Foreign Office. The question of the eastern coast of the Adriatic—once historically Roman, and later dominated by Venice—was a burning issue. It seemed irrelevant, at least in Italy, to observe that the newly formed federation of young Slav states did have economic and racial claims worth consideration. The old enemy, Austria, had merely been exchanged for a new and no less threatening one, Jugoslavia. The war and the sacrifices had been endured in vain.

Even then, however, there were in Italy some quiet and philosophic minds who thought differently. One of the most notable of these was the historian Guglielmo Ferrero, and it is significant that he lived in exile in Switzerland until his death in 1942. Ferrero's mind had the transcendent qualities inherent in true Italian genius; it would naturally prove antipathetic to the Fascismo that was so soon to permeate Italy. Such men go voluntarily into exile rather than be stifled. I like to believe that in his exile he is sustained by a silent salute from the divine poet, that famous exile of six centuries ago. Perhaps Dante, in 1920, was hearing Ferrero's quiet voice more plainly than did the latter's wildly shouting contemporaries. It was the era of the rebirth of nationalism—the most violent and retrogressive nationalism the modern world had yet seen.

Parliamentarianism had already sunk to a new low. Debate was debate only in name. Parties had split, and then subdivided. Bills were still introduced, but could be carried only by strange alliances. Leaders, finding that they could not depend on reasoned support, accepted doubtful accomplices, in return for whose temporary aid they must eventually relinquish their once zealously held principles.

The time was nearly ripe for Mussolini. This once ardent radical-socialist had put his political creeds in reverse. A fiery supporter of the pro-Ally party, he had fought at the front and boasted that his body carried the scars of a hundred wounds. Invalided home, he assumed one of the minor Cabinet portfolios, which he was bringing up to a certain efficiency. Personal stories enhanced his reputation. On wintry mornings, when the rest of Rome huddled and shivered, he would strip to a bathing suit and swim the Tiber. The build-up was progressing rapidly; soon the Superman would appear.

From Rome, to Florence, to Milan. Thence to the reclaimed French provinces of Alsace-Lorraine. Strassbourg and Metz, those two lovely cities neither completely French nor completely German, but rather typifying the culture of the great river which pursues its majestic course northward from the Swiss mountains to the Lowlands with sovereign indifference to the enmity on the east and the west of it.

In Strassbourg, the manager was a woman who looked French but spoke with a pronounced German accent. She conceded her joy over the return of her province to France. (She came of a family that had regarded the German occupation since 1870 as usurpation.) "But," she said, "there are some things we hope may be retained from the old occupation: cleanliness, order, efficiency. In clinging to those advantages one does not have to love France less. . . ."

After Strassbourg and Metz came Belgium, Holland, and finally London with a series of five concerts at the Queen's Hall.

[277]

I appeared at two of these. The exciting tour was over. It was a relief to draw a long breath, and the cancellation of a South American contract by mutual consent was a welcome reprieve. This transaction was a somewhat complicated affair. The contract, which had been made some years before, I had been unable to fulfill owing to the entry of the United States into the war and my service overseas; and it had been held over until after the cessation of hostilities. The snag that now emerged was that the original terms, calling for payment in French francs, had been agreed on at a time when the franc was still at par. By June 1920, however, the franc was worth less than half its original value. My European agent who had made the contract felt sure until the last moment that a proper adjustment would be made; and, at one time, this seemed likely. But the lengthy exchange of correspondence and cables ended in an impasse, with Latin America obstinately holding out for literal enforcement of the now inequitable contract. I was careful not to enter into the discussion, but was relieved when the contract was finally canceled. It meant a rest after a season in which I had played about one hundred engagements.

CHAPTER THIRTY-FIVE

 ARY and I took advan-
tage of the holiday to spend the summer in England, part of it
on the coasts of Devon and Cornwall and part in a tiny dower
house on a large estate hidden among the Shropshire hills.

One day before we left London Hugh Walpole had lunch with
us. Success was already changing the spare schoolmaster into
the ample figure that was to become so popular on the lecture
stage. His two Russian novels, best-sellers in his country and
ours by the end of the war, had greatly enhanced a reputation
already solidly begun with earlier books—"although," he said
somewhat ruefully, "I shall never quite live down *Fortitude!*
I have developed a sixth sense that warns me of the approach of
the typical clubwoman. You know—the kind that always man-
ages to assume the role she particularly admires, and—what is
worse—compels you to listen to her revelatory confessions. They
always pick on *Fortitude,* and are sure it is autobiographical.
Denials do no good. I don't even try to stem the tide any longer."
Mary exchanged glances with me: how lucky that we had not
even mentioned *Fortitude!*

Walpole was a real help with our summer plans. When he
learned that we expected to spend some weeks in Devonshire,
making side trips to Cornwall, he said: "You must pay me a
visit. I have a little fisherman's cottage at Polperro."

"When will you be there?" Mary asked.

"Oh, I shan't be there—not for some time, at least." And with
that charming casualness which is the mark of the true Britisher,
he added, "Do you mind? The fisherman and his wife will take

care of you. I'll write them. It's primitive but quite comfortable, and the village itself is well worth seeing. Say you'll do it!"

No conjugal conference was necessary; we agreed without delay, assuming as nearly as we could the same casual tone. We did our best to pretend that it was our habit to descend on houses minus their hosts.

After we had spent several days in Sidmouth, that coast town full of prim reminders of the early girlhood of Queen Victoria, Walpole's note arrived reminding us of his invitation. We thereupon set forth in a hired landaulet of antique vintage—appropriate, where a modern car would have violated the spirit of that quaint setting. Our pace was leisurely, restful, rewarding. That lovely coast line, changing so abruptly from the lush green of Devonshire to the sculptural rocks of Cornwall, invites lazy contemplation and reflection. There can be little or no true enjoyment of the road if the traveler has an eye on the clock. The white plaster houses gave way to gray stone villages. Cornwall has a bleak but poetic quality. Polperro itself was a miniature citadel growing out of the coastal rocks. The streets were too narrow for anything as wide as a car, so we made our way on foot, bag and baggage, to Walpole's narrow house.

The fisherman and his wife were on hand to greet us. Apparently they were quite accustomed to this absentee hospitality. If they had their reservations about the habits of their author-employer and the odd appearance of his guests, they said nothing. One of the charms of England is that you are permitted to be a nonconformist provided you do not violate the sanctity of unchangeable habits.

Everything about the house was perpendicular, and it looked about ten feet wide. You felt that if it were laid on its side and equipped with wheels it could serve as a railroad car. We went up the narrow ladder that served as staircase and made our way into the front living-room where tea awaited us.

After tea, we decided on a walk of exploration along the rocky coast. The fisherman nodded tacit approval over his lazy pipe. "Mayhappen," he observed, "you'll take a bathe. First thing the master he always does. There be some good sandy coves all along."

[280]

I looked at Mary. The chilly waters of the Channel were, I knew, something less than tempting to her. But she was always game for adventure, and I hastened to get our bathing suits and towels. Where were we to dress and undress, Mary asked. Were there any bathing houses?

"Just drop your clothes behind a rock," said the fisherman patiently, as though advising backward children.

How we complicate our lives, I thought, by letting the conventions obscure our simplest problems! The walk, the swim (which was brief, for the water was cruelly cold), and the return home to a simple dinner were all parts of an idyllic interlude.

By lamplight we made an entertaining survey of Walpole's not inconsiderable bookcase. In each of the first editions of his own books was a dedication from himself to himself: "To Hugh, from his best friend"—or "Well, old man, you tried something that didn't quite come off; still, the attempt was worth while"— or "From Hugh—to Hugh; keep it up; this is more like something I hoped for—and Mrs. T. is certainly an improvement on the Duchess." It was, Mary remarked, a delightful and subtle way for our host to be present, after all.

The house in Shropshire, to which we moved after Cornwall, was one of those typical Elizabethan structures of white plaster and black beams, over whose front purple clematis sprawled in affectionate profusion. A squad of efficient maids left by our clairvoyant landlady ran the house, and incidentally us, in conformity with British country habits. It was an admirable arrangement. The squad was officered by Mrs. Gertrude Moon, the cook, whose decisions, Mary confided, no one would dream of questioning. Once when I begged for some change from the invariable lamb or mutton joints hedged round with cabbage, boiled potatoes, and vegetable marrow, Mary silenced me with a word. "It is easier," she declared, "to change our tastes than to move these people from the narrow gauge of their ways. So content yourself, curb your Continental appetite, and remember the privilege of living in the haunts of the Shropshire Lad. Think of the imagination shown in the very names of these villages—

[281]

Clunton and Clunbury,
Clungunford and Clun,
Are the quietest places
Under the sun—

as Housman wrote."

"That's just it," I retorted. "They've used up all their imagination on place names, and have none left for the culinary art!"

"At least," Mary reminded me, "they let themselves go at teatime. See the array awaiting us now in the garden." There were strawberries and clotted cream, crumpets, cake, and sandwiches. "I tried to explain to Mrs. Moon that we were not accustomed to such lavish teas. But do you think that did any good? She merely looked at me with pained surprise, said, 'Yes, Modom.' And the afternoon rite remains unchanged."

"And that holds good for early morning tea, too."

"You've noticed that? The facts that it is left untouched morning after morning, that I have repeatedly said we didn't want it, make no impression at all. It is brought up every day, as regular as clockwork."

I had, I confessed, taken mine this morning. So, it seemed, had Mary! It was one of those dark, overcast days when the clouds, always lower in the British sky than elsewhere, hang with a drugged heaviness. Shamefaced, we agreed that the tea had helped. "But I warn you," prophesied Mary, "that I, who am a habit-hater, will become a pest in the future if this one is allowed to get hold of us. In the meantime, their secret triumph is no less sweet because it goes unmentioned."

Our neighbors in the large Georgian mansion on the estate were a typical county family, a hyphenated name making up for the absence of a title. They were distant until they learned that both Mary and I sported tennis racquets, whereupon we were urged to become almost daily guests. In England's summer, tennis is a quotidian affair. It is conducted in the most leisurely manner and everyone joins in—old and young, stout and slim. It is not uncommon for an octogenarian to take his place among the four and, racquet in hand, calmly wait for the ball to land in the limited sphere of his activity. Mary, who has a good forehand drive, would often get impatient with the leisurely tempo and interject a sudden shot out of reach of the slow-moving players. This always evoked astonished applause and polite cries of "Oh—jolly good shot!" But you felt, even if you didn't hear, "We'll let it pass this time, but see that it doesn't happen again." Then Mary would curb her rebellious activity, and the game would resume its leisurely pace.

The Capel-Cures (I guess at the spelling) were a curious family, typical of the England that was, is, and ever shall be a puzzle to those who love and seek to understand her. The inconvenient comfort they enjoy, their stubborn resistance to the interchange of ideas, tempt one to charge them with complacent hypocrisy. But the suspicion is unjust. The English are, in reality, a race of romantic poets; but they distrust the spoken word as a mistranslation of their deepest feelings. Only with Nature or with animals does an Englishman let himself go. Even toward children the cool and distant code of manners must be preserved. You often wonder about this enigma of a happy childhood with none of the outward signs of tenderness and affection to which we are accustomed. But in spite of all this inarticulate masquerade, you sense their belief in the dignity of the individual regardless of his station. We certainly felt it with our Mrs. Moon. Her acquiescence in orders was a masterpiece of compliance without submission—the sort of compliance that many a junior officer must get when he is dealing with an experienced top-sergeant. Nor was it any different with the Capel-Cures. At the tea-table—that rewarding entr'acte in the mild exertions of the tennis court—Mrs. Capel-Cure manipulated the tepid conversation with a master hand. All controversial subjects were ignored. It was an intricate game, Mary claimed; each of the players trying to utter the greatest number of words with the least discernible meaning.

Not being too apt at this sort of thing, both of us often trespassed on forbidden territory. There were no penalties—we were Americans, and therefore indulged. But the conversation was firmly steered back into safe channels. There was one uncomfortable moment when they learned that I was a musician. Over the tea-table hovered the tradition of ancient churchyards whose burial grounds were open to all "excepting only actors, musicians, and vagabonds." Mrs. Capel-Cure hastened to the rescue.

"How interesting!" she exclaimed, without conviction. "I knew a musician once. I've forgotten what his name was but he used to give concerts . . . and even travel . . ." Her voice trailed off. But the situation was saved: the authoritative tea-table of the manor house had recognized this odd pursuit. Presently Elgar's name was mentioned. He was now Sir Edward Elgar—a distinction that cloaked his questionable calling in respectability. Was his music known in America? I replied that nearly twenty years ago I had had the honor of giving the first performances in our major cities of his violin concerto. The word "concerto" was evidently foreign to their ears. One of the ladies—she prided herself on being a step or two in advance of the others—asked brightly if it were part of *The Dream of Gerontius.*

Fortunately the conversation soon veered to more familiar topics. Mrs. Capel-Cure and her coterie described the annual bazaar that was shortly to take place on their grounds. It sounded dreary and ominous, but we were urgently invited to attend. Mary's glance said, "It'll be awful, but we've got to do it." And we submitted with good grace.

The bazaar *was* awful. It must take centuries to learn to produce at one time and in one place the variety of unusable objects that were assembled for sale. But they were all bought with determined zeal, and there was always the consoling suspicion that the possession of this junk was only temporary—its new owner would, in turn, donate it to some future bazaar. In England, superannuated articles are never destroyed or given away; they migrate from home to home through the agency of bazaars.

In the Capel-Cures' house, musical talent had been mustered. It was chiefly vocal. Ballad after ballad was warbled to the accompaniment of a discouraged piano whose tuning was a masterpiece of indefinite pitch. I played a game with myself, trying here and there to detect true quarter-tones. The singers struggled valiantly on. They were neither looked at nor listened to by the perambulating crowds. But they were, I suppose, a traditional part of the affair. I saw Mary looking a little wilted and fought my way to the tea-table where tea had been steeping for hours—a potent brew. But this was a moment for something drastic. At the cost of threepence a cup I procured two cups. Perhaps tannin poisoning was around the corner, but I noticed that Mary finished her cup as quickly as I did mine. We suddenly felt better; anyway, it was close to the time when we could reasonably make our escape.

The pony and cart which was our sole means of transportation trundled us home. In the late afternoon light the narrow, winding lanes take on a mysterious and magical quality. Each turn reveals a picture that recalls some well-remembered phrase of English poetry. Behind this hedge, through that open doorway, you seem to catch figure after figure from imperishable literature. It is fiction and poetry become fact. On that drive back, even the bazaar shed some of its boredom. But we decided that the English country bazaar should remain unique in our experience.

CHAPTER THIRTY-SIX

BY October 1920 we were in New York again. After the lazy, sweet monotony of an English summer, this city of feverish speed makes an overpowering impact. In spite of every resolution to the contrary you find yourself joining the irresistible rush.

"Look out," Mary warned me; "you'll be penalized if you're found for more than fifteen minutes in any one place!"

It was too true to be funny. The city screamed with noise that pierced your eardrums, the heaven-storming structures rose ever higher, and, far below, in the depths of the rock foundations, one heard the convulsions of underground traffic. But the skyline remained, as always, a thing of wonder. It would, I thought, be impossible to live here, were it not so utterly impossible not to live here.

The change in the aspect of the streets ceased to surprise you. It was a chronic, not an ordinary, affair. In the orchestral world, also, changes were going on. The Philharmonic was having one of its customary crises. After nearly eighty years was it to fold its tents and steal away? The two-party musical system had prevailed for so long—the Philharmonic versus the Symphony—that it seemed unthinkable that one of these famous rivals might no longer be there. But this was to leave out of the reckoning the vitality inherent in the old Philharmonic organization; it was not its first or only eclipse. And it was to come back in all its militant splendor, its chief weakness being not a lack but a plethora of leadership.

Meantime a new orchestra had been formed with Artur Bodanzky as leader. He was a delightful and sensitive musician and I always looked forward to playing with him. This short-lived musical group was not without an influence on the future, for it was undoubtedly responsible for the concerts of The Friends of Music.

The periodical *Vanity Fair* was playing up musical events as well as sartorial styles both male and female, and it ran a series of jingles about musicians. Some of these still run in my head.

> Said Artur Bodanzky
> To Papi, "Old manzki,
> Your tempos are snappy!"
> "I thank you," said Papi.

The singers were lampooned also:

> Said Culp to Caruso,
> "You sob! Pray why do so?"
> "I just love to gulp,"
> Said Caruso to Culp.

Nor were violinists neglected. One trembled at what was to come.

> Said Spalding to Elman,
> "You play very well, man!"
> "Your humor is scalding,"
> Said Elman to Spalding.

I don't know whether Mischa ever saw this doggerel. In any case, I think he emerges from it better than I do.

Shortly after this, Elman's gracious generosity toward a colleague was strikingly exemplified. A piece of mine called *Etchings,* a theme and variations of considerable development, came to his attention. After studying it with loving care, he performed it many times with the sweep, the tonal beauty, and the eloquence for which he is famous. It was an exposition to delight any author. I was present when he played it at Carnegie Hall. Sitting a few rows ahead of me in the crowded auditorium was his old master Leopold Auer, still vigorous in spite of his years. Elman was clearly in his best form that evening, and the house thundered its enthusiasm. And a few evenings later he played *Etchings* at our home. The multitudes were reduced to individuals, but his performance and his success were repeated.

We were then living in East 67th Street. The apartment was not large, but it contained a music room of sizable dimensions, and we used often to have chamber music there. It was spontaneous and informal, and often had a haphazard charm impossible to capture in the more studied renditions given in a public hall. We were never at a loss for recruits for the first and the second violin stands, nor were cellists scarce. But the experienced viola-player was always at a premium. In the quartet world he is cherished and coddled in the same way that the orchestral world pampers its oboe-players.

One evening we had Thibaud, Heifetz, and Paul Kochanski, besides myself, as violinists. Hans Kindler and Felix Salmond were the cellists. Léon Sametini was our one and only viola-player; he was a fine fiddler in his own right, but his prowess on the viola condemned him, for that evening at least, to the contralto role. On this occasion we played chamber works until the early hours of the morning, climaxing the session with Schubert's great quintet in C major for two cellos. This supreme work is unkind to any piece that has the misfortune to follow it; its sensuous beauty, its opulent tonal splendor, make any ensuing music sound pale. "You open the pages of Schubert's music," remarked Thibaud, "and Vienna itself comes in at the door!" And Ossip Gabrilowitsch once told me that he had an innate suspicion of people who do not love Schubert.

That genius has indeed been one of the enigmas of tonal history. By all man-made rules, Schubert's talent—deprived of the formal training received by other composers—should never have borne fruit. And I suspect that, if by chance all our documentary evidence of his life were to get lost, or be destroyed, some future musicologist would argue—as the Baconians do about Shakespeare—that Schubert simply could not have written Schubert's music because his technical education had been so slight.

The early twenties brought a revolution in the field of mechanical music. Up to that time the phonograph had reigned supreme. The sales of records of semi-popular pieces and songs ran into the hundreds of thousands in a single year, and the royalties paid to the favorites easily surpassed the returns from a profitable concert season.

At that time I was under contract with the Edison Company, a strong competitor of Victor, especially in the United States. Victor, affiliated with the English company called His Master's Voice, had practically a monopoly of the foremost names of the operatic and concert stage. However, it was an advantage to figure in a catalogue almost free of violinistic rivals; and the advantage was demonstrated in the twice-yearly royalty checks that regularly increased in size. Then, in the early 1920's, with the sudden appearance of radio the public abandoned its old toy for a new one, and the figures on our royalty checks were suddenly diminished. It seemed to happen overnight.

Atwater Kent, who pioneered in radio sets of moderate price, was also a pioneer in putting semi-serious concerts on the air. It was quite a novel sensation to be engaged for an hour's recital, which was broadcast all over the country. It was exciting, and not a little nerve-racking. My years of experience in making records were a great help. In recording, however, when something goes wrong, you do have a chance to correct it; whereas when you are on the air it is now or never!

The Atwater Kent program enjoyed a wide hook-up, and we were informed in feverish accents that audiences of astronomical dimensions were listening in. Impressive, of course . . . but somehow it did not sound convincing in the chilly studio atmosphere. If the artist is to be stimulated to his best, one auditor *right there* is worth two million supposititious listeners off in the ether!

When broadcasting from New York we had as announcer Graham McNamee, then on the threshold of his famous career. Already he had that faculty of communicating electric enthusiasm (could he really feel all this for music?) that made him the most acclaimed narrator of sports events. From the ring in his voice when he announced a concert, you would have thought that Beethoven and Bach were as dear to his heart as the exploits of a Dempsey or a Tunney.

Occasionally, when concerts far afield prevented my broadcasting from a metropolitan center, we had some odd experiences

[289]

with local announcers. In Oklahoma City, for example, the spokesman for the evening's radio recital appeared that morning at our hotel. It would be difficult to imagine anyone less fitted for the task. Nervously fingering the program, he confessed that he was utterly unable to pronounce the titles and the names of the composers. Would we kindly coach him? I turned him over to Benoist, who struggled with him for hours. They went over and over the words with laborious care; the titles and the authors' names got spelled out phonetically; by dint of endless repetition, syllable after syllable was drummed into the announcer's unreceptive ears—and by late afternoon my frustrated accompanist was exhausted.

"Do you think he got a glimmer?" I asked.

Ben shook his head. He had, he declared, performed his good deed for the day—for the week—for months to come; but it was no use. "I promise you," he warned me, "some juicy revelations this evening!"

Oddly enough, the main part of the program progressed without untoward incident. I could see by Ben's expression that he was almost disappointed as the pleasantly innocuous voice repeated with parrot-like precision the unfamiliar names and words. But disaster was to overtake us before the hour was up. The script contained a reference to my Guarnerius violin. At this point, our narrator's nervousness obviously increased. His color heightened, his voice grew tense, he clutched his script. "And, ladies and gentlemen," he said, "this famous violin was made in the year 1735 by the great rival of Strad-ee-vayrius—none other than Joseph—er—*Gonorrheas!*"

Ben and I didn't dare look at each other; we were due to play again in a few seconds. The next piece started with a long sustained note requiring steady control of the bow—a control that was conspicuous by its absence. A convulsion of suppressed laughter traveled the length of my arm, and the bow rippled from frog to tip. Fortunately our announcer was totally unaware of his enormity.

"How did I do?" he asked, at the close of the proceedings.

"Inimitably!" I assured him. "I am only sorry we haven't got it on wax—it ought to be heard again."

"Poor old Guarnerius!" reflected Ben, in an aside. "After a checkered career during his natural life, including prison terms and general insecurity—it's really too much. He doesn't deserve to be disturbed in his grave nearly two hundred years later by being proclaimed a social disease!"

Though we fully expected repercussions from this profanation of the air's purity, it passed completely unnoticed. All that happened was that a young lady who sat in the audience chamber beyond glass partitions, and who came afterwards to present her thanks for the performance, said to us, "But I didn't quite get the name of that famous violin-maker?" Ben pointed to the typed program notes; he didn't trust himself to speak.

There are many occasions on which you do not, or should not, trust yourself to speak. One is that period in the greenroom at the end of a concert, when enthusiastic invasions produce compliments of doubtful meaning. The neophytes who crowd in are glib with phrases they have picked up here and there, and the results are often surprising.

One evening the wife of a college professor approached me fairly bristling with the accolade she was determined to bestow. I had given her, she informed me, an unforgettable evening. She had heard them all—a roster of eminent names tumbling from her lips. "But the fact is, Mr. Spalding, that they are all technique and no soul—whereas you," and she paused for breath, "you are all soul and no technique." Silence was the only possible reception for this astonishing disclosure.

In the city of Worcester, Mass., after a sonata recital with Ossip Gabrilowitsch, I had another entertaining experience. The program consisted of sturdy music: three sonatas by Brahms, Mozart, and Beethoven—cherished examples of a lovely literature. The audience in Worcester was, you felt sure, both familiar with and fond of these works. The applause was of the most excited kind, and the whole atmosphere invited an artist's best efforts. Following the performance there was a small reception which Ossip and I attended. The élite of Worcester's intellectual life was present and, for the most part, the comments were generous and knowing. But there was one lady (the wife of a college professor) whose courage outstripped her discretion. She

[291]

had been deeply moved by the music. "I was so glad," she said, "that you included some French music in the program. . . ." French music? I puzzled, repeating to myself the three obviously Teutonic names. What *was* she talking about?

"Yes," she went on, oblivious of my blank expression; "strange though it may seem to you, Mr. Spalding, I had never heard any of Moh-tsar's delicious music until that adorable Yvonne Printemps introduced him to us last year in New York!"

This jewel was altogether too precious not to share with Ossip. But I knew he would never believe me; he must hear it at first hand. So I called him over and begged the intrepid Egeria to repeat what she had just said. She was only too eager to comply. I saw Ossip's tired eyes open wide; his lips tremble to interrupt with a premature "But—" I nudged him sharply, and he caught himself in time. "Madam," he said, with a courtly bow when the lady had finished, "I shall never forget what you have said to me. You have read into Moh-tsar's music a new, a wholly original, meaning."

Gabrilowitsch had a matchless way of fusing the percussive tone of the piano with a stringed instrument so that at times their racial differences were completely reconciled. Those sonata concerts with him—so abruptly ended by his illness and death—remain among the most delightful memories of my life. And the rehearsals were equally rewarding. When we were preparing for the first series he asked me which I enjoyed more, rehearsals or concerts? There was no catch in the question—he wanted a simple statement of fact. Without pausing to think, I answered quickly, "Rehearsals, of course."

"Capital! So do I. I thought you would. As a matter of fact, I reverse the general pattern: to me a concert is a preparation for the next rehearsal."

When we played together in Buffalo I wanted Gabrilowitsch to meet my old friend Philip Wickser. I knew they would take to each other, not because they were alike in temperament or in technique of living but rather because of a fascinating contrast. It was one of the experiments in human counterpoint that succeed.

Wickser is a lawyer; he had gone through Harvard Law

School with my brother, and we have been warm friends ever since. His mind is essentially pragmatic, realistic, irritatingly logical. His approach to music and to painting, which is original and self-taught, was made by a literary route. He had always been a booklover and an omnivorous reader. By dint of frequent private concerts and careful listening he built up for himself a familiarity with great musical literature—both symphonic and chamber music—always with emphasis on the instrumental field. His love of music is completely unregimented, either by technical training or by ready-made opinions from newspaper criticism. His taste in painting runs to the French ultra-moderns with such aggressive gusto that it baffles conservative Buffalo to understand what he likes to hang on his walls. And some of his most radical excursions in this field must be, I suspect, a little trying to his wife, who regards them with more patience than pleasure. His wine cellar matches his library in distinction, and must be the envy of many a connoisseur.

In sum, this paradoxical figure, compounded of acute mental activity and physical inertia, represents one of the rarest types, a real amateur of the arts. I told Ossip all about him. "By all means," he said, "I want to meet this fellow Wickser. There are all too few of them about."

Accordingly, we three had lunch together on the day of the Buffalo concert. Of late the glory of Mozart had burst upon Phil in its full radiance. This is always a blinding revelation, especially to those lovers of music who have for a time failed to penetrate the superficial crust of the rococo conventions. With his new-found vision, Phil wanted to talk only of Mozart, and wasted no time in steering the conversation to the subject he wanted to probe. As a matter of fact he doesn't probe—he vivisects. Ossip was, of course, delighted; for him, too, Mozart was the supreme master.

"It is in its essence," he said, "the purest expression of music that has ever been. Children get it, profound people get it; but you have to be both profound and simple to really understand it."

"Then you would give Mozart first place?" Phil asked.

"Without a moment's hesitation," replied Ossip.

"And you, Albert?" turning to me.

[293]

Well, I was on a spot, for—though I yield to no one in my admiration of Mozart—the conversation had been altogether too unanimous; the absence of any dissenting opinion made for flat and unseasoned fare, especially for Phil. So I spoke up for Bach. "In musical architecture," I said, "the B minor Mass stands like the Parthenon."

"But even the Parthenon," said Ossip, "has its limitations. Consider this point: Bach is supreme in the world of polyphony, which practically ended with him. He proposes and disposes of a universe that is complete and yet limited. Will you be shocked if I confess to a certain fatigue caused by the very finality of his logic? His contemporary, Handel, though a lesser composer, was in one sense a greater one, for his music has ventilation which is lacking in Bach."

"You mean," I interjected, "that quality which in painting is called space composition?"

"Yes. The musical ideas breathe and have their being more freely."

"Let's get back to Mozart," suggested Phil.

"Above all, Mozart," I went on. "If he had not had the advantage of studying Bach, he would have had to invent him. Part of the wonder of Mozart was that he reinjected polyphonic treatment in an era that was turning its back on it."

That evening the Mozart sonata seemed to outshine its colleagues Brahms and Beethoven, the insistent calls for a repetition of the Rondo outweighing the thunderbolt of the *Kreutzer*. When Phil came back to the greenroom, Ossip chuckled to us both. "Well," he said to Phil, "you see, we won with Mozart!"

Ossip's rather frail body housed a dynamo of energy that drove him forward even after he had had warnings of approaching collapse. In that last year he had the following Herculean tasks: His regular duties as conductor of the Detroit Symphony Orchestra had been expanded to include special performances of opera as well as the subscription concerts; his personal appearances as virtuoso had not diminished—they had increased; and in addition to all this, he had undertaken to perform in a single season seventeen pianoforte concertos—covering almost the entire field of this literature—with the young National Orchestral

Association led by Leon Barzin in New York. This was work to daunt a Goliath, and Ossip was no Goliath; on the contrary, he was a frail David. But there were no limits to his unconquerable spirit, and the phonograph records made in his last season reveal one of the sweetest psalmists who ever sang on the keyboard. His restless quest of perfection had never heard the word "fatigue."

One night, after an arduous sonata concert and long rehearsals, I was ready to relax and call it a day. Not so Ossip. To my dismay I found him propped up in his berth with the gigantic score of *Tristan*. He was to conduct it a few days later, in Detroit. Forgetting his many years' seniority, I talked to him like a Dutch uncle, but to no avail.

"I must work how and when I can. Sleep will come by and by if I concentrate on this," he said, pointing to the score. "It will elude me if I turn off the light now and try counting sheep. No, Albert, it's no use; you can't lead me back to the nursery. But thanks just the same." It was lovable and suicidal at the same time—*how* suicidal, I didn't quite realize at the time.

These Gabrilowitsch stories advance my own narrative by more than a decade—to the middle thirties. But my memory has an anarchistic urge to violate the limitations of precise chronology. Events and people are associated in one chain of thought which defies both geography and the passing of years.

CHAPTER THIRTY-SEVEN

IN 1925 Mary and I digressed from our usual habit of spending the summers in England. The magnet that deflected us was a small stone house hidden away under tall pine trees on the crest of one of the mountainous ridges of the Berkshire Hills in western Massachusetts. It had been built by Charles Freer of Detroit, the railroad magnate whose business successes had been only an apprenticeship to his real vocation—the study and collection of Oriental art, chiefly Chinese. The museum in Washington, D. C., which bears his name is the realization of that mission.

He was born in Kingston, New York, in circumstances bordering on actual poverty. His taste in art had its beginnings in a passionate love of the beauties of Nature. This particular hilltop—then a woody wilderness—had been the goal of many a trek to enjoy the lovely view that takes in the many miles of valley southward. This hill rises abruptly to the west of the town of Great Barrington, and, once you are deep in its forest fastness, it is difficult to believe that the varied activities of three or four thousand people are going on below.

Freer had to go to work at an early age. One of his first jobs on the railroads—which were eventually to make his fortune—was in the modest capacity of brakeman. One of the officials of the line traveling on the same train once noticed that the young employee was engrossed in a book. Whether this was an infraction of the rules, or whether he was prompted by friendly interest, the official stopped and asked Freer what he was reading. The young brakeman looked up (probably jumped up) and said: "It is a book on Whistler—James A. McNeill Whistler." This was, we must remind ourselves, before Whistler was generally known to the American public; but, fortunately, the railroad official happened to have heard of him. "Whistler?" he repeated, surprised to find that the young man's book was not a Nick Carter. "Yes, sir," said Freer, gaining confidence. "We are going to hear more and more of this artist as time goes on. With the first money I can save, I am going to buy one of his etchings."

It would be pleasant to think that this early love of art supplied the impetus for Freer's economic achievements. Perhaps it did; the possibility is so apt, poetically, that it should at least be suggested.

Towards the end of his life Freer returned to the Berkshire hilltop of his boyhood dreams. He was then badly crippled by an illness that was soon to prove fatal. He bought some land on the crest of the hill and had plans drawn for a house of informal design. The stone for its construction was quarried from the ground it was to stand on; the hill being, in reality, a moraine left from the last glacial period.

Freer never lived to enjoy this home; he died when it was barely completed. It was left to his assistant and collaborator in his great collection, Katherine Rhoades, who is a warm friend of ours, and it was from her that we rented and eventually bought the house. After we saw it we never wanted to live anywhere else.

The house presents a modest appearance but has rooms of generous proportions. Though conveniently near the town, it feels remote from everything but Nature. Its greatest glory is its array of majestic pine trees, carefully stripped of their lower branches and approaching the sky before spreading their canopy of green shade. It is a place around which the circle of contentment has been drawn.

We found that most of our neighboring friends and acquaintances lived about eight miles to the north of us, in Stockbridge. They rather raised their eyebrows at the little industrial town of Great Barrington, and we were often chided on our imprudent choice. Midway between the two towns there is a miniature Alpine pass flanked by a rocky elevation called Monument

Mountain; Alexander Sedgwick called this "The Great Divide." Why had we put ourselves beyond the Divide? We patiently explained over and over again that it was the attraction of a particular site, a particular house, that had drawn us, rather than the choice of an élite community.

One day at luncheon I found myself next to a charming lady who militantly posed this question: "And just what prompted you, Mr. Spalding, to settle in Great Barrington?"

Having carelessly failed to catch the lady's name, I rashly replied: "I'm not sure. . . . Perhaps merely to avoid Stockbridge!"

The temperature dropped suddenly, though I then had no idea why. But when I told Mary of this passage of arms—"And who," she demanded, torn between amusement and horror, "*who* did you think was talking to you?"

I didn't know. Who?

"Only a member of the Inner Circle of Stockbridge—Mrs. Sedgwick herself! Really, you *are* impossible!"

In time, owing to Mary's unfailing tact and Sedgwick magnanimity, we succeeded in living it down. We may have been granted, too, some of that special indulgence accorded to people who live in what I call the "Hoboken of the Berkshires."

Life in this pleasant, rolling countryside moves at a more leisurely pace than prevails in most of our other vacation areas. We used almost daily to round off the afternoon with some tennis. I was so bold, at about that time, as to enter my name in the annual club tournament. Now my tennis is respectable for a fiddler, though hardly of a quality to carry me far. But the participants that year were all only moderately good, and I had the luck to push through to the finals. At this point I met the previous year's holder, who played a soft but irritatingly steady game. He quickly had me facing defeat. The score was one set and five games to two in his favor. Perhaps a little too sure of his victory, my opponent unconsciously relaxed a little; at the same time I lashed out with the sort of shots that come off only occasionally. Luck was with me, however, and those shots found the lines and the corners, where formerly they had been going wild. Much to my surprise, I won the match.

This minor triumph had an amusing sequel. The win was,

apparently, a popular one, particularly with Joyce, the club steward. And he saw to it the following season that I had one of the best lockers, and busied himself as an unexpected press-agent on my behalf. One day I heard him being interviewed over the telephone by the local correspondent of the *New York Times*. After covering the golfing news, he conveyed this amazing intelligence: "Mr. Spalding has just come in from the tennis courts; he is our best player!" (A gross exaggeration; this year there were any number of better players.) "Yes, the name is S-P-A-L-D-I-N-G. . . . Yes—Mr. *Albert* Spalding. . . . Yes—I believe he does play the violin, too. . . ."

When I told Bill Tilden this story he could not resist using it—probably elaborating it. As it got retold, my victory gained in size appallingly and I acquired an altogether unjustified reputation for tennis prowess. When ultimately it reached *Time Magazine,* I was astonished to learn that I was the New England champion! It is quite impossible to stem this kind of avalanche. Denials are of no use; they merely create firmer belief.

The summers came always too swiftly to a close. Once the days begin to shorten, time seems to telescope itself, and before you know it another concert season is at hand.

CHAPTER THIRTY-EIGHT

THE eight or nine calendar months devoted to concertizing followed an almost unchanging pattern during the nineteen-twenties—three to four months in Europe, and four to five months in the United States. A good press agent must find me peculiarly disappointing, because I do not confine myself to a record of triumphs in capital cities. Some of my most cherished memories find their way to an humble locality among poor people who live contented but unheralded lives. An experience rich in human values can often be found in a village—and sought in vain in a metropolis.

Arriving one morning at the little wayside station of Heide in Schleswig-Holstein, I found Herr Biel awaiting me on the platform. Biel was a merchant of sorts, purveying sporting goods as a livelihood, but his real vocation was music. He was the moving spirit in the local society that had engaged me, and in addition he was a spectacle to behold: trousers too tight for the legs they enclosed, a coat straining its buttons to meet amidship, and above it all a collar that choked you to look at. From it you could not say that his head emerged—rather, it spread out like an estuary from a river in flood. The neck descended in layers over the constriction of that collar. But Herr Biel's reddened face oozed kindly enthusiasm and concern. How was I? How were the concerts going? How was the Gnädige? (He had never met the Gnädige, but no matter.) And how was Herr Benoist? Benoist was with me to answer for himself and did so quite properly. His German is as fluent as mine is halting. I quickly saw that Herr Biel was nervous. What was it? I was soon to know.

"And how," I asked, as we were driving to the hotel, "did you like the program?" At once I knew that I had touched on the source of his nervousness.

"*Aber,* Herr Spalding, I hardly know how to tell you—such presumption—we have changed the program."

"Changed the program?" I echoed.

"That is," continued Biel, becoming, if possible, even redder in the face, "we have *added* to it."

"Added to it?" I echoed again, apparently able to converse only in borrowed terms. "But it is already such a long program."

"Ah," said Biel, "but you forget what a long time we have to wait until we can hear you."

This was said so ingenuously that I was touched, even if not convinced, and smilingly pointed out that there were major works of Handel, Brahms, and Schubert, and the Franck sonata —pretty substantial fare for one evening.

"What," I asked, "did you think of adding?" His hesitation made me go on, "Come, come, don't be nervous! Tell me!" Then it came.

"The *Chaconne* of Bach."

I was about to answer *"Ausgeschlossen"* ("Out of the question"), but I was afraid of producing apoplexy in the anxious little man. After a dismayed pause, I finally consented.

His joy brought on muscular reactions which can hardly be described. Have you ever noticed the way some dogs, notably English bulldogs, not content with tail-wagging, wiggle everything from the chest down? So Herr Biel wiggled. And for the first time since we had met, he perched a too-small bowler on the top of his bald scalp. I thought it opportune, in order to ease the situation, to tell him of the anecdote of Ysaÿe playing many years ago in one of our smaller towns. The Bach *Chaconne* figured on the program. Ysaÿe was in fine form, the concert went splendidly, a large audience had been enthralled, and a well-earned supper was looked forward to with zest. Among the enthusiasts who had flocked to thank and congratulate him was a little man whose appreciation was qualified by deep disappointment, for a late train (he had come many miles to attend the concert) had made him miss the early part of the program, and, above all, the *Chaconne* which he had longed all his life to hear. Ysaÿe was astounded, interested.

"You have never heard the *Chaconne!*" he said.

"No, Master, never."

"And you have traveled how far to hear it?"

"Two hundred miles."

"Very well," said Ysaÿe, forgetting hunger and supper, "come with me. I shall play Bach's *Chaconne* in my hotel room for you alone."

If you had ever seen Ysaÿe eat his supper—especially after a concert—you would recognize what this meant. The little stranger from two hundred miles away couldn't possibly have realized what a miracle was being promised for his special benefit. Ysaÿe, when he told me the story, said that he was strangely moved, and that in this unique performance, played to a solitary person whom he had never seen before and was never to see again, he poured out his whole heart. "It was," he said, "far better than I had played it a couple of hours before."

"*Tiens,*" he added, "*j'avais même oublié que j'avais faim. Et, mon petit* [in an expansive mood he sometimes used to call me his little one], *je t'assure que j'avais rudement faim.*"

"I wish I had been there," I told him. "It must have been unforgettably beautiful."

"Yes," said Ysaÿe, "it was beautiful. But do you know what that sacred pig said to me when I finished?" I couldn't imagine. "That little species of a vegetable who had cheated me out of my supper—I had ordered a good one, too, and even if it had been kept, it was probably cold by then—that camel whose mother was a monkey merely asked me if *that* was the *Chaconne* of Bach?

"I told him it was indeed. I was too astonished to say more. 'Well,' said that hangman, that assassin of all his ancestors, 'I don't think much of it!' And for that," concluded Ysaÿe, "for that I had sacrificed my beautiful supper."

Biel was very sober, much too sober, when I had finished the story. I had expended a good deal of energy in translating it into my lame German, stumbling now and then and being assisted by a word here and there from Benoist. Still it had, I thought, its humorous side, and I wanted at least the polite rejoinder of a laugh, even if it was a hollow one. Only the gravity of the sacrilege, however, had struck Biel.

"I can assure you," he said, the tone of his voice suddenly taking clerical orders, "that such a thing could never occur to you or Bach in Heide."

I heard Benoist muttering something extremely Rabelaisian, cloaking it in French which, it was to be hoped, Biel could neither hear nor understand.

There is a kind of protocol which governs the entire day of an engagement in one of these small provincial cities. We are installed in the somewhat primitive hotel, immaculately clean, a trifle meager in heating capacity, and with a menacing frugality that makes Benoist all but snort when I politely assure the catering committee, *Alles in bester Ordnung.*" Ben, whose sybaritic tastes and Falstaffian philosophy have gained him a worldwide reputation, and who has an infallible eye for detecting any threat to comfort, views my amenities with deep distrust. He has already appraised the rooms and his verdict is apparent although as yet unspoken. Already he is shivering at the prospect of a morning pilgrimage through drafty halls to the coeducational bathroom, to say nothing of the winding corridors that lead to that chamber of convenience (always indicated in Europe by a double zero). And the beds— Oh, the beds! How to describe them? Imagine a widened drinking trough brought in from the public square where from time immemorial it has quenched the thirst of local horses. Strips of sagging tape serve as the bedsprings. Over this a thin matting (they call it a mattress, God forgive them) indents itself until it resembles a discouraged waffle. Does it sag in the middle? No, it doesn't sag—it toboggans! It is topped, of course, by the inevitable feather monstrosity, the pride of Mittel-Europa. This forbidding luxury always contrives to sweat the torso while the extremities freeze.

The little placard over the bell says, as it always does, ring once for the waiter, twice for the chambermaid, and three times for the valet. In the Heide hotel all three roles are assumed by one individual, the wide-eyed Zimmer Mädchen with flaxen, almost albino, hair braided and wound tightly round her head. She comes running in answer to Benoist's insistent ringing. Her perpetual expression of astonishment becomes, if anything, more bewildered when he explains that we want woolen blankets.

"Ach! The Herrschaften don't like feathers?" She can hardly believe it.

"No," insists Ben, firmly, "and what is more, we wish the bedding to be carefully tucked in."

The girl is by now completely mystified and Benoist proceeds to give her a lesson in what he considers proper bed-making. By this time her resistance is completely worn down and, quite against all her instincts and principles, she agrees to humor the strange barbarians.

We descend for the midday meal presided over by the Bürgermeister. The musical element of the town is fully represented. *Gemütlichkeit* receives something of a jolt when we do not take Schnapps; this is an essential part of the ritual, and our refusal acts as a snag to the preliminary toasts which were carefully prepared. We mitigate the offense by explaining that we never indulge in any alcohol before a concert. Then, too, our hosts reflect, do they not come from that strange land of Prohibition? So the atmosphere of cordiality returns. We are invited to express our admiration for the wonders of the Kiel Canal, over which we have traveled; for the industrious shipbuilding we have observed; for that new greyhound of the sea, the *Bremen,* on which we presumably made the ocean crossing. Here, as a matter of fact, we were embarrassed to explain that sailing dates had deprived us of that privilege, a misfortune we hoped soon to repair, and a chorus of *"Ach! Schade,"* commiserated with us.

The Bürgermeister, an amiable and well-informed man, exerted himself with both food and conversation. He had had an excellent musical training in his youth and no one could help realizing how much of his leisure was given to this form of art. Weekly meetings at his house of a string quartet in which he participated. . . . Also, besides his official duties, he wrote the weekly musical and dramatic reviews for the local paper. One could see that the people of Heide had versatile talents. Witness the Bürgermeister! Witness the chambermaid!

There were many polite questions about music in America. About our conservatories . . . were they, indeed, good? They were? So much the better! Was chamber music played? It was? How gratifying! And our orchestras. Their capabilities had been spoken of. Were they really so fine? How astonishing! Of course, with the advantage of the importation of German Kapellmeisters and also much of the orchestra personnel from middle Europe. . . . I found myself rather tactlessly murmuring something about the promising talents of certain gentlemen with strangely un-Teutonic names—Toscanini, Koussevitzky, Monteux, and Mengelberg—and saying that for wood winds the French were— But I checked myself in time and covered my retreat with more welcome remarks regarding Furtwängler, Muck, the Damrosches, and Theodore Thomas. The road to heresy had happily been avoided.

An afternoon pilgrimage, chiefly on foot, had been planned, but I pleaded for some hours of rest and practice. (The *Chaconne* was staring me in the face and I hadn't played it in some months.) Reluctantly the Mahlzeits are said and we are wished a "gute Ruhe" until the evening.

"There is," I remark to Benoist when they have gone, "a great deal of this that is tiresome, but also a great deal of rewarding sweetness in their spontaneous reaction to music."

"There is," he agreed. "Still, I do wish that the women wouldn't all wear their corsets upside down. In no other way could they possibly achieve such figures."

"And," I continued, "not a man over thirty who hasn't a bald head. As a matter of fact, their heads are not merely bald, they're positively lacquered."

Ben, whose fast-disappearing hair is a source of painful concern to his vanity, is at once on the defensive and points out the advantages of a naked dome.

"Therein," he cites, "be wisdom, judgment, and, above all, conclusive evidence that one's virility has had industrious and fruitful employment!"

[305]

Decidedly, it is time for me to be ashamed of my generous crop of hair.

I shouldn't have worried about the length of the program. In fact, a complete reversal of the musician's general preoccupation about too long a program is in order in Germany, especially in the small towns. Herr Biel was quite right in adding the *Chaconne,* and I cannot recall having played it with more enjoyment and more absorption than I did that evening. It would be interesting to appraise the contribution an audience makes to a performance. There is no denying that it is considerable. I felt it very deeply in the playing of the *Chaconne* that evening and it prompted the inclusion of certain effects that I have never forgotten, and which I continue to use in many a more important center. After the theme, the many minor variations, and the resolution to the first wonderful variation in D major, I have always been hypnotized by a wish that at this moment I could exchange my violin for Bach's favorite instrument, the organ. Here the music has weaved its way through the majestic theme and the pattern of a design, now intricate, now dramatic, to the doors of a cathedral. It had always seemed to me that no change of bow, however legato, no instrument, in fact, except the organ, could give this phrase just the note of sustained repose that it demands. That evening in Heide I had the illusion that my violin was, in effect, an organ. Such is the power of suggestion that, as I felt the doors of the church slowly open, I could all but smell the incense burning, and see the light dimmed but glowing with the glory of the old stained glass. I have never since played or heard this phrase without something of this picture returning. And for it, I bow my grateful acknowledgment to the deep and almost religious concentration of that audience in the modest little town of Heide.

CHAPTER THIRTY-NINE

Iₙ rehearsing and restudying
one's old repertoire, it is always essential to have plenty of new
material at hand. The preparation of a new work is not only
important in itself; it freshens one's survey of well-worn works.
And the presentation for the first time of a concerto or sonata
never fails to be an adventure. Quite a respectable array of such
adventures has marked my calendar with red-letter days. Some
performances fall short of one's hopes; but the work lavished on
them is never less than rewarding.

To one of these first performances I owe not only a delightful
friendship, but also my first introduction to Budapest and Hungary. It was not a world première, for the piece had been performed in Europe; but for the United States it was the première
of Dohnányi's Concerto.

This fascinating Hungarian musician won his spurs not only
as pianist and conductor, but also as composer. His creative work
is rather in the conventional post-romantic pattern, the struc-
tural treatment offering more than an occasional reminder that
Dohnányi is a disciple of Brahms, whom years ago he knew and
revered. But it has, besides, a personal note altogether his own.
The Violin Concerto is not a pathfinder in unknown moods; it
follows trails already blazed. But it is lovely music, admirably
written for the instrument and shrewdly scored. I had already
played it in Boston and Chicago, and performances were scheduled for New York and Brooklyn with the New York Symphony
under Walter Damrosch.

Dohnányi, who had for many years been absent from the

American concert stage, was due to make his pianistic reappearance. When he arrived in New York he learned that I was to play his concerto the following week. Apparently he was delighted, for he lost no time in looking me up. "Would it be agreeable to you and to Damrosch," he asked, "if I were to conduct the first playing in New York?"

I was, of course, enchanted, and so was Damrosch. To have the composer wielding the baton always adds luster to a performance. But the composer is not always the best interpreter of his own works. I found Dohnányi the pianist, and Dohnányi the composer, far superior to Dohnányi the conductor. He had little of the top-sergeant in his make-up and did not impose on the orchestra the exemplary discipline he imposed on his own fingers or his own writing. The concerto fared better in Boston and in Chicago than in New York. When, in Brooklyn, Damrosch resumed the reins, the driving became at once smoother, the scoring more transparent, and the rhythms less sluggish.

A few evenings later, the Erno Dohnányis came to our apartment for an evening of chamber music. He had a new quintet for piano and strings that we were anxious to hear and play. This lovely work—one of his finest creations—was inspiring to know. Not less inspiring was its composer at the piano; there, he was at his unsurpassable best—a pianist's pianist, a musician's musician!

Mrs. Dohnányi had been, I was told, an actress of distinction, greatly acclaimed on the Viennese stage. It was patent that she felt no regrets for her career. Her eyes were fixed on her husband; quite clearly, she adored him.

Dohnányi said to me: "You have never played in my country?"

This was true, and it was an omission I was anxious to repair at the first opportunity. Aptly enough, as I told him, plans were under way to include Budapest in my following season's tour of the Continent.

"Excellent," said Dohnányi, "but be sure to let me know when it is to be. I want to lend a hand in your first Hungarian concerts."

This was no less than a royal summons; I did not need to

learn from him that he occupied the throne in the Magyar capital's music.

A fiddler's first visit to Budapest is like a Moslem's first visit to Mecca. You suspect that the porter who trundles your bags at the station, the taxi-driver who contravenes every law of safety, and even the newsboy at the street corner, are merely marking time in these pursuits—that when his day's chores are over he will turn to his real love, the violin, and shame many a professional with his skill.

Budapest, the proud twin city that straddles the Danube, is not beautiful. Its flamboyant and pretentious architecture screams imperfections, and you wonder why you like the city so much. But, before you know it, you find yourself joining in the chorus of indiscriminate praise. Its position is superb. The hills and promontories rise above it and sweep down to the broad river— to the Danube which is not "blue" in spite of the Strauss waltz. It is brown, and it flows into a sea that is called Black but is reportedly green.

The Hungarians are generally good-looking. Dark-haired and fair-skinned, they do not look Latin, or Teuton, or Slav. They constitute an alien island of humanity amid the three distinct types of Europeans, and you marvel at the necromancy of ancient migrations that produced this phenomenon. The five-hour trip from Vienna is not merely the crossing of a border—one may cross continents and traverse oceans without finding its parallel.

In Budapest we had rooms at the Ungarica Hotel overlooking the river. The disproportionately high ceilings made us feel that we ought to be mounted on stilts. We found that we were not strangers here. Dohnányi's favorable report had been spread far and wide, and his good word was invaluable to us.

The concert manager, Barczy, who was also head of the well-known publishing house of Röszavolgy, called on us immediately. Tall and spare, he had a face as shriveled as a dried prune; its corrugations must have defied his razor's best efforts. But when it relaxed in a smile, his face was a study in ugly amiability. He spoke in English—haltingly, and with engaging disregard of literal meanings. Each attempt on our part to shift to German was politely but firmly ignored; English was to be our medium of communication. Barczy outlined the concert schedule in Budapest and in province towns.

"With Dohnányi play, and you play, there will be out-of-house sold. He say you play good! They have in him belief. He no say where not so! Jenö Hubay he come to all concerts. You know Hubay?" Not personally. "Pity it not summer. Summer not good for concerts, but fine for Americans!" We looked puzzled. "In summer, we know, all Americans eat mice. Only in Hungary you get good mice. You like, no?"

Mary was the first to regain her wits, and with her best smile she agreed that we were great eaters of *maize*. "Only we call it 'corn' in America," she explained.

But Barczy clung to his own term. "Yes," he said, "beautiful mice in Hungary. You come again in summer, for to eat, not to play!"

Food was such an agreeable subject that we continued the discussion. Mary grew quite lyrical about the spicy, wine-flavored apples comparable only to our finest northern New York State brands. She has a voracious appetite for fruit, which had been severely rationed during our recent journeys in Scandinavia and Germany, and our arrival in Austria and Hungary had set her off on an apple debauch; she ate apples in any and every form. It was plain that Barczy was delighted with her. "You come to dinner tonight? Mrs. Barczy—she cook apples. Also some friends."

Despite the sinister implication, we agreed. When we came to dress for dinner, it was not in evening clothes. Throughout Central Europe, neither "black tie" nor "white tie" seems to find favor for evening events. I have never been able to discover why the afternoon cutaway is considered more comfortable; probably it is chiefly a matter of time-honored custom.

The Barczys' apartment was somber, with its dark, heavy woodwork, its funereally curtained windows, its massive and overcrowded furniture. No light was permitted to invade this interior—no color—not even (you suspected) any ventilation. Amid these gloomy surroundings the smooth, blonde placidity of Mrs. Barczy seemed oddly out of place. At first glance she

appeared years younger than her husband. You could scarcely believe that the years which had so corrugated his face could have slipped by without marring the eggshell smoothness of hers. That careful smile never expanded beyond a Mona-Lisa-like simper; it was clear that she had isolationist views on disturbing emotions. She greeted us with distant courtesy in a monotonous, high-pitched voice muted against stridency; you were sure that its tepidity would endure forever. Introductions followed. There were younger people who looked older, and older people who had once been younger; Mrs. Barczy alone was timeless.

Among the guests was a priest, a certain Father Damiene, an interesting and puzzling person. It was hard to tell just where his manifold activities began and ended. He represented the Vatican—not quite a Legate, nor yet a Nuncio, but some sort of spokesman for the Holy See. He composed popular tunes from time to time; he was also connected with the Röszavolgy firm, and took part in that firm's concert management. His tastes were as catholic as his religion, his conversation spiced with Rabelaisian touches, and his puckish tolerance of human frailties conflicted disconcertingly with his cloth. His fund of anecdotes was inexhaustible. You had no doubt that he shared his fellow countrymen's reverence for Dohnányi the musician; but you felt also that for the man himself he had a special affection, because of the somewhat peculiar status of the present Dohnányi marriage.

"Both the Dohnányis," he explained, "have been married before. Both former unions resulted in children. Mrs. Dohnányi, if you will remember, was the wife of the famous violinist Hubermann."

Yes, we had heard that.

"But the tender passion is no respecter of laws, conventions, or sacraments." The old eyes twinkled. "Of course, since they were all Catholics, there could be no question of divorce."

"What, then, was the solution?" asked Mary.

"Ah, gracious lady, it is a little difficult—a little complicated—to explain; but I will try. Until the close of the war the situation had, certainly, its irregularities. Mrs. Dohnányi the First had been for some time (together with her children) living apart

[311]

from her husband, making her home in Berlin. She would not have considered divorcing him; nor would he, a true son of the Church, have thought of suggesting it. Frau Hubermann, likewise, was no longer living with her husband. It is to be hoped that the two friends did not find life too lonely. You know that at the end of the war we endured a Hundred Days' revolution— a hundred days of terror and disorder, a hundred days of Bela Kun."

Father Damiene paused for a moment. He drew out a scarlet handkerchief and trumpeted an unimpeachable B flat.

"It is consoling to reflect that during that nightmare one couple at least were enabled to reach happiness. For divorce and remarriage immediately became attainable commodities; the dual transaction took less than twenty-four hours. And Dohnányi and Frau Hubermann hastened to avail themselves. . . ."

"But," protested Mary, "was it recognized? When the Hundred Days had passed and law and order returned—and with them the authority of the Catholic Church—what then?"

"It *was* a dilemma," admitted Father Damiene; "but a dilemma has never baffled the Universal Church. Infallibility overcomes it, in one way or another."

"And how," persisted Mary, curiously, "did it overcome this one?"

The priest was pleased with his audience. "The Church," he said, "was faced with an accomplished fact. Certainly it could not countenance flagrant sin; nor could it tolerate divorce. It decided that this unhallowed union must be solemnized in the Cathedral. And this was done."

"And the former marriages were annulled?"

"No, indeed! That would have been impossible; you see, there had been children. But another formula was found." Father Damiene paused again. "Erno Dohnányi was married, *as a bachelor,* to Frau Hubermann, *as a Jungfrau.* It was all quite satisfactory!"

The Dohnányis lived in a pleasant villa a few kilometers outside the city. We had lunch with them there the following day, and he and I spent the afternoon rehearsing the sonatas to be played at my first performance in Budapest. I had thought to include Dohnányi's delightful sonata, but he insisted on keeping the first program for Beethoven, Brahms, and Franck. A lesser musician would have been less modest.

Dohnányi's playing had a rapturous quality of improvisation, whether he addressed himself to old or to new compositions. Often it was technically imperfect, for he now devoted little time to practicing. But even the occasional false notes contributed to the effect of careless grace, and his unfailing rhythm and musicianship were always a joy. He apologized for the waywardness of his fingers and promised to discipline them in time for the following night's concert. I warned him that I should probably dislike better playing. Obviously, however, he did devote himself to some pianistic calisthenics the next day, for that night his performance more nearly approached the virtuoso level.

The concert hall was crowded. Only those who have experienced it can realize fully what a first appearance in Budapest means to an artist. Other congregations applaud as warmly, shout as vociferously; but here there is a quality of concentration, of absorption, of intensity, that provides an invisible column of strength. It is theirs to give, and yours to take. You do not ask why it is so; you merely accept it. And instinctively you know that here is a moment that justifies the interminable effort of artistic endeavor.

The concerts followed in rapid succession. The orchestral appearance (at which I played the Brahms concerto) and my own recital happily confirmed the début. Characteristically, a certain part of the public insisted that my temperament owed much to my Magyar blood. In vain I tried to discover for myself some Hungarian ancestor; it seemed churlish not to be able to satisfy a public so warm!

CHAPTER FORTY

ONE of the provincial towns to which the concert tour was to take us was Kecskemet, some hundred-odd kilometers south of Budapest. Barczy planned that we should travel by automobile, with Father Damiene as our special guide and mentor. The car was an open Mercedes of indefinite vintage. The road was rough, the car's springs inelastic; but the trip was interesting. The long Hungarian plains slope southward from the Austrian Alps on the northwest, and from the Carpathians on the northeast. The scenery would have an agrarian monotony but for the white plaster villages that punctuate the landscape. The farm buildings were low—not more than one or two stories—and served admirably as a bleached background for the dark beauty of the peasantry. Evident in these small rural communities was an intimately leveling process between man and beast. The cow, the goat, the pig, the poultry, paraded the common courtyard as though they owned it. From village to village, as far as the eye could see, stretched the endless and fertile plains. Wheat, barley, and corn colored the broad expanse with wide brush-strokes of green and russet. You felt very close to the soil here.

Breaking the silence, Father Damiene said, "It is a primitive life, but not a hungry one."

It was true. And, you reflected, there was probably—in these tiny rural units—far less concern over the loss of Transylvania to Rumania than one found in the metropolitan center. Insufficient rainfall would be a more immediate, a more pressing, calamity. When I suggested this, Father Damiene concurred.

"You cannot expect peasants," he said, "to apprehend the academic niceties of 'self-determination' on a national scale. The horizon of their world is extremely limited—limited, indeed, to the soil on which they live, on which they work."

"Yet they are called upon to fight and die for another world—for a world beyond," I said.

"Oh, that!" The priest shrugged his clerical shoulders. Evidently he accepted many things with a tolerant skepticism. "Politicians decide; the people must abide. In this particular case Transylvania, which was formerly part of Hungary, contained a large Rumanian minority. That province now belongs to Rumania. In spite of a certain amount of repatriation—forcible repatriation, I must say—it now contains a large Hungarian minority, chafing under their new rulers. The problem has not been solved; it has merely been shifted."

"It is certainly a burning question in Budapest—not to be escaped."

"Well," sighed the priest, "the new map of Europe was easy to trace on paper, but it has produced a good many burning questions. Perhaps the Transylvanian one has the fiercest flame. But for the peasants, at least, the heat of the sun holds more potentialities for good or evil than the political furnaces of city and industrial life."

We were approaching Kecskemet, picturesquely situated on the Tisza River which, complementing its western neighbor the Danube, finally merges its tributary waters with that noble stream. As though in deference to the Hungarian plateau, which is the granary of Central Europe, the two arteries first run from north to south; then, having fulfilled their mission, they join hands and turn abruptly eastward for the plunge into the Black Sea.

Kecskemet was a quaint town. Unpretentious buildings, mostly of plaster, herded themselves together with a comfortable disregard for unity of design. A child might easily build a miniature counterpart with blocks. The place was not beautiful, but it had a naïve freshness that was altogether engaging. As we entered its rather narrow streets I noticed that the entire city was decked with flags. Besides the national emblems, I saw the Stars and Stripes prominently displayed.

"All in your honor!" announced Father Damiene, pausing to relish our surprise before going on to explain. "Today happens to be the birthday of the Hungarian patriot Kossuth who, as you know, owed his liberation in 1851 to an American man-of-war. In welcoming a great violinist, the town of Kecskemet has decided to make it a double feast!"

It was touching, it was naïve; it seemed to suit the occasion.

"Where is the concert to be?" I asked.

"In the large hall of the Calvinist College. It is a very nice hall. Most of the concerts are given there."

I looked at him in surprise. A Protestant island in this Catholic sea? Father Damiene nodded.

"But," I suddenly recalled, "you yourself have kindly offered to turn pages for Mr. Benoist. Were you aware that the concert was to be in heretical surroundings?"

The Vatican's representative was apparently undisturbed. "And why not?" he parried calmly.

The remainder of the afternoon was filled with arduous duties. It was, I thought, a doubtful advantage for an artist to be so signally honored. A large reception was held at the Town Hall, where we were welcomed by the local dignitaries. The wife of the Prefect was a lovely young woman—a blonde, which is rare among the Magyars. She spoke excellent English and was, I learned, the daughter of Hungary's Regent, Admiral Horthy.

"In this Kingdom without a King," I said to her, "it is really your father who is monarch."

She smiled, neither an acquiescence nor yet a denial. The Prefect's wife was discreet. "Hungary," she said, "has learned to do without so many things. For the time being, at least, a vacant throne is not too great a problem."

Many toasts were proposed in the famous Tokay wine of Hungary, as well as in a still more fiery liquid, product of the province, a heady, potent apricot brandy. At last Father Damiene rescued us.

"Can we go to the hotel to change?" I asked.

But this, it appeared, would not do; Kecskemet hospitality

would not tolerate it. Instead, we were next driven to a private house, where a large family greeted us as though we were old friends. Mary was embraced by at least four generations. More liquor was pressed upon us, but we summoned the necessary firmness to refuse it. A room had been set aside for us—vacated, I felt sure, with real inconvenience by this overlarge household; one longed for the impersonal convenience of even the simplest inn.

Mary retired first, promising that the freshening-up process would be dispatched with military speed. She was as good as her word. But when she emerged her eyes danced with suppressed laughter.

"Is there running water?" I whispered, for both Benoist and I had to shave.

There was, she assured me grimly, running water—both hot and cold. "But it runs on two legs; it is darkly feminine; it neither knocks at the door nor hesitates to enter. But it smiles— and that helps!"

"How about . . ." I was going to probe other mysteries, but Mary clairvoyantly anticipated my question.

"You will find it all there. Every conceivable gadget for 'sanitation.' Only—the water runs by foot. No pipes. All quite feudal. But pocket your embarrassment and remember that we did not come to Kecskemet to be pampered with Ritz luxury. The 'running water' will not notice you; she is used to it. Anyway, you and Benoist have the better of the bargain."

I couldn't quite see how.

"At least," she went on, "you can take your time shaving and dressing, while *I* have to be polite to four generations downstairs. I can see already the family photograph albums. . . ."

The problem proved less formidable than Mary had threatened. The "running water" came and went, as she had predicted; but in deference to decency there was a knock on the door. We had barricaded it with a chair while making a lightning change of trousers. For relief of another sort, Benoist and I took turns standing sentinel. The experience was not without its excitement, and Ben aired to the full his vocabulary of one-syllable French words.

[317]

The Calvinist hall was gaily decked with Hungarian and American flags. In this sanctuary of the sternest of faiths we found the most un-Protestant audience you could imagine. The author of the doctrine of predestination would have been horrified by the profane scene. For here was playing on the fiddle—instrument of the Devil; dresses in gay colors—unbridled temptation to the eye; shameless young women in evening dress displaying beauties not good for man to look upon; vociferous enthusiasm, an affront to sobriety. And above all, prominently seated on the podium, a representative of that Babylonian woman the Church of Rome. Damnation. . . .

But the concert was exciting, Father Damiene complacent. Our enthusiastic welcome of Lajos Kossuth to America in 1852 was being returned with compound interest. When it was all over we were all both hungry and tired, and the long ride back to Budapest was still ahead. Mary was more tired than hungry; Father Damiene, more hungry than tired. Father Damiene's claims prevailed. He directed the driver to an eating place dear to his palate. It was less than a restaurant, but more than a lunch counter. The outer room, ill lighted, disclosed a scene which only Toulouse-Lautrec could have painted. It was crowded with dim figures who were neither eating nor drinking, but stood or squatted in a circle in the middle of the room. Drawing nearer, we saw that a cock-fight was in progress, and we hastily made for an inner room where there was less drama. Here we enjoyed an unhurried Hungarian supper of heavy dishes.

And so at length to our midnight journey. Under his arm Father Damiene carried a bulky package holding some bottles of the famous apricot brandy. It was, he explained, a parting present from this grateful town. I eyed this largesse doubtfully. With frontiers to cross, I had been trying to reduce baggage to a minimum and I had no wish to burden myself with a miniature cellar. Would Father Damiene, perhaps, be so good as to accept custodianship of this gift? Permanent custodianship. Father Damiene would; indeed, it was evident that he had expected just that.

A farewell lunch the following day with the Dohnányis was enlivened with the stories of our adventures at Kecskemet.

"Did you not know," said Dohnányi, "that Kossuth was a Calvinist? At least, he had his education at a Calvinist college. It was all most appropriate. Appropriate, too, that you should celebrate the day with the local apricot brandy."

"But a little trying," I reminded him, "as a preparation for concert work."

"No more trying than one of your American cocktails, and far less injurious to the stomach!"

Reluctant good-bys were said. We made plans for a return visit. From the long windows of the Ungarica Hotel, Budapest suddenly assumed that beauty for which it is unwarrantedly famed. But there is no loveliness like that of a plain woman who is suddenly transfigured; it has an exciting element unknown to the static calm of classic good looks. All at once you find irregular features smiling themselves into your heart. In such fashion, on that day, smiled Budapest. It would have been unbearable to tear ourselves away with no prospect of a return.

On the piano in our hotel room stood the open score of the Beethoven concerto. Dohnányi noticed it. "Where and when are you playing it?" he asked.

"In Hamburg, at the Beethoven Festival."

Dohnányi's eyes glistened. "And with Muck?"

"Yes, with Muck. It is always an experience."

"Ah, Muck. . . ." His voice trailed off. His thoughts were far away.

INDEX

[321]

[322]

Spalding, Albert (Cont.)
first visit to Holland, 102-108;
later visits, 109-14; Berlin concert, 115-16; first trip to Russia,
117-45; to Finland, 146-52; return to St. Petersburg and
friendship with Pugno, 153-
60; concerts in other Russian
cities, 162-69; concerts in Norway, 170-79; in Denmark, 179-
94; in Finland again, 195-97;
Russia again, 198-204
in Florence at outbreak of First
World War, 205-206; and in
U. S., 206-207; concerts
throughout U. S. (1914-17),
208-209; on our entry into
War, enlists, 210-12; begins association with LaGuardia, 213-
15; embarks for overseas service, 215-16; on the *Carmania,*
217-22; in Paris, 222-24; first
flight, 227-28; transferred to
Italy, 231-32; trains under La-
Guardia, 232-33; to Paris to
plan joint trip to Spain, 233-
37; in Barcelona for supplies,
238-44
in Rome, 246-47; dines at Padua
with the King, 247-52; depu-
tizes for LaGuardia in making
speeches, 254-55; trained as
flight observer, 256-57; demobilized, 257
concerts in Italy, 258; return to
U. S., and marriage, 258-59;
concert tour of U. S. begins,
258-65; in California, 266-69;
to Europe with N. Y. Sym-
phony Orchestra, 270-78; in
Paris, 270-72; Riviera, 273-74;
Genoa, 274-75; Rome, 276-77;
summer in England, 279-85;
musical evenings in N. Y. C.
apartment, 288; making phono-

Spalding, Albert (Cont.)
graph records, 289; broadcast
recitals, 289-90
buys house at Great Barrington,
296-98; earns reputation as tennis star, 298-99; reminiscences
of Heide, 300-306; trip to Hungary, 307-19; to Hamburg to
play under Muck, 4-6, 319
Etchings, 287
Spalding, Mrs. Albert (wife of the
author), 109-12, 114, 150, 216,
237, 258-59, 271, 273-75, 279-
85, 286, 296-98, 310, 311, 312,
317
Spalding ancestry, 16
Spalding, Boardman (brother), 8,
26-27, 29, 31, 34, 91, 293
Spalding, James (grandfather), 15,
16
Spalding, Mrs. James (grandmother), 8, 12, 14, 18
Spalding, J. W. (father), 8, 16, 18,
19-21, 22, 28-29, 34, 49, 135,
136, 205, 211
Spalding, Mrs. J. W. (mother), 8,
10, 15, 16, 17, 18, 19-21, 22,
25, 34, 39, 85, 204, 211-13
Spalding (A. G.) & Brother, 20
Springs, Sergt. Elliot, 215
Stanislavsky, 168
Stanley of Alderley, Lady, 66
Stein, Mme. Wanda, 199
Stockbridge, Mass., 297-98
Stokowski, Leopold, 274
Stolypin, Alexander, 128-29, 141,
155-57
Stolypin, Peter, 128, 129
St. Petersburg, 121-45, 153-60, 198-
203; U. S. Embassy in, 138-39
Strassbourg, 277
Strozzi, Princess, 37
Swann, Captain, 211, 212, 213, 218-
19